The abstract reflections of theologians and philosophers have often had little impact on the work of practicing business managers. O'Brien, Collier, and Flanagan's *Good Business* seeks to bridge that gap. . . . The authors provide a useful summary of basic concepts (such as human dignity, the common good, justice, subsidiarity, and solidarity) and survey some of the issues that surround them. But beyond that they do a rare thing, which is to make a serious and determined attempt to explain how these basic concepts might play out in the practical management of business enterprises . . . illustrated by a set of case studies that helps to ground theory in application.

—Robert G Kennedy
University of Saint Thomas
Saint Paul, MN

In an era when so much of business ethics treats only issues within the firm, O'Brien, Collier, and Flanagan's *Good Business: Catholic Social Teaching at Work in the Marketplace* employs Scripture, tradition, and contemporary Catholic social thought to provide a lively and more expansive vision of what businesses are called to be. An excellent resource for the classroom.

—Daniel Finn
St. John's University, Collegeville, Minnesota

O'Brien, Collier, and Flanagan's *Good Business* strikingly illustrates how Catholic social teaching challenges the overemphasis on individualism and profit for a few in contemporary American capitalism. In eight chapters the book develops and applies . . . Catholic social teaching to the structure of economic life. . . . The authors admirably bring together theory and practice by relating in each chapter a different approach to economic enterprises illustrating . . . the [teaching] developed in that chapter.

—Charles E. Curran
Southern Methodist University

Created by the publishing team of Anselm Academic.

Cover image © gui jun peng / Shutterstock.com

Printed in the United States of America

7059

ISBN 978-1-59982-169-6

GOOD BUSINESS

Catholic Social Teaching at Work in the Marketplace

Thomas O'Brien

Elizabeth W. Collier

Patrick Flanagan

Publisher Acknowledgments

The publisher wishes to thank the following individuals who reviewed this work in progress:

Scott Paeth
DePaul University, Chicago, IL

Jennifer Reed-Bouley
College of Saint Mary, Omaha, NE

Christopher Vogt
St. John's University, Queens, NY

Contents

Preface

When the topic of business ethics is raised, someone is sure to make the joke that business ethics is an oxymoron. After everyone nods and has a good laugh, the discussion turns to a litany of recent moral offenses perpetrated by businesses. Usually, a long list of negative case studies is offered as proof that modern business leaders treat ethics as irrelevant. These interactions often conclude with the refrain that modern businesses somehow must behave immorally and anti-socially in order to exist in the dog-eat-dog world of competitive capitalist markets. The most disconcerting part of the scenario is that many business leaders and business school students are among the first to make this joke and among those who laugh the loudest at its telling.

This cultural bias treats the marketplace like some kind of lawless moral dystopia that is entirely irredeemable. In other words, it considers the modern capitalist marketplace as an utter failure—an utter moral failure—and a kind of curse on human society. It implies that society would be much better off without it. Not surprisingly, when presented with this argument, the same business leaders and students who laughed the loudest and proved the most adept at conjuring examples of the sins of capitalist businesses, in the next moment, sober up and sing the unbridled praises of the marketplace. They recast the capitalist marketplace as an abundant provider, a lab for human creativity, the last bastion of genuine freedom, and the best of all possible commercial worlds.

The authors of this book consider both extreme cynicism and unquestioning esteem misguided and dangerous attitudes when evaluating the moral worth of the capitalist marketplace. Many business ethics textbooks unconsciously play into the hands of both the cynics and the sycophants by focusing too much on case studies that highlight evils in the marketplace and not enough on those that highlight outstanding moral leadership. One could easily finish reading a standard business ethics textbook and conclude that business is an amoral enterprise at best and that the only reasonable attitude is either to give in to the culture and become amoral oneself or to abandon any hopes of becoming a business leader for fear of becoming ethically bankrupt.

To combat the impression that the business context is rife with bad behavior that can barely be kept in check, this book uses predominantly positive case studies that highlight many wonderful things that businesses do around the world. The text assumes readers are aware that capitalist businesses can behave badly and sometimes engage in very destructive behavior and certainly does not shy away from bringing up some of these examples as it discusses the principles and theories of Catholic social thought. However, a primary aim of this book is to spark the moral imagination of students by demonstrating the ethical impulse behind many capitalist enterprises around the world today. In this way, the book aims to serve as an instructional and inspirational volume that motivates future business leaders to pursue enterprises that are successful both morally and financially.

This book expounds on the major themes that arise from the substantial and august body of work known as Catholic social teaching. Each chapter examines one of the central theoretical themes of Catholic social thought and applies it to contemporary business practices and critical issues that arise in the global economy today. Each then presents two actual business cases and encourages readers to insert themselves into these situations to explore solutions that make sense in the light of the high moral standards set by the Catholic social tradition. It is the hope of the authors that this approach will inspire readers and broaden their moral imagination regarding what a business should be and how it should operate within the novel conditions of global markets.

Introduction

Thomas O'Brien

The Tradition of Applied Ethics

Before applying Catholic social teaching (CST)to business enterprises and the marketplace, it is important to survey the field of applied ethics and to review how Catholicism has informed that tradition from its own perspective. Ethicists evaluate human activity to determine the relative goodness or evil (right or wrong) of an action that has either taken place or is being proposed. Applied ethics is a subset of ethics that focuses on applying ethical principles and theories to a specific set of circumstances. So, for instance, medical ethics is a type of applied ethics that applies established ethical principles and theories to circumstances and dilemmas that arise in hospitals, clinics, and medical research facilities. Business ethics, also a type of applied ethics, applies established ethical principles and theories to the circumstances and dilemmas that arise in the marketplace.

Undoubtedly, applied ethics has been around since the beginning of human society. People seem to naturally assess the fairness of their interactions with others, and they normally do so by using common sense and practical measures to determine who was helped or harmed, and by how much, in various controversial situations. Over time, people became more sophisticated at evaluating and categorizing ethical offenses and this refinement developed into the discipline of ethics. The first section of the introduction will introduce the basic outlines of that discipline and some important technical terms that will appear throughout the book. It will be followed by a discussion of the way Catholics have interpreted these standard ethical perspectives. Finally, the introduction will offer a brief overview of the history and development of CST, relating this more specific tradition to the broader discipline of ethical analysis.

The Basics of Applied Ethical Reasoning

Systems of applied ethics fall into two general categories: decision-making systems and character-based systems. Decision-making systems answer the question, "What should I do?" Those using these systems aim to make the right decision when faced with a moral dilemma by applying a guiding principle and choosing the best option. They tend to focus on the task at hand and, therefore, do not address longer-range goals of moral development and perfection. Because these systems emphasize achieving the right or good in a single moment in time, the principles must be applied again and again as moral dilemmas arise. A number of the theories described in greater detail in the following pages, such as consequentialism and Kant's categorical imperative, fall under the decision-making category.

In contrast to decision-making systems, character-based systems answer the question, "Who should I be?" or "Who should I become?" Although often used to resolve moral dilemmas and guide practical action in a current situation, the real value of character-based systems lies in their capacity to foster moral growth and promote character development. These systems tend to lead people to focus on longer-range goals associated with the moral improvement of individuals or societies. Normally, people using these systems employ a scale of increasing moral achievement as a map that points one toward a final goal of ethical perfection.

Consequentialism

Consequentialism is a decision-making ethical theory that focuses on the results, or consequences, when evaluating the moral worth of a particular course of action. Consequentialists ask questions such as, "What happened?" or "What is likely to happen?" when they approach an ethical dilemma. They are most interested in maximizing the beneficial outcomes and minimizing the harm done to everyone involved in a particular circumstance. Consequentialists tend to be relatively indifferent to abstractions such as principles, virtues, or moral imperatives. Instead, they have a more practical interest in assuring that the outcomes of a particular case will increase the overall welfare of those impacted by the consequences.

In its application, consequentialist logic is very similar to the logic of comparison shopping, in which the shopper chooses between various products by comparing their features. Ultimately, comparison shoppers choose the product that they believe will maximize their happiness after weighing and comparing the options available. In a similar way, consequentialists face moral dilemmas by comparing various courses of action and choosing the one they think will produce the greatest satisfaction, happiness, or utility. This weighing of consequential options is especially effective and convincing when one has reliable information about what actually did happen or what is likely to happen in a given case. It proves much less useful in novel or unprecedented situations or when the outcomes of actions are otherwise not easily predicted.

The term *consequentialism* describes a category of ethical approaches that can be further broken down according to how broadly one defines the group of people affected by a moral dilemma. If the group consists of only oneself, then this kind of consequentialism is called egoism. This standpoint focuses solely on whether the expected outcomes are going to be good for a person or a group of people to whom the primary decision maker is closely associated. It is not so much an ethical theory as a description of self-interested behavior. Some confuse *egoism* with *egotism*, an exaggerated conception of one's own importance. While egoists might have a big ego, they might just as easily have poor self-esteem. Sometimes *egoism* is also confused with *selfishness*. While egoists might behave in very selfish ways, it should be noted that some of the most generous corporate actions, i.e., philanthropic gifts to the arts and social welfare, are motivated by egoistic concerns—promoting the company in the eyes of the public.

An egoist chooses the options with the best results for oneself and one's close associates, which is a fairly good description of the way most people make decisions in their daily lives. Most individuals do not normally make choices based on how an action will impact other people outside their own identity group, or for that matter, the entire global family. Think, for example, of college students who choose a major because of how it will promote their personal career aspirations and improve the lot of their family rather than because of its benefit to the wider community. Egoism becomes an ethically problematic stance only when the pursuit of one's own interests conflicts with the welfare of others.

Egoism itself is not an ethical theory with a developed logic and a loyal following among scholars. It is really just a descriptive term pointing to behavior that is essentially self-interested. On the other hand, consequentialism describes a category of ethical analysis that tries to take into account the good of all those being influenced by a decision. One ethical theory within the consequentialist family is known as utilitarianism. This doctrine demands that people choose the option that will result in the greatest possible balance of good over evil for everyone affected by it. Utilitarians want to maximize the overall utility of decisions so that human society flourishes as a result. They evaluate both the number of those affected as well as the quality or intensity of the goodness and harm experienced.

In this way, utilitarianism consists of more than mere majoritarianism, which is based on a simple exercise of counting heads and claiming that the interests of the majority always trump those of the minority. Nevertheless, utilitarians sometimes find themselves at a loss to condemn cases in which a minority is being oppressed in a way that significantly benefits a much larger majority. Therefore, the classic ethical dilemma presented to stump utilitarians is one in which the enslavement of a relatively small minority results in a much higher standard of living for a much larger majority. Utilitarians would acknowledge that slavery is a bad situation; however, because only a relatively small number of people experience it and because the good is so generally distributed, they have difficulty condemning it without going outside of their normal logic, which usually considers only results as legitimate in making an ethical evaluation.[1]

Deontology

The word *deontology* comes from the Greek root *deon*, which means, "duty or obligation." Deontologists focus on evaluating individual cases based on certain expectations about the principles people should apply when making decisions about what to do in a given dilemma. These expectations can take the form of universal moral principles, such as the principle to avoid harming others, which can be found in virtually every major moral system. However, deontological moral expectations can also be tied to more specific and local roles that people play in a certain society. So, for instance, soldiers may still be held to the universal moral duty to avoid gratuitously harming others, while at the same time, may be duty bound to follow orders that require them to maim and kill an enemy of the nation so as to maintain the good order of the state.

In its application, deontological logic resembles the logic of the job description in the business world, in which the supervisor evaluates the performance of workers by comparing their actual work record to the expectations in the job description. If employee performance does not measure up to the expectations in the job description, the employee is deemed deficient. Similarly, if the behaviors of those acting within an ethical dilemma do not measure up to the various principles that the deontologist deems critical in that situation, then those behaviors are judged morally suspect.

A critical difference between consequentialists and deontologists is that most deontological systems emphasize the application of principles and the examination of intentions. While consequentialists look exclusively at the concrete results of actions, deontologists often view these results as distractions because of their unpredictability. For this reason, results cannot be considered the sole criteria in the moral equation.[2] Consequentialism takes an inductive approach, much like the experimental sciences. Something is good or bad depending on the results or data that come from practical applications of an idea. Conversely, deontology takes a deductive approach, much like the theoretical sciences. The

---

1. It should be noted that utilitarians have responded to this "slavery objection" in a variety of ways. Most often, they simply claim that only fictitious idealistic versions of slavery could ever be justified in a utilitarian analysis. These authors assert that situations in which people were actually enslaved would result in a society that was much worse off than one in which people were justly remunerated for their labor. See R. M. Hare, "What Is Wrong with Slavery," *Philosophy and Public Affairs* 8.2 (1979): 103–21.

2. Consequentialists respond to this criticism by claiming intentions themselves are the truly unpredictable part of the moral equation.

goodness or evil in any given circumstance can be inferred from a set of universal principles shown to be true in all circumstances.

Immanuel Kant (1724–1804) was one such deontologist. He believed that the moral worth of an action could be assessed only by considering the intentions of the actors in a case. He maintained that the only acceptable action in any given circumstance was one that yielded a maxim, or principle, that could be universalized—one that would be endorsed by any and all reasonable observers.[3] This first formulation of what Kant called the categorical imperative eventually yielded a second formulation that seems very close to the Golden Rule that schoolchildren have learned for generations: "so act as to treat humanity, whether in your own person or in that of any other, in every case at the same time as an end, never as a means only."[4]

Virtue Ethics

Virtue is an ancient ethical concept that assigns moral value to both behavior and character traits that conform to notions of "the good." A virtue is a trait of either a person or an action that makes that person or action stand out as morally good. Virtue ethics determines the morality of an action by assessing how well people's behavior and character conform to these standards of perfection. Virtues can be applied to behavior—in which case, they function as a kind of practical moral wisdom. So, for instance, one particular course of action might be honest, courageous, and forthright while another might be cowardly, deceptive, and cunning. The ancient Greek philosophers referred to this as *phronesis*, an application of virtue as a practical guide to behavior.

In a similar way, virtues can also be applied as character traits to describe a person and assign that person a standing in the moral universe. Therefore, people who regularly boast excessively about their own meager achievements might be branded arrogant, while those who do not seek excessive attention despite their outstanding achievements might be seen as exhibiting the virtues of modesty and humility. The ancient Greeks knew this as *arête*, using virtues to analyze the character of individuals.

According to virtue ethicists, the ultimate purpose of all this virtuous behavior is *eudaimonia*, or human happiness. The ancient Greek philosopher Aristotle (384–322 BCE) used the term *eudaimonia* to describe the deep satisfaction that someone ought to feel at the end of a life well lived—that is, a life lived according to the virtues. For Aristotle, a life lived according to ethical

---

3. Kant's First Formulation of the Categorical Imperative: "Act only in accordance with that maxim through which you can at the same time will that it become a universal law." Immanuel Kant, *The Groundwork of the Metaphysics of Morals* (Mississauga, ON: Broadview Press, 2005), 81.

4. Ibid., 88.

principles was equivalent to living the happy life. Happiness was not achieved through the accumulation of wealth, the exercise of power, or the gaining of recognition and fame. Rather, Aristotle observed that happiness seemed almost entirely dependent on the moral worth of the decisions one made throughout one's life. Conversely, those whose lives lacked *eudaimonia* almost always had vices such as greed, avarice, selfishness, cowardice, and pride. Therefore, happiness was achieved through moral discipline, and the pursuit of happiness was, at the same time, the pursuit of the good.

Western religious traditions take up ancient Greek notions of virtue and appropriate them for use within their moral systems. For this reason, virtue ethics exists in Judaism, Christianity and, to a lesser extent, Islam in ways that closely resemble the original formulations. For example, the Catholic Church lists four cardinal virtues as essential to the Christian life: prudence, justice, fortitude, and temperance.[5] In addition to the Abrahamic traditions, the notion of virtue survives in almost every major religious tradition as well as in the smaller, local ones. For instance, the *sanatana dharma* in Hinduism is one example of virtue in a major non-Western religion. According to the *sanatana dharma*, all Hindus have a duty to adhere to the following virtues:

- Altruism: Selfless service to all humanity
- Restraint and Moderation: Sexual relations, eating, and other pleasurable activities should be kept in moderation
- Honesty: One is required to be honest with self; honest with family, friends, and all of humanity
- Cleanliness: Outer cleanliness is to be cultivated for good health and hygiene; inner cleanliness is cultivated through devotion to god, selflessness, nonviolence, and all the other virtues.
- Protection and reverence for the Earth
- Universality: One shows tolerance and respect for everyone, everything, and the way of the universe.
- Peace: One must cultivate a peaceful manner in order to benefit oneself and others.
- Reverence for elders and teachers

Justice

Morally evaluating economic relationships almost always raises issues associated with fairness and equity, and therefore, a discussion of justice ensues. In modern

---

5. *Catechism of the Catholic Church*, no. 1805, *http://www.vatican.va/archive/ccc_css/archive/catechism/p3s1c1a7.htm*.

philosophical discourse, justice is understood from many different perspectives, but the one most applicable to business ethics is *distributive justice*. Theories of distributive justice guide the allocation of the benefits and burdens of economic activity in order to achieve some acceptable level of fairness and equity. The mode of reasoning for the principles of allocation is analogous to a "lifeboat" exercise that encourages participants to imagine themselves adrift on an ocean with insufficient resources for everyone's survival. The participants must decide who gets the resources and what standards should guide the decision making. Such exercises, like theories of distributive justice, shed light on the values and moral priorities of a group and how they get implemented in ways that privilege some and disadvantage others.

Generally speaking, there are six schools of distributive justice: strict egalitarianism, resource egalitarianism, desert-based justice, libertarianism, utilitarianism, and Rawlsian justice. Egalitarian principles stress equality and the need to establish structures that ensure impartiality.

Strict Egalitarianism

Strict egalitarians demand that everyone in a society receive exactly the same income and resources. Although a very simple and straightforward requirement, such a demand has never proven practically realizable in actual circumstances. It is very difficult to enforce absolute equality in circumstances in which individual strengths and weaknesses are diverse and in environments in which the constant introduction of novel elements throws the equilibrium off kilter.

Resource Egalitarianism

For that reason, most egalitarians are limited-resource egalitarians, demanding equal distribution of only certain resources in a society. For example, many resource egalitarians believe that in a truly just society, all people would begin life with essentially the same set of basic resources, such as nutrition, housing, clothing, education, and so on. What one did with that initial set of basic resources supplied gratis by the state would determine one's fate in that society.

Desert-Based Justice

In this way, resource egalitarians are similar in spirit to certain other schools of justice that believe people should be rewarded for their activities in accordance with their contribution to the social product. These desert-based principles focus on effort, ingenuity, and productivity, recognizing that some members of society deserve a larger share of society's benefits because of their more substantial role in building and maintaining the social order. In other words, if someone works hard at something society values, then that person should be richly rewarded. On the other hand, if someone contributes little, or contributes only in ways that are not valuable to that society, then that person should languish in poverty. Desert-based principles like these, however, do not account for the randomness, chaos, messiness, and unpredictability of human life and society. Some people who work very hard and contribute a great deal to society still fail due to unforeseen circumstances such as illness, accidents, or the collateral damage inflicted by family members who need their assistance.

Desert-based principles also do not have a developed notion of social value and social utility. They assume that societies always value things that are beneficial and useful, when clearly this is not the case. Societies frequently reward wasteful, useless, and even counterproductive activities. One only needs to look at the economic meltdown of 2008 to identify banking executives who were richly rewarded for contributing to this disaster. From the perspective of justice, do people who contribute to waste, destruction, and frivolity still deserve outsized compensation? Furthermore, societies often undercompensate for activities they claim to value highly. For instance, aspects of US society tell its military personnel that they are held in the highest esteem; however, soldiers earn little more than most service-sector workers, and many veterans struggle to get basic health care needs met. Does US society value the destructive "contributions" of bankers more than the self-sacrificing service of military personnel?

Libertarian Justice

Libertarian notions of justice place greater emphasis on freedom and less on the capacity of a society to engineer equality through law, policy, and regulation. In fact, libertarians are skeptical that equality can be achieved through the imposition of laws, regulations, and other restrictions on otherwise free commerce. Therefore, from a libertarian perspective, justice is achieved only within a society that guarantees the state will not interfere with individual pursuits, assuming those pursuits are themselves not interfering with the rights of others to pursue their own goals. The state should protect individual rights to acquire, control, and transfer property but, otherwise, should play no proactive role in ensuring, supplementing, or regulating the use of property.

Libertarianism, sometimes called empirical negative liberty, is based on the notion of radical self-ownership, which tends to run counter to more generally accepted ideas of mutual rights and responsibilities that members of a society owe one another. On a practical level, the concept of radical self-ownership denies the obvious social construction of the self and of one's role in the larger context of society. In truth, people don't own themselves. Selfhood is beholden to a myriad of human relationships that teach, influence, assist, resist, challenge, counsel, and so forth. These human relationships include known relationships with family, teachers, friends, doctors, lawyers, counselors, and others. However, a fuller accounting of our socially constructed selves would reveal a vast hidden world of unseen and unknown actors who have had some kind of influence on our lives and who together comprise an incalculable impact on people.

Utilitarian Justice

One theory of justice that takes the larger web of social relationships very seriously is utilitarianism, an ethical idea briefly introduced earlier. Utilitarianism is a consequentialist system that seeks the best and most useful results for everyone concerned. This basic ethical ideal of general welfare can easily be scaled to include entire societies or even the global community. Therefore, justice for a utilitarian consists of choosing the policy alternatives that will result in the greatest good for society as a whole. Taken at face value, utilitarianism seems laudable; however, sometimes utilitarianism has difficulty condemning alternatives that clearly sacrifice individual rights and liberty, when it judges those alternatives as resulting in the greatest overall good for the majority of the members of society. In the lifeboat exercise, someone following a strict utilitarian analysis might justify throwing someone (or even a small group) overboard if that meant the rest would be more likely to survive and even thrive while awaiting a rescue.

Rawlsian Justice

Finally, without going into too much detail, there is the *difference principle* and John Rawls's theory of justice, which is based on the welfare of the least well-off in society. John Rawls (1921–2002) was a philosopher who spent most of his career at Harvard teaching and writing about the principles that would inform a genuinely just society. According to Rawls, the relative justice of a society can be determined by the fate of its poorest and most marginalized members. The more just a society is, the better off the poor in that society will be, relatively speaking. This theory led some to accuse Rawls of being a strict egalitarian in disguise and his system of justice mere window dressing over a core of utopian socialism. Rawls responded that a strictly egalitarian system might be the most just, but the real test consisted of comparing the lots of the least well-off in different systems. It might be the case that a society that tolerated some disparity in income could actually result in a more productive economy overall and, therefore, end up distributing more wealth to the poorest members of that society. Rawls asserted that differences in income and wealth were only tolerable when it benefited the poor in some way. Hence, capitalism might be more just than socialism but only if it could be shown that the poor fared better in that system than in the collectivist egalitarian ideal. The main weakness of Rawls's theory of justice is that it is a thought experiment rather than a practical theory. While some have attempted to use his theory in concrete situations, its real purpose is to draw attention to the meaning of justice and the demands that it places on society.

Teleology

An introduction to common approaches to applied ethics would not be complete without discussing the family of theories known as teleology. Like many other ethical terms, this one has its etymological roots in ancient Greece. *Telos* is a Greek word meaning, "final purpose, goal, or end." Therefore, this ethical perspective concentrates on the ultimate purpose of human striving. It asks the question, "What is the ultimate goal of human life and how does one arrange intermediate goals, purposes, and ends so that they align with that ultimate purpose?" Many confuse teleology with consequentialism because both focus on "ends" and "goals," but these systems are distinct in that they seek entirely different goals. Consequentialism is concerned with the immediate results of an action, sometimes referred to in philosophical circles as the *efficient cause*. Teleology is concerned about only the immediate results to the extent that they are properly ordered toward a larger purpose, sometimes referred to as the *final cause* by medieval philosophers.

Teleological systems demand that humans order their actions toward a long-term, transcendent purpose or goal, and frequently, that goal takes the form of an exemplar or a model of perfection. One can find many examples of exemplars in the religions of the world. In Christianity, Jesus is the model of perfection, and Christians are frequently referred to as followers of Christ. Christians are encouraged to model their behavior after the example of Jesus, and this becomes a type of shorthand method of determining the moral path for Christians. In the present, one can see teleology at play in the popular Christian meme printed on a wide variety of T-shirts and bracelets—*WWJD*—"What Would Jesus Do?" More precisely, teleology is concerned with who Jesus was and how one can become more Christ-like through a more mindful approach to everyday behavior. Christian discipleship, therefore, serves as one of many examples of teleology in a major world religion.

Not all teleological systems are religious. In fact, one of the most popular psychological theories of ethical development has teleological elements. Lawrence Kohlberg, a psychologist at Harvard University in the 1970s, claimed that every person who progresses toward moral maturity does so by moving through a series of predictable stages. Kohlberg derived this theory of moral development, in part, from the work of his mentor, Jean Piaget, who used stages to describe human cognitive development. Kohlberg's system as a whole assumes the existence of such a thing as moral maturity and the highest standard against which all other stages can be compared and judged. The highest stage in Kohlberg's theory, stage 6, is a level of moral perfection that few have achieved.

Catholic Interpretations of Applied Ethical Reasoning

The ethical theories outlined previously constitute the foundation of most conversations about business ethics today. Although almost every Catholic university in North America teaches some form of business ethics, few resources specifically analyze this field from the perspective of the Catholic moral tradition. This section of the introduction will give a brief overview of the Catholic moral tradition, pointing out the areas of agreement and divergence from those theories discussed in the previous section, "The Tradition of Applied Ethics." Before the book addresses the Catholic social tradition and how it applies to businesses and the economy, it is important for the reader to understand how Catholics analyze the behavior of individuals acting in commercial markets. The social tradition is, in part, an outgrowth of the broader moral tradition, and it frequently references elements of the moral tradition when making its arguments for certain policies and practices.

Divine Command

An obvious way that the Catholic moral tradition differs from secular traditions has to do with the belief in God and the conviction that God is concerned about human behavior and the consequences of that behavior. Catholics believe that God even demands certain types of behavior and that believers face divine approbation and punishment, depending on the quality of choices they make when faced with moral dilemmas. In many circumstances, the reason a Catholic may deem something right or wrong may depend on whether something is approved or rejected by God.

The belief in divine command raises the question of how one determines the will of a God who is believed to be above and beyond human understanding. The answer, in short, is revelation. Catholics believe that, while God is beyond the normal confines of human comprehension, aspects of the divine will and mind have been revealed so that humans might better know what is expected of them. Catholics believe that God has pulled back a part of the veil of human ignorance that conceals the otherwise overwhelming presence of the divine so that they might catch a glimpse of those things required for their salvation.

One way God is revealed is through Scripture, and the portion of Scripture that first comes to the mind of many Christians when they think of morality is the Ten Commandments (Exodus 20:1–17).[6] Christians and Jews share the story of the giving of the Ten Commandments, and it offers a good example

---

6. A more complete discussion of the Ten Commandments can be found in James F. Keenan, *Moral Wisdom: Lessons and Texts from the Catholic Tradition* (Kansas City, MO: Sheed & Ward, 2010), 99–116.

of one type of moral revelation, in which God made the divine will abundantly clear by etching ten moral proscriptions on the relatively permanent medium of stone tablets. Moral direction for Christians is drawn from the New Testament as well as the Old Testament and can be found in nearly all of the various literary forms found in the Bible—poems, song lyrics, myth, history, chronicles, letters, proverbs, parables, prophecies, and gospels.

For Christian ethics, the most compelling Scriptures recount the life, ministry, death, and Resurrection of Jesus. The four Gospels retell similar, though not identical, versions of his life. As mentioned previously in the section on teleology, Jesus provides the primary Christian model of moral perfection, and observant Christians try to conform their lives to the example he set. Catholics expand on the teleological thrust of their moral universe by including saints, who also serve as models of exceptional virtue. In addition to Christ's ethically archetypal behavior, the Gospels preserve many important moral sayings that help guide the character and behavior of Christians. Followers of Christ are regularly admonished to love one another, show forgiveness to offenders, demonstrate mercy toward the poor and marginalized, abandon lust for power, and serve one another. Christian ethicist Joseph Fletcher, in his book *Situation Ethics,* went so far as to say that all of Christian morality could be reduced to the simple command to love.[7]

Magisterium and Tradition

Although divine command constitutes an important element of the Catholic ethical tradition, it is not the only source of moral authority. Catholics believe that God's will is also revealed in the ongoing tradition of the Christian community reflecting on moral duty and acting in inspirational ways to improve the lives of others and establish institutions that serve the poor and vulnerable. The term *magisterium* comes from the Latin root for teacher, *magister,* and refers to the teaching *charism,* or vocation, of the church.[8] The Catholic tradition believes that God confers the teaching vocation in special ways to theologians and members of the hierarchy. Therefore, when Catholics refer to "the teaching church" they refer to these groups of clergy and theologians who have been gifted and tasked with the vocation to teach the divine truths. Moral theology is one of the important subdivisions of the magisterial office in Roman Catholicism.

Given the importance of magisterial tradition in the Catholic Church, many of the moral beliefs and practices espoused by Catholics have their source in the

---

7. Joseph Fletcher, *Situation Ethics: The New Morality* (Louisville, KY: John Knox Press, 1966), 69.

8. A more complete discussion of *magisterial* authority in the Catholic Church can be found in Francis A. Sullivan, *Magisterium: Teaching Authority in the Catholic Church* (Mahwah, NJ: Paulist Press, 1983), 24–51.

Church's recorded history, laws, policies, doctrines, and documents. In fact, the Catholic social tradition had its origins in book-length documents issued by the Church known as encyclicals. Applying the broader moral tradition to individuals and groups dates back to the beginning of the church in the first century of the Common Era. Documents such as *The Shepherd of Hermas, The Didache, The Epistle of Diognetas,* and the countless sermons of the earliest Christians offer documentary evidence of the centrality of the moral life for these first believers.[9] In these texts one discovers recurring moral directives to care for the poor, feed the hungry, clothe the naked, avoid avarice, renounce power and wealth, share property, and treat even the lowliest with honor.

Over the course of almost two millennia, the church has continued to reflect on the moral duties of its members and eventually an impressive body of work emerged with relatively consistent principles, theories, and practices that have become the distinctive timber of a uniquely Catholic ethical voice. Catholic moral thought stresses the need for actions to be consistent with the natural purpose laid out by God the Creator. Therefore, the Catholic moral tradition has a strong natural law tradition that judges actions based on the degree to which they conform to a divine will that can be discerned from nature itself. Catholic ethics also demonstrates profound respect for individual conscience and the formation of a virtuous character. Conscience introduces the idea that God directs the thoughts and actions of believers and that each person has access to this divine guidance, which is referred to as conscience. As stated before, Christian ethics can have a teleological focus, for it demands that followers conform their lives and actions to the perfect model of Christ. Catholics have taken up this teleological impulse and expanded on it by introducing saints—people who were outstanding Christ-like examples in their lifetime. Eventually, all of this reflection on the moral life was written down and codified in practical manuals and church laws. Catholic moral thought, therefore, is not only theoretical, but also practical and pastorally focused. In the rest of this section, three key aspects of the Catholic moral tradition will be reviewed more closely.

The Natural Law

The natural law in Catholic moral theology is the belief that a moral order exists independent of human creative intervention. Natural law theologians do not view ethics as a product of human culture but rather as something humans discover in the same way that they discern the laws of other preexisting orders like those in the physical universe. In this way, the best analogies for the logic of the natural law are the physical sciences. The natural law infers what is right and wrong from observable evidence in the world of human society, which natural

---

9. All of these texts and more can be found at the Early Christian Writings website, *http://www. earlychristianwritings.com/index.html.*

lawyers treat as a given of nature itself.[10] This may seem counterintuitive to most modern readers, who have been brought up in an age of ethical relativism. Popular media generally treat ethics as a merely personal bias: what one person deems right or wrong is grounded solely in personal choice. While many recognize that society may influence personal moral choices, those social influences themselves are conditioned only by history, habit, and human psychology and are not in some way necessary or built into the "nature" of human society. The natural law, therefore, is an entirely different perspective on the purpose of human behavior and the development of particular character traits.[11]

Natural law theology claims that everything that exists has a specific purpose within the natural order and that the entire natural order itself is purposeful and ordered toward achieving a certain end. In the case of Catholic natural law, that purpose is union with the divine. Natural law morality claims that there is a moral order ordained by God and that humans have access to and can understand this order by observing how humans behave in community—inferring right and wrong from the behaviors and character traits they witness. This ethical worldview deems things "natural" because they lead to the general welfare of the group and contribute to overall human flourishing. Likewise, "unnatural" acts frustrate welfare and human flourishing, thus obstructing the beneficent divine will. What is good is—at the same time—natural, because it fulfills its intended purpose of being in harmony with the will of the divine. As a matter of course, those things considered unnatural are evil because they frustrate their intended design or purpose.[12]

Therefore, in addition to Scripture and tradition, Catholic moral theology also has been informed by the notion that all personal, interpersonal, and social behaviors are structured according to a divinely created natural order, which is governed by natural laws that set parameters on human behavior. The natural law, like all other ethical systems, suffers from limitations and flaws in both the construction and implementation of the theory. One of the main sticking points for natural law theologians is demonstrating how their particular rendition of what constitutes "natural" and "unnatural" is not simply a sophisticated veneer over what ultimately amounts to personal biases for or against certain character traits or behaviors. So, for instance, in the past, natural law has been invoked to condemn homosexual behavior, a position that was generally accepted as doctrine before Vatican II. However, during the latter half of the twentieth century,

---

10. Richard M. Gula, *Reason Informed by Faith: Foundations of Catholic Morality* (Mahwah, NJ: Paulist Press, 1989), 222.

11. For a more in-depth overview of how the natural law is distinct from relativistic notions of post-modernity, see Steven Brust, "Ancient and Modern: Natural Law and Universal Moral Principles," *Catholic Social Science Review*, 14 (2009): 65.

12. For a more extensive treatment of this theology, see Charles E. Curran and Richard A. McCormick, *Natural Law and Theology: Issue 7 of Readings in Moral Theology*, (New York, NY: Paulist Press, 1991).

a significant constituency within the Catholic Church began to raise questions about this categorization and assert the goodness of human sexuality in general, calling for the tolerance of many sexual expressions that had been heretofore declared anathema. Those listening to these voices had to either reject the natural law in its entirety or redefine what is and is not "natural." This led many to rightfully accuse the natural law of being philosophical window dressing on relativistic personal prejudice.[13]

In spite of these recent challenges to its credibility and authority, the natural law remains an important element of the Catholic moral imagination. Even many Catholic theologians who reject the particulars of the natural law still hold fast to the idea that humans and their societies are governed by a kind of moral order—one that has consequences not only for physical life in this world but also for eternal life in a heavenly realm.

Conscience

Whether in a Catholic context or not, references to conscience abound in contemporary culture, but when pressed to define or describe this concept, many struggle to come up with an adequate response. Generally speaking, conscience describes that internal voice possessed by each individual that serves to guide and correct behavior and form one's moral character. It is a person's moral compass or, to use a more contemporary illustration, a moral GPS.

For Catholics, conscience is God's way of speaking to individuals at the deepest level of their being during times of duress and especially when confronted with choices of good versus evil. It is inviolable and must be respected, even when the choices that ensue are not endorsed by the official teachings of the Catholic Church.[14] Although an autonomous function of an individual's authority within the moral sphere, conscience is not entirely alienated from external authority. For Catholics, the external authority of official church teaching can and should play a positive role in forming and guiding conscience.[15]

The act of conscience has three distinct steps: *synderesis,* moral science, and conscience.[16] The Greek term *synderesis* highlights the innate, or instinctual, moral impulse of the human person.[17] It directs attention to that moment in the

---

13. John J. McNeill, *The Church and the Homosexual* (Boston, MA: Beacon Press, 1993), 89–108.

14. See Charles Curran, *Faithful Dissent* (Kansas City, MO: Sheed and Ward, 1986), for an extended case study on the inviolability of conscience.

15. For a more complete discussion of conscience in the Catholic tradition, see Jayne Hoose, "Conscience in the Roman Catholic Tradition," in Jayne Hoose, ed. *Conscience in World Religions* (Notre Dame, IN: University of Notre Dame Press, 1999). See also Keenan, 27–44.

16. This three-part structure is taken from Gula, 131.

17. For more about the meaning and development of the idea of *synderesis*, see Robert A. Greene, "Synderesis, the Spark of Conscience, in the English Renaissance," *Journal of the History of Ideas,* 52, no. 2 (Apr.–Jun. 1991): 195–219.

moral dilemma when a person first senses something is wrong. *Synderesis* is a visceral moment before any reflection or reasoning has come to the fore to analyze the situation and synthesize a response. It is an awareness, an emotion, a reaction, a feeling of suddenly being thrust into a situation in which the stakes are high, someone is intending to harm another, and that person has the means to carry out that intention. *Synderesis* is followed by moral science, the step during which a person takes the time to question the situation at hand, make sure that his or her initial reactions were on target, evaluate the situation more thoroughly, and deliberate on what is right and wrong in that given situation. Finally, after one has felt strongly that something is wrong and has thoroughly deliberated about the moral response, one confronts the choice of whether to follow through with the right course of action or not. It is this moment of judgment—a moment always informed by the virtues—that is rightfully labeled *conscience*.

Catholics believe that over the course of a lifetime of difficult choices, conscience has a formative influence on a person's character. Eventually, moral choices become matters of integrity—a person either acts in character or out of character.[18] *Character* identifies the responsive orientation of a person. It becomes a way of seeing and responding to the world. A person's character determines whether that person sees the world as a hostile or friendly place, whether that person acts in a way that is loving and helpful or fearful and selfish. Character is a predisposition but not the sole determinant of behavior in any given situation. Character functions as a personal hermeneutic—a way of seeing, interpreting, and valuing the world. The theology of conscience reminds Catholics that most of what people see does not lie before their eyes but behind them where they interpret these images to fit into a framework of meaning. Conscience influences an individual's choices, while at the same time is formed by them. Catholicism is very conscious of the need to take care in forming a person's conscience so as to direct it toward the divine will.

Practical Moral Reasoning

Although Catholic moral theology has its roots in the life and ministry of Jesus and his earliest followers, it becomes an actual discipline under the more practical circumstances of the penitential rites that developed in the church in the fourth century and beyond. Penance is the sacrament of reconciliation in which individuals seek forgiveness for transgressions against others or against God. This process was made into a ritual practice over the course of the first few centuries of the church. The first documents recording the practice were the Irish Penitentials, which were created by missionary monks who had gone to Ireland to convert and minister to the Druids but who found themselves

---

18. Gula, 139.

instead thrust into social roles for which they had not been fully prepared. When the Romans drove out the Druid shamans, they unknowingly also drove away those who adjudicated conflicts within these communities. The shamans were also the judges who heard cases, discerned who was at fault, and meted out fair and just consequences. With the disappearance of the shamans, the communities frequently fell into chaos, and many began turning to the monks to fill the vacuum in law enforcement and justice. The penitentials were records of the "trials" held by the monks, listing the offenses and the punishments imposed.[19]

Eventually, the Church used the Irish Penitentials in other contexts, and they became more complex and sophisticated over time. They were ultimately incorporated into the sacramental practice of reconciliation, in which Catholics attempt to sacramentally right wrongs they have committed. The majority of these wrongs, or sins, are moral in nature or has moral elements. For this reason, a good deal of moral theology in the Catholic tradition has a practical thrust: it is meant to be used as a guide in the confessional where the priest meets in confidence with the believer and helps that individual understand right and wrong, good and evil, as they exist in that context. In order to perform this important task, priests need training in moral reasoning and, more importantly, in practical moral reasoning—the type they can readily apply and explain to people who may have little background in philosophy or metaphysics.

Over the course of centuries of development, the Catholic Church established a practical method for approaching moral cases and eventually employed a kind of casuistry, or case-method approach, in which the case at hand could be compared to paradigm cases that had already been resolved. This moral method has similarities to the casuistry used in legal practice today in which settled cases serve as precedents to help argue a solution to a legal dilemma. While not as commonly taught in seminaries as it once was, casuistry is still used by pastoral theologians to help prospective Catholic ministers understand how to approach common moral quandaries they are likely to encounter in their specific context. So, for instance, ministers training to work in a hospital will take courses that deal specifically with issues arising from that context, and students will be exposed to countless actual cases in which doctors, nurses, patients, and their families have been confronted with perplexing ethical quandaries. For this reason, Catholic moral theology is, in many respects, a kind of professional ethic; it is practically oriented toward pastoral application in the professions. Likewise, this book addresses practical and applied issues within the context of the business environment.

---

19. Timothy E. O'Connell, *Principles for a Catholic Morality* (Minneapolis, MN: Seabury Press, 1978), 12–13.

The Catholic Social Tradition

Just as the Catholic moral tradition provides an ethical vision for the human person in relation to others, so the Catholic social tradition gives an ethical vision for society. It acknowledges that the structure of a society has an impact on the welfare of those within it. A poorly structured society can do great harm; while one built on sound principles can help members flourish and advance. The principles that undergird CST are rooted in Scripture and the writings of the earliest followers of Jesus. The chapters of this book will go into greater detail about the development of the individual principles and their ancient roots in Scripture and tradition. This introduction will instead examine the more recent history when these previously disparate principles were collected into a thoroughgoing social theory.

Historical Development of Catholic Social Teaching

Catholic social teaching as a systematic social theory has its roots in the Catholic transition from a mindset wedded to the medieval economic, social, and political establishment to one that embraced, at least in part, the liberal, industrial, and democratic structures that were replacing the *ancien régime*. Since the Protestant Reformation beginning in 1521, the Catholic Church had progressively lost its grip on the levers of political, social, and economic power across the Western European landscape. Feudal systems were giving way to modernity in virtually all of the major urban centers of Europe. Only small towns and rural areas persisted in the old ways of life, and even these areas were showing signs of the impact of the new social, political, and economic order.

When the French Revolution in 1789 overthrew the last major citadel of the old order, the Catholic Church's last significant ally among the old European aristocracy disappeared almost overnight. Throughout most of the ensuing nineteenth century, the Church experienced a split between those who nostalgically attempted to maintain allegiances with the old, dying aristocratic class—along with the social principles that upheld that order—and those who tried to demonstrate that a harmony existed between the best principles of the new democratic order and those of the Gospels. This second faction within Catholicism would eventually prevail and become the progenitors of the emerging CST.

A number of notable individuals and movements within Catholicism had an enormous influence on the Catholic Church as it made this difficult transition to more modern notions of proper social order. Among these early voices were the Social Catholics, and one of the first proponents of a more open approach to new social, political, and economic ideas was Frederick Ozanam, a literature professor at the Sorbonne in Paris. In his years as a student, he founded the

Society of St. Vincent de Paul, an outreach to the urban poor who were predominantly industrial workers. He stressed the need for the Church to have a voice of its own and, therefore, an existence independent of the modern state. At the time, this was a radical departure from the Church's traditional position that the only legitimate state was the confessional state—one that embraced Catholicism and gave the Church a place in the halls of power. Ozanam was among the first to assert that one could be both a loyal Catholic and a believer in the efficacy of modern liberal democratic institutions.[20]

Unfortunately for Ozanam, he would die before ever seeing this vision of a modern Catholic Church realized. Pius IX, who had become pope just a few years before Ozanam's death, would lead the Church in a reactionary direction, working against all things modern and progressive during the three decades of his reign. While the rest of Europe shed the last remnants of feudalism and monarchy, Catholicism would remain a bastion of conservatism, attempting to convince its followers that a return to the medieval church-state union was still possible. During this same period, from the middle of the nineteenth century to the end of Pius IX's reign in 1878, others in the Church continued to work diligently to realize a Catholic Church that challenged, rather than merely rejected, the modern state.[21]

Under the leadership of the Bishop of Mainz, Wilhelm Emmanuel Von Ketteler, the Social Catholics began to develop a more theologically complete vision of the issues the Church needed to address and the principles it should espouse in order to challenge the emerging liberal states. Von Ketteler and his cohorts fought for the prohibition of child labor, the limitation of working hours, the separation of the sexes in the workplace, the closing of unsanitary workshops, Sunday rest, care for disabled workers, and state inspection of factories. They also maintained that charity was not sufficient to meet the needs of modern society and was conceived of too individualistically in a modern context. They did not believe that private property was an absolute value and argued that the state needed to rein in laissez-faire capitalism through regulations and taxes. They rejected both individualism and collectivism as solutions to the role the state should play in society, stressing instead the *via media*, or "middle way," to balance these conflicting visions of the ideal society. They emphasized that citizens had duties as well as rights in relation to the state, and they promoted the traditional theological notion of the common good as the guiding principle of the state.[22]

---

20. Thomas O'Brien, "Pioneer and Prophet: Frederick Ozanam's Influence on Modern Catholic Social Teaching," *Vincentian Heritage Journal* 31, no. 1 (2012): 29–46.

21. For a concise overview of this era, see Owen Chadwick, *Oxford History of the Christian Church: A History of the Popes, 1830–1914* (New York, NY: Oxford University Press, 1998), 93.

22. Marvin L. Mich, *Catholic Social Teaching and Movements* (Mystic, CT: Twenty-Third Publications, 1998), 5–28.

A Documentary History

Eventually, these ideas would be incorporated into the inaugural official document of modern CST, *Rerum novarum* (*RN*) (On the Condition of Labor), issued by Pope Leo XIII in 1891. The first in the long series of Catholic social encyclicals, it was concerned with the harsh conditions industrial laborers were forced to endure, both at work and in their squalid homes. It was critical of capitalism, while at the same time, fearful of socialism. Like his Social Catholic predecessors, Leo XIII imagined the ideal state would steer a middle way between the extremes of socialist collective control and capitalist laissez-faire. He believed that peace and harmony could be achieved between the rival social classes in society if the rich owners would only reach out generously to the poor workers. He advocated self-help organizations for the workers through the establishment of unions, or as he termed it, "associations." *Rerum novarum* insists that these unions or associations have a religious as well as a social purpose. In the end, Leo XIII laments the passing of the medieval guild system, which comes across as somewhat nostalgic to a contemporary reader. Subsequent encyclicals will, for the most part, abandon the idea of a proper medieval order to society.

It is hard to overestimate the impact *Rerum novarum* had on Western society and its notions of church, state, and economic organization. Most Catholics did not expect the pope to espouse such ideas. The grand majority of Catholics believed that a papal encyclical would continue the tradition of condemning all modern developments in social structures and maintaining their old, aristocratic alliances through carefully worded praise of the feudal order. Instead of siding with the old elites of the landed aristocracy or the new elites of the captains of industry, the Church chose to align itself with the concerns of the poorest in nineteenth-century European society—the urban industrial worker. After shedding their disbelief, people of the world, both Catholic and non-Catholic alike, found themselves surprisingly edified by an official document of the Church. *RN* quickly became a rallying cry for labor organization, outreach to the poor, and opposition to the abuses of capitalism. Over the ensuing decades, it would become the catalyst for positive social, political, and economic change in Europe and around the world.

However, in time, *Rerum novarum* began to show its age. It had addressed issues and promoted solutions that most developed countries incorporated into their customs and laws during the first couple of decades of the twentieth century. In the meantime, new, equally critical issues had emerged that had not existed at the end of the nineteenth century. Innovations and new social ideals had also come to the fore, and these needed to be analyzed and challenged. By the time of the Great Depression, the world was ripe for an update of this seminal document, and Pope Pius XI delivered with *Quadragesimo anno* (The Reconstruction of Social Order) in 1931. Despite being the second document, it set the stage for the Catholic social tradition to continually update the insights of the Church on social, political, and economic issues. Had it not been for *Quadragesimo anno, Rerum novarum* might have gone down in the annals of Catholic theology as a wonderful, yet singular, moment of inspiration. Since *Quadragesimo anno,* the popes have considered it a duty of their office to regularly evaluate and comment on the major events and movements of the era and to offer a moral perspective on these developments. The following is a list of some of the Catholic Church's major social teaching documents:[23]

1891—*Rerum novarum, RN* (On the Condition of Labor), Pope Leo XIII

1931—*Quadragesimo anno, QA* (The Reconstruction of Social Order), Pope Pius XI

1937—*Divini redemptoris, DR* (On Atheistic Communism), Pope Pius XI

1937—*Mit brennender Sorge, MBS* (On the Church and the German Reich), Pope Pius XI

1961—*Mater et magistra, MM* (Christianity and Social Progress), Pope John XXIII

1963—*Pacem in terris, PT* (Peace on Earth), Pope John XXIII

1965—*Gaudium et spes, GS* (Pastoral Constitution on the Church in the Modern World), Second Vatican Council

1967—*Populorum progressio, PP* (The Development of Peoples), Pope Paul VI

1971—*Octagesimo adveniens, OA* (A Call to Action), Pope Paul VI

1971—*Justice in the World,* Synod of Bishops

1981—*Laborem exercens, LE* (On Human Work), Pope John Paul II

1987—*Sollicitudo rei socialis, SRS* (On Social Concern), Pope John Paul II

1991—*Centesimus annus, CA* (One Hundred Years after *Rerum novarum*), Pope John Paul II

2009—*Caritas in veritate, CR* (Charity in Truth), Pope Benedict XVI

The rest of this book will unpack the Church's social teaching by examining recurring themes and applying these to the marketplace, using specific examples from various levels of business structures. The text focuses on eight key themes in this tradition. CST can be adequately understood through a careful analysis of these themes and the organic connection and interdependence that exists among them. The eight themes, reflected in the titles of the eight chapters in this book, are human dignity, common good, stewardship,

---

23. These documents are available at the Vatican's website: *www.vatican.va.*

option for the poor, economic justice, subsidiarity, solidarity, and rights and responsibilities.

Like many business ethics texts, this text not only engages decision making at the level of the board of directors and the CEO, but also analyzes the experience of employees in the warehouse, in the workshop, and behind the cash register. The marketplace is the responsibility of all participants, even if some play more elite and privileged roles than others. Many inspiring stories about business practices exist, and this is reflected in the case studies featured in the chapters. Most business ethics textbooks use cases to show how businesses have failed to meet the basic standards of morality. While this text does refer to cases like these, it also includes many cases that are meant to spark the moral imaginations of readers and possibly inspire them to emulate instances of moral business practice as they prepare themselves for business-related careers in corporations, nonprofit organizations, and government.

Chapter 1

Human Dignity in a Technological Age

Thomas O'Brien

Introduction

As I was composing this chapter, I sat at my desk multitasking as I often do in order to gather my thoughts, rest my brain, get unstuck, or just relax the synapses. There I was, bouncing between outliner, word processor, computer game, and buying bicycle parts, when it occurred to me that technology has made my life essentially different from the lives of even my most recent ancestors. In fact, it has made my life fundamentally different from what it was just twenty years ago.

I have always loved bikes and always wanted to tinker with them, but short of giving up my academic aspirations and going to work as an apprentice at a bike shop, I had little access to bicycle parts and the necessary repair and maintenance information to fulfill that vision. Today I have all this at my fingertips as I click a button to order parts that will transform my klutzy three-speed cruiser into a single-speed commuter. Technology has not only changed my bicycle, it has also genuinely transformed me by providing easy access to any and every bike part, a wealth of "how-to" and "do-it-yourself" information, as well as the blogged experiences of others trying to do the same thing with their bikes. In this case, technology has played a humanizing role supplying the tools for me to become a genuinely active producer of bikes, rather than merely a passive consumer.

Although not all encounters with new technologies can be characterized as positive, let alone successfully humanizing, enough of them must be in order to explain the enthusiastic demand for these products and services. However, the rapid and relentless advance of modern technology also poses myriad challenges to the ways people conceive, perceive, and make sense of the world. Cutting-edge technologies are both pervasive and invasive; they touch every aspect of life whether one is aware of it or not. The spread of technology in modern Western societies raises questions not only about appropriate use, efficient application, and useable interface but also about technology's capacity to alter the ways people think about themselves and other humans.[1]

Many argue that advanced technology is at a critical crossroad, where its power to alter the environment and one's very self is such that each new advance has a sort of ontological, or fundamental, potential to transform the definition of what it means to be a human living on this planet in the context of a community of humans and other living creatures.[2] Many also claim that as technology progresses further and as the definition of the self becomes more and more distinct from the relatively stable conceptions of humanity that have held sway for eons, the understanding of human dignity will likewise evolve.[3] The key lies in the capacity to develop technologies that are both efficient and humanizing, effective and dignified.[4] Some would claim that technologists focus more on the former than the latter and that questions about humanity and dignity will always require the attention of those creating and consuming the latest technological advances.

The Historical Roots of the Human Dignity Tradition

The belief that humans, by their very nature, are valuable in ways that are both quantitatively and qualitatively different from all other creatures has been a consistent theme since the dawn of Western philosophical and theological traditions.[5] This conception of the human as uniquely valuable has formed the foundation for most ethical systems in Western culture and has undergirded

---

1. Oswald, Bayer. "Self-Creation? On the Dignity of Human Beings," *Modern Theology* 20, no. 2 (April 01, 2004): 286–87.

2. Similar arguments are being made in other academic disciplines. See David Gurnham, "The Mysteries of Human Dignity and the Brave New World of Human Cloning," *Social & Legal Studies* 14, no. 2 (June 2005): 197–214.

3. Others have recently made similar claims: Elaine Graham, "The 'End' of the Human or the End of the 'Human'? Human Dignity in Technological Perspective," in *God and Human Dignity* (Grand Rapids: William B. Eerdmans, 2006), 263–281; and Christoph Schwöbel, "Recovering Human Dignity," in *God and Human Dignity*, 44–58.

4. UNESCO has recently called on developers of advanced technologies to consider the impact of their creations on human dignity and human rights. "Reflections on the UNESCO Draft Declaration on Bioethics and Human Rights," *Developing World Bioethics* 5, no. 3 (September 2005): 197–209.

5. J. Prescott Johnson, "The Idea of Human Dignity in Classical and Christian Thought." *Journal of Thought* 6 (January 01, 1971): 23–37.

conceptions of social justice and human rights.[6] All Western governments rely on this conception of the human to support their most important laws and democratic structures. In fact, it is hard to overestimate the importance of the notion that all persons share a dignity that is equal and inviolable. If some stroke of dark magic were to erase this concept from humanity's collective memory, it is not hard to imagine human existence devolving into the solitary, poor, nasty, brutish, and short state of war that Thomas Hobbes wrote about in *Leviathan*.[7]

Biblical and Theological Roots of Human Dignity

Western theories of human dignity have their theological origins in the creation stories of Genesis, which present the human as the climax of God's creative activity. In addition, Genesis affirms that humans are purposefully created to resemble God and that this semblance is rooted in the dominion humans have over the rest of creation.

> Then God said: Let us make human beings in our image, after our likeness. Let them have dominion over the fish of the sea, the birds of the air, the tame animals, and the wild animals, and all the creatures that crawl on the earth.
>
> > God created mankind in his image;
> > in the image of God he created them;
> > male and female he created them.
>
> God blessed them and God said to them: Be fertile and multiply; fill the earth and subdue it. Have dominion over the fish of the sea, the birds of the air, and all the living things that crawl on the earth. (Genesis 1:26–28)

The second chapter of Genesis begins the long scriptural exposé of the dimensions of human nature, explicating both the glorious and the dangerous elements of what God has bestowed on this special creature. Humans have choice and the power to guide their own destinies, but these characteristics carry with them the potential to choose foolishly and the capacity to inflict great evil.[8]

---

6. Martin A. Bertman, "The Theoretical Instability and Practical Progress of Human Rights." *International Journal of Human Rights* 8, no. 1 (Spring 2004): 99.

7. Thomas Hobbes, *Leviathan*, edited with introduction by J. C. A. Gaskin (New York: Oxford University Press, 1996), 84.

8. Oswald Bayer more fully explores the negative side of this will to create in his article, which attempts to theologically unpack the human impulse to "self-create" in the age of advanced genetic technologies. Oswald Bayer, "Self-Creation? On the Dignity of Human Beings," *Modern Theology* 20, no. 2 (April 2004): 275–90.

It is because of this frightening potential for evil that Christians believe God sent Jesus in order to redeem humanity from the grip of sinfulness. Jesus reminds his followers that every hair on their heads has been counted and that the God who cares about all living creatures cares for humans more than any other creature (Matthew 6:25–34). Jesus reinforces the notion of human dignity by taking a special interest in the poor and explicitly choosing to live, preach, and minister to the poor rather than associate with social peers and the upper classes. Many Christians believe that Jesus' preferential association with the poor highlights the truth that it is human nature and not wealth or social status that gives humans value in the eyes of God (Mark 9:33–37). This interpretation sees Jesus as opting for those who have no wealth or status because the poor represent humanity stripped of the artificial and superficial value placed on humans by social structures. The poor represent naked humanity— both literally and figuratively.

From these and other scriptural seeds springs Christian theological anthropology. When viewed from the context of the entire witness of the creative event, Christian theologians have concluded that, in a special way and unlike other creatures, "human persons are willed by God: they are imprinted with God's image."[9] Each human carries the spark of the divine, which endows persons with dignity, purpose, and grace. It also entitles every person to treatment befitting this unique status. The belief that the human is a sacred being, who uniquely represents the divine, demands a response of reverence by those who hold this belief. The same reverence is expected when a believer encounters an icon or celebrates a sacrament. Every person is deserving of reverence; treating humans as anything less than, or other than, an image of the divine is a type of desecration of this singularly sacred symbol.

Philosophical Roots of Human Dignity

Although the Bible provides a powerful witness to the Christian notion of human dignity, theology is not the only source for this fundamental moral insight. Numerous philosophers over the centuries have established their ethical systems on the foundation of the special and immeasurable value of human life. One obvious relative of human dignity theory is Immanuel Kant's categorical imperative, which he defined in his *Groundwork of the Metaphysics of Morals*. Kant bases his ethical theory on the idea that the moral justification for an action lies in whether it could be tolerated by all other rational creatures in all other conceivable settings. In other words, one has to act in

---

9. John Paul II, *Centesimus annus* (1991), *http://www.vatican.va/holy_father/john_paul_ii/ encyclicals/documents/hf_jp-ii_enc_01051991_centesimus-annus_en.html.*

such a way that the maxim of one's action could be made into a universal law of nature.[10] In his second formulation of the categorical imperative, Kant affirms that people should always treat other rational creatures as ends unto themselves and never merely as a means to an end.[11] Using precise philosophical language, Kant makes essentially the same point about the dignity of human life as the Genesis narratives, that is, "every human person has an inherent worth from the very fact that they are rational creatures."[12]

In the twentieth century, the existential philosopher Gabriel Marcel took up the cause of human dignity. Marcel distinguishes between those people who are "available," or aware of the full human presence of others, and those who are "unavailable," or not fully present to the humanity of others. The *unavailable* person reduces other people to "examples" or "cases" rather than seeing them as whole and unique individuals. In the *unavailable* state, other selves are encountered as objects—as a "He" or a "She" or even an "It."

> The other, in so far as he is other, only exists for me in so far as I am open to him [sic], in so far as he is a Thou. But I am only open to him in so far as I cease to form a circle with myself, inside which I somehow place the other, or rather his idea; for inside this circle, the other becomes the idea of the other, and the idea of the other is no longer the other *qua* other, but the other *qua* related to me. . . .[13]

Encountering the other person as a "Him" or "Her" means treating that person, not as a presence, but as absence. According to Marcel, treating the other as a "He" or "She" rather than a "Thou," renders one incapable of seeing oneself as a "Thou," and in deprecating the other, one deprecates oneself.

The *available* person, on the other hand, encounters another self in his or her full subjectivity—as a "Thou." Marcel writes, "If, on the contrary, I treat the other as 'Thou', I treat him [sic] and apprehend him *qua* freedom. I apprehend him *qua* freedom because he *is* also freedom and not only nature."[14] This *available* person "cannot think in terms of *cases*; in its eyes there are no cases at

---

10. Immanuel Kant, *Groundwork for the Metaphysics of Morals*, ed. Lara Denis (Toronto, ON: Broadview Press, 2005), 81.

11. Ibid., 87. "Now I say: the human being and in general every rational being exists as an end unto itself, not merely as a means to be arbitrarily used by this or that will, but in all his actions, whether they concern himself or other rational beings, must be always regarded at the same time as an end."

12. Paul Borowski, "Manager-Employee Relationships: Informed by Kant's Categorical Imperative or Dilbert's Business Principle," *Journal of Business Ethics* 17 (15) (November 1998): 1626–27.

13. Gabriel Marcel, *Being and Having*, Trans. Katharine Farrer. (Westminster, UK: Dacre Press, 1949), 107.

14. Ibid., 106–107.

all."[15] Persons who are *available* to others have an entirely different experience of their place in the world in that they acknowledge their interdependence with other people. Relationships between *available* people are characterized by presence rather than absence; in the communication and communion between persons, they somehow transcend the physical gulf between them without merging into an amalgam of some kind. According to Marcel, "It should be obvious at once that a being of this sort is not an autonomous whole, is not in [the] expressive English phrase, self-contained; on the contrary such a being is open and exposed, as unlike as can be to a compact impenetrable mass."[16] To be *available* to the other is to be present to and for the other, to put one's resources at the other's disposal, and to be an open and permeable character. In the words of Catholic social teaching (CST), Marcel's *available* person recognizes the human dignity of others.

Human Dignity in Catholic Social Teaching

Catholic social teaching develops the philosophical and theological perspectives on human dignity together. Because of the historical circumstances within which these documents were drafted, the theory of human dignity was developed in relation to philosophical concepts about the dignity of human labor. The earliest documents of this tradition develop the theology of the *imago dei*[17] (image of God) in the context of neo-Thomistic natural law philosophy.[18] Humans not only are iconic representations of the divine, but also their work is analogous to God's creative activity. When a person mixes his or her labor with raw physical material to create a product, then "on it he leaves impressed, as it were, a kind of image of his person" (*Rerum novarum*, no. 15). Thomistic philosophy establishes personal ownership of property either through "occupancy" or by means of labor. Using this philosophical foundation, the Church claimed that dispossessed laborers, like early industrial factory workers, had been robbed of their dignity precisely because they did not enjoy the full fruits of their labor. CST affirmed that the role of the government consisted in

---

15. Gabriel Marcel, *The Philosophy of Existentialism*, Trans. Manya Harari (New York: Carol Publishing Group, 1995), 41.

16. Gabriel Marcel, *The Mystery of Being*, vol.1, *Reflection and Mystery*, Trans. G. S. Fraser (London: The Harvill Press, 1951), 145.

17. *Imago dei*, is a Latin phrase that can be found in a passage in the book of Genesis in which God creates humans in the image of the divine. It is used to highlight the belief that humans stand out as exceptional elements in the created world. This exceptional status is the foundation for treating all humans, no matter their social standing, as equal and uniquely valuable in the eyes of the Divine Creator.

18. Neo-Thomism, a distilled version of Thomas Aquinas's philosophy, was developed by the Catholic Church in order to make Aquinas's thought accessible to people with ordinary intelligence. This simplified Thomism was used to train and prepare clergy after the Council of Trent in 1565.

restoring the rights and property of the laborer without negating the property rights of the owner of capital.

Nowhere is the union of the philosophical and theological perspectives on human dignity clearer than in the social encyclicals of Pope John Paul II. In the 1981 encyclical *Laborem exercens* (On Human Work), John Paul II combines traditional creation theology with the personalist philosophy of Max Scheler, which informed his own teaching and writing as a professor of moral theology and social ethics.[19] The encyclical is an extended theological and philosophical reflection on what he calls the objective and subjective meaning of work. For John Paul II, work attains its fullest meaning not in its objective sense, that is, not in the work done and the products produced, but rather in the subjective sense, that is, in the persons who do the work and the humanization that results from the doing of the work. "As *a person, man is therefore the subject of work.* As a person he works, he performs various actions belonging to the work process; independently of their objective content, these actions must all serve to realize his humanity, to fulfill the calling to be a person that is his by reason of his very humanity" (*LE*, no. 6).

Modern Applications to the Business Setting: Emerging Technological Challenges to Human Dignity

In his article, "Why the Future Doesn't Need Us," Bill Joy, computer guru and cofounder of Sun Microsystems, takes on futurists who imagine only utopian results from the ongoing development of certain powerful technologies. Joy sees just the opposite. He fears these technologies could just as easily lead to a dystopian or even disastrous future.[20] He claims that the power of emerging technologies has the potential to be exponentially more lethal than any technology humanity has encountered before—even nuclear energy. Joy fears that certain emerging technologies present humankind with a Pandora's box brimming with temptations that could lead to dire consequences in spite of the best of intentions. After spelling out in detail the various ways that robotics, nanotechnology, and genetics could doom humanity, Joy concludes that technologists and the businesses that produce cutting-edge products must embrace an ethic of relinquishment, refusing to pursue certain lines of inquiry because these have the potential to inflict such enormous harm.

---

19. See the official biography of Pope John Paul II at the Vatican website, *http://www. vatican.va/news_services/press/documentazione/documents/santopadre_biografie/giovanni_ paolo_ii_biografia_prepontificato_en.html.*

20. Bill Joy, "Why the Future Doesn't Need Us," *Wired* 8.04 (April 2000), *http://www.wired.com/ wired/archive/8.04/joy.html.*

Many people found Joy's "new Luddite"[21] reasoning compelling. He was, after all, the last person one would expect to propose that businesses and engineers freeze development on some of the most promising technological advances. If one of the world's leading names in technology speaks out against the trajectory of this industry, then the rest of the less technically inclined population had better sit up and take notice. Indeed there are dangerous technologies that have the potential to destroy and even obliterate, but some technologies go even further toward eclipsing existing notions of human dignity, even when they do no physical harm.

For some, something about Joy's recommendation to relinquish technological development did not seem right from either a moral or a philosophical perspective. First, relinquishment as a strategy runs headlong into the essential curiosity of human nature. Resisting the impulse to know and investigate does not seem to be a drive that can be repressed indefinitely. Repressing this impulse also raises the question of how to impose and police this ethic globally across an immense geographical expanse as well as the myriad of cultures that might not accept its logic. More importantly, would an ethic of relinquishment harm the contemporary understanding of human agency[22] and, in turn, ideas about human dignity? Relinquishment seems to assume ubiquitous incompetence or, even worse, a tendency toward evil in human nature. Is humanity such a blundering horde? Is it so inclined toward its own destruction? Does humanity not trust itself with this powerfully important task?

In the end, Joy's thesis seems to be informed by some of the same concerns voiced by the original Luddites—that humans are meddling in matters beyond their limited understanding and metaphorically "playing God."[23] What John Caiazza calls "techno-secularism," which includes "an ethical vision that focuses on healthful living, self-fulfillment, and avoiding the struggles of human life and the inevitability of death," also informs Joy's perspective.[24]

---

21. The original Luddites were factory workers in early nineteenth-century Britain who demonstrated their opposition to being displaced by new industrial machinery by attacking the factories and destroying the machines. Since that brief outburst of violence, the term *Luddite* has been used to describe anyone who reflexively opposes new technologies, especially those who raise fears that the new technology will destroy a way of life and usher in a dystopia of one sort or another.

22. Human agency is important here because Joy's argument might lead one to conclude that humans cannot be trusted to behave in ways that will result in human flourishing. An ethic of relinquishment could be used to conclude that humans do not have the capacity to be responsible for their own destiny—this would constitute an abandonment of the idea of human agency and that humans should have control of their own future.

23. For a more thorough critique of this perspective see Cynthia S. W. Crysdale, "Playing God? Moral Agency in an Emergent World," *Journal of the Society of Christian Ethics* 23, no. 2 (June 2003): 243–259.

24. John C. Caiazza, "Athens, Jerusalem, and the arrival of techno-secularism," *Zygon* 40, no. 1 (March 2005): 9.

It attempts to supplant the abstract, reflective, and noninstrumental answers offered by the more reflective disciplines of science,[25] philosophy, and religion with the magical mindset of the technological fix or, from Joy's perspective, the technological disaster. Whether one envisions technological utopia or dystopia, the theory informing those conclusions remains the same: technology magically transforms the world, leaving humans either blissfully happy or facing miserable decay in its wake.

Science, philosophy, and religion tend to be critical of the totalistic claims of techno-secularism.[26] The common assumption that improvements in wealth and technology inexorably lead to better, happier lives has been questioned by philosophy and religion for eons. Now the sciences are providing polling data that supports these less empirical assertions[27] and calling into question the assumption on the part of futurists that advances in technology could lead to some prospective Eden or, for that matter, a destiny marked only by perdition and anguish. The reflective disciplines recognize that happiness is a complex human condition and that the excitement induced by technological advances simply proves too fleeting to deliver on the promise of true and lasting satisfaction. Religion and philosophy have long held that happiness can be found in a life well lived, which often has more to do with establishing and nurturing right relationships than access to wealth or technology. As Barbara Strassberg points out in her essay, "Magic, Religion, Science, Technology, and Ethics in the Postmodern World," technology will have an important, but not a solitary, or singularly deterministic role to play in the way human society shapes its future.[28]

Moral dilemmas abound in the production and application of modern technologies, and some technological fields do not seem to offer a clear-cut ethical path forward. Like Joy's article, the following section of this chapter will examine three broad technological categories, evaluating their trajectories according to the standards set by the ideal of human dignity. It will assess challenges and threats to key aspects of human dignity theory and explore possible alternative

---

25. Science is included among the group of reflective disciplines because of the increasingly abstract nature of some of the inquiries of scientific theoreticians. For a more complete discussion of the increasingly close relationship between these two odd bedfellows, see Ervin Laszlo, "Why I Believe in Science and Believe in God: A Credo," *Zygon* 39, no. 3 (September 2004): 535–539.

26. For a more detailed discussion of the dangers of technological and cybernetic totalism, see Michael W. DeLashmutt, "A Better Life Through Information Technology? The Techno-Theological Eschatology of Posthuman Speculative Science," *Zygon: Journal of Religion and Science* 41, no. 2 (June 2006): 267–87.

27. James Surowiecki, "Technology and Happiness," *Technology Review* 108, no. 1 (January 2005): 72–76. *Computers & Applied Sciences Complete, http//www. ebscohost.com.*

28. Barbara A. Strassberg, "Magic, Religion, Science, Technology, and Ethics in the Postmodern World," *Zygon: Journal of Religion and Science* 40, no. 2 (2005): 307–32.

trajectories. Each case will entertain future possibilities, hopefully without getting caught in the trap of either utopian or dystopian thinking. Balance will be maintained by recalling that the future of humanity will likely be as thoroughly and richly human as its past and, therefore, determined by more than merely the development of new technologies.

Biotechnology

In effect, humanity is damned if it goes ahead with the production and use of a technology and yet also damned if it follows Bill Joy's recommendation and relinquishes development of it altogether. Nowhere is this truer than in the flourishing field of biotechnology, with its constantly changing borders between life and death, its ever-increasing capacity to alter the quality of life through genetic manipulations, and now even its capacity to create new life forms as the understanding of these sciences progresses.[29] Each of these technological trajectories confronts ethicists with a definition of human nature that is far more protean than the one they are used to endorsing and defending. This, in turn, makes applying human dignity theory to cases involving the latest biotechnology advances more problematic.

In her article, "Created Co-creator and the Practice of Medicine," Ann Pederson states, "at both the beginning and end of life, new technologies are changing the way we define life and death."[30] Here she refers to a constellation of technologies applied earlier and earlier in the lives of children, and later and later in the lives of seniors, in order to extend and preserve life. For instance, artificial womb technologies,[31] among many other advances in neonatal care, preserve the lives of children who, not so long ago, would have certainly faced death or disability due to premature birth. While the preservation of life seems morally unproblematic, the application of these technologies has raised many unanticipated issues. On a number of occasions, for example, these technologies have helped to save the life of a child born to a drug-addicted mother, who subsequently abandons the child. According to Renee Denise Boss in the *Journal of Palliative Medicine:*

---

29. Modern biotechnology also raises the issues of the affordability of health care in the United States and how the financially exclusive system of distribution is, in itself, an affront to human dignity. For a more lengthy discussion of these issues, see R. McDougall, "A Resource-Based Version of the Argument That Cloning Is an Affront to Human Dignity," *Journal of Medical Ethics* 34, no. 4 (April 2008): 259–261.

30. Ann Pederson, "Created Co-Creator and the Practice of Medicine," *Zygon: Journal of Religion and Science* 39, no. 4 (2005): 801.

31. Frida Simonstein, "Artificial Reproduction Technologies (RTs)—All the Way to the Artificial Womb?," *Medicine, Health Care and Philosophy: A European Journal* 9, no. 3 (2006): 359–365.

Decisions to limit life-sustaining therapies for neonates are regularly made together by parents and physicians who agree that the predicted quality of life is extremely poor. Why then, when parents abandon a baby whose quality of life is also predictably grim, are those in charge unable to make decisions to limit that infant's suffering? [32]

Another example is the dilemma created by the excess embryos produced when infertile couples use *in vitro* technologies. Although the gift of life given in these cases to otherwise barren couples again seems morally laudable, embryos produced by this method will most likely be stored in a freezer until they become unviable. [33] What is the status of those lives and what is the moral value of a procedure that produces so much of this kind of waste? [34] If the end result is death after a decade in the deep freeze, then is it ethically acceptable to use these embryos in scientific experiments or to harvest stem cells from these otherwise doomed embryos? More importantly, these cases present an affront to human dignity no matter what course of action is taken, whether that consists of indefinite storage, destruction, or experimentation.

Just as thorny as the technologies applied at the beginning of life are those applied at the end of life in order to extend, preserve, or enhance the quality of life for individuals who, in another age, would have already died. One cluster of technologies receiving a great deal of attention recently has been artificial life systems, like feeding tubes, and artificial lungs, hearts, kidneys, and other vital organs. Biomedical technology has rapidly become adept at keeping the physical body alive—so rapidly, in fact, that it has occasionally outstripped the human capacity to reflect on its obvious consequences. New classifications have appeared in the literature in order to account for these newfound powers. Terms such as *brain dead* and *persistent vegetative state* now join the old medical standbys such as *coma* and *unconscious*, in order to help determine the right path to take when confronted with an unresponsive, but ostensibly alive, body. [35] When people say that they value life, what sort of "life" does that mean? Does a body with functioning organs qualify as human life? As the

---

32. Renee Denise Boss, "End-of-Life Decision-Making for Infants Abandoned in the Neonatal Intensive Care Unit," *Journal of Palliative Medicine* 11, no. 1 (2008): 109–11.

33. Marcia Clemmitt, "Couples Reluctant to Abandon Their Frozen Embryos," *CQ Researcher* 16, no. 2 (2006): 710.

34. For a more extended discussion of this issue, see Giuseppe Benagiano and Maurizio Mori, "Evolution of Thinking of the Catholic Church on the Beginning of Human Life," *Reproductive BioMedicine Online* 14 (2007): 162–68.

35. For more background on the historical evolution of this medical terminology, see N. D. Zasler, "Terminology in Evolution: Caveats, Conundrums and Controversies," *NeuroRehabilitation* 19, no. 4 (December 2004): 285–92.

capacity to preserve and extend organ function continues to improve, won't the number of people preserved in these states of suspended animation increase? Will there be a day when society warehouses the living dead? Is that the same as valuing life?

Valuing life, or at least a certain quality of life, is the promise offered by the latest genetic therapies. Most genetic manipulation is presently geared toward preventing and correcting inherited diseases and syndromes in order to improve the quality of life.[36] Again, it is rather difficult to find anything morally suspect about this kind of technological intervention. However, some applications of genetic science pursue the more controversial goal of "enhancing" and "improving" the personal traits of individuals who fall within the normal limits of human functioning.[37] This kind of genetic manipulation raises many questions, especially when such modifications are made to the germ line; and they become more than simply alterations for that particular individual, but traits inheritable by subsequent generations.[38]

Given the embryonic stage of development of this science, society is not at the point of confronting actual cases, and scientists assert that it will be decades before such questions need to be answered. Nevertheless, many talented and well-funded technologists are pursuing technologies that will allow individuals to live longer, run faster, jump higher, be smarter, be musically gifted, and so on.[39] Even if only a few of these projects ever come to full fruition, humanity will confront a flood of ethical concerns. For instance, who gets access to these technologies?[40] Right now the vast majority of technologists working on these projects work for companies interested in making money off of these long-term ventures, which suggests that access to these genetic modifications will be limited to those who can afford to pay. Is it possible then, that in the future a group of wealthy families will launch a branch of humanity that is qualitatively different from the rest of the population?[41] Even worse, is it possible that in this same future humanity will also face real genetic

---

36. James S. Larson, "Medicine, Government, and the Human Genome," *Journal of Health & Human Services Administration* 24, no. 3/4 (Winter2001/Spring2002): 323–25.

37. Elizabeth Fenton, 2008. "Genetic Enhancement—A Threat to Human Rights?" *Bioethics* 22, no. 1 (January 2008): 1.

38. David Heyd, "Human Nature: An Oxymoron?" *Journal of Medicine & Philosophy* 28, no. 2 (April 2003): 166.

39. Fenton, 7.

40. Dov Fox, "Luck, Genes, and Equality," *Journal of Law, Medicine & Ethics* 35, no. 4 (December 2007): 712–726.

41. For a lengthier discussion of these issues, see the *Tikkun* interview with Michael Sandel, "The Problem with Genetic Engineering," *Tikkun* 22, no. 5 (September 2007): 40–85. Academic Search Premier, *http//www. ebscohost.com.*

discrimination against disabled individuals or even against those who simply do not possess extraordinary engineered traits?[42]

This rapidly increasing capacity to produce, preserve, extend, clone, and manipulate human life raises questions about the very concept of the unique and mysterious gift of individual human existence. In his article "Genetic Frontiers: Challenges for Humanity and Our Religious Traditions," Philip Hefner points out that "the most critical challenge is to our understanding of human nature and values."[43] The degree to which humans can choose the beginning and end of life, as well as desirable traits for themselves and their children, will in large part determine the extent to which they conceive of human life as a product rather than a gift.[44] The ability to choose life or death and even which desirable traits to keep and which undesirable anomalies to delete as is done for avatars in online gaming platforms, ontologically transforms the human from a mysterious subject of infinite worth into a manipulable consumer item of definite and marketable value. The question becomes how to prevent this devolution of human dignity and recover a sense of the "priceless" quality of human life[45] given the trajectories of current technological development.

Cybernetics and Robotics

Today the success of knee replacement surgery depends in no small part on advances in cybernetic and robotic technologies. Because of these advances, those who undergo this surgery can expect to feel up to almost any task at the end of recuperation. However, a mere twenty years ago the prognosis for the full recovery of knee function would have been much less certain; and only forty years ago, a person would face the prospect of spending retirement years hobbling around with a painful, gimpy joint. Such is the pace of advancement in reverse-engineering the human body using nonbiological materials.

---

42. Karen Eltis, "Genetic Determinism and Discrimination: A Call to Re-Orient Prevailing Human Rights Discourse to Better Comport with the Public Implications of Individual Genetic Testing," *Journal of Law, Medicine & Ethics* 35, no. 2 (Summer 2007): 282–83.

43. Philip Hefner, 2007. "Genetic Frontiers: Challenges For Humanity and Our Religious Traditions," *Zygon: Journal of Religion & Science* 42, no. 1: 183.

44. Relying on the founding secular philosophical traditions that inspired the US Constitution, Robert George makes more or less the same point in his short articles in the journal *Social Research*. Robert P. George, "Ethics, Politics, and Genetic Knowledge," *Social Research* 73, no. 3 (Fall 2006): 1029–1032.

45. Maureen Junker-Kenny, "Valuing the Priceless: Christian Convictions in Public Debate as a Critical Resource and as 'Delaying Veto' (J. Habermas)," *Studies in Christian Ethics* 18, no. 1 (April 2005): 55.

Once again, many rightfully feel grateful for these kinds of technologies and ask what could possibly be ethically problematic with pursuits that yield so many wonderful benefits. However, robotics and, to a greater extent, cybernetics raise questions about blurring the distinction between human and machine.[46] Replacing more and more of the given biological self with chosen, nonbiological parts threatens the concept of human nature and, therefore, of human dignity. These issues become logarithmically more convoluted when the discussion focuses on replacing the human brain by transferring the scanned contents of consciousness to software that can be loaded into a computer.[47] In these cases, technology and techno-futurists challenge the meaning of the term *human*, begging the question, "At what point does the term *human* no longer accurately describe these cybernetic creations?"[48]

Returning to the example of a person with a brand-new knee, probably no one would question her humanity after her operation; there would be little or no superficial evidence that something fundamental had changed. Even if she had multiple joints and organs replaced, most would not struggle to identify her core humanity. In fact, the technologies used in these cases are designed to fool people into thinking the new mechanical parts are no different than the originals. But what if her biological brain was replaced? And what if, years down the road, obvious problems with the "brain" changed her behavior in public and she had to be taken in for a software reboot? Is the person still a human in this instance— or is this just an illusion? Does the person have a mind, or is "he" or "she" just a very clever software program?

The founding belief of most cybernetic endeavors is that humans will eventually be able to construct a better version of themselves—a faster, stronger, smarter, and, therefore, happier version. For Christians, this scenario raises theological questions about God because it relegates God to the role of the maker of an inferior product. In essence, human ingenuity surpasses the divine. In so doing, it poses the conundrum of the created surpassing the creator, thereby negating the very notion of a superior being. It also raises questions about the dignity of human nature similar to those raised by genetic engineering.[49] If science can engineer humans, either genetically or mechanically, then the value of the human lies not in the human *qua* human, but in the excellence of scientific technique and the number and quality of features

---

46. For a discussion of this issue from the perspective of someone who does not think cybernetics necessarily results in this sort of blurred moral vision, see Henk G. Geertsema, "Cyborg: Myth or Reality?" *Zygon: Journal of Religion & Science* 41, no. 2 (2006): 289–328.

47. Christof Kochand and Guilo Tononi, "Can Machines Be Conscious?" *IEEE Spectrum* 45, no. 6 (2008): 55–59.

48. Raymond Kurzweil, *The Age of Spiritual Machines* (New York: Penguin Putnam Inc., 1999).

49. See Bayer, 286–287.

that one possesses.[50] Cybernetics must face the question, "How does humanity avoid the commodification of itself and, therefore, the demotion of its own nature as it progresses further and further down the road toward its technological future?"

Environmental Impact

So far this chapter has focused on the intended consequences of actual or proposed technologies. In this last section, the focus shifts to the unintended consequences of technological advance—environmental destruction. Most of the technologies used on a daily basis are highly beneficial, and many people would find it hard to imagine a world without these conveniences. However, each of these technologies comes at a cost to the ecosystem. Aggregating these relatively small costs for an ever-increasing population of billions of people leads to concerns. For example, I am very conscious of my own energy consumption, yet I know that this is not sustainable over the long haul.[51] The gas heat I enjoy in the winter, the air conditioning I use sparingly in the summer, the electricity generated in a nuclear plant, the computer I use to write this chapter, and even the bike I use to commute, all depend, to varying extents, on a model of energy use and resource consumption that can be sustained for only a few more decades.[52]

Virtually every imaginable technology has some environmental impact that, if multiplied exponentially over the entire human population, could have potentially grave consequences for life on the planet. Twenty years ago, the environmental movement regularly pointed out that Earth could not support "another America," suggesting that if the peoples of the undeveloped world began to mimic the production and consumption patterns of people in Europe and North America, then the planet was doomed. Per capita energy use and pollution rates were such that Americans were destroying the planet at a pace many times that of the average citizen in the developing world. Today, however, one rarely hears this phrase anymore because reality has quickly caught up to the direst prognostications. During this twenty-year period, China alone has produced tens of millions of new middle-class consumers, and some economists project that by 2015 China will have more than 300 million citizens

---

50. Some philosophers in what is being termed the post-humanist school of thinking believe that it is necessary to begin imagining the dignity of the cybernetic person. In this way, they are speaking of a kind of post-human dignity. Nick Bostrom, "In Defense of Posthuman Dignity," *Bioethics* 19, no. 3 (June 2005): 212–214.

51. Mathis Wackernagel et al., "Tracking the Ecological Overshoot of the Human Economy," *Proceedings of the National Academy of Sciences* 99 (14), 9266–9271.

52. Some would claim that there are already signs that humanity has reached such limits. For just one example see Moises Velasquez-Manoff, "Diet for a More-Crowded Planet: Plants," *Christian Science Monitor* 100, no. 162 (July 16, 2008): 14.

living according to the standards of the Western middle class.[53] Whether Earth could support another America, it now is, due to the ever expanding global population growth and the massive expansion of the middle class, especially in China and India.

Fortunately, there appears to be growing awareness of the impact of humans on the environment, and a small but significant minority realizes that it might have dire near-term consequences. The question, from the perspective of CST, is how this awareness might challenge the traditional notions of human dignity. First, are humans really distinct from the rest of creation given the growing realization of radical dependence on the symbiotic web of relationships called nature? Second, given their destructive potential, are humans really the crowning achievement of this creation? Third, how can the species that has caused so much environmental degradation be understood as the stewards of this same Earth?

For reasons noted previously, contemporary ecotheology challenges traditional notions of human dignity, especially aspects of the tradition that stress human moral exceptionalism—the notion that humans have a unique moral value in comparison to all other creatures. Frequently, this challenge is only implied; the radical novelty of ecotheology's ideas about humanity and its relationship to the rest of creation is rarely explored in depth. Most ecotheologians recognize the inadequacies of traditional Catholic/Christian anthropologies in relation to the epic environmental challenges the planet faces. However, many of those same theologians, in the next instant, recall the tremendous value of these same traditional notions, which have been the source and sustaining inspiration for many of the most noble and progressive movements of the last few centuries.

The question confronting Christians then is whether this is an either/or dilemma: do humans either choose traditional conceptions of human dignity—and in so doing risk sacrificing life as we know it on this planet—or choose novel conceptions of human moral equivalency and risk undermining the moral and legal underpinnings of most of the Western religious and civil tradition?

Addressing this question requires identifying models of Christian ecotheology and examining the definition of humanity that emerges from each.[54] Five major categories of ecotheology emerge: traditional anthropocentrism, stewardship anthropocentrism, eco-justice, ecocentric deep ecology, and meta-ethical value theory. Traditional anthropocentrism, familiar to anyone conversant in traditional Christian moral doctrine, makes strict distinctions between the

53. Peter Ford, "Consumer tidal wave on the way: China's middle class. (Cover story)," *Christian Science Monitor* 99, no. 25 (2007): 1–12.

54. There are many examples of other categorizations of ecotheology, such as Laurel Kearns, "Saving the Creation: Christian Environmentalism in the United States," *Sociology of Religion* 57, no. 1 (1996): 55–70, and Raymond E. Grizzle and Christopher B. Barrett, "The One Body of Christian Environmentalism," *Zygon* 33, no. 2 (June 1998): 233–253.

inestimable, intrinsic value of human life and the calculable, extrinsic value assigned to the rest of creation. It casts God as a monarch, or a feudal lord, and, therefore, subjugating the rest of creation. Humans are understood as subjects of the royal divinity whose duty is to respect and obey the will of God.

Stewardship anthropocentrism maintains the distinction between human life and the rest of creation to some degree but places greater moral weight on the value of nonhuman creatures than traditional anthropocentrism.[55] This perspective falls short of equating the value of human life with the value of the rest of creation; however, it does advance Christian theology toward a more inclusive value theory that takes the natural world into account.

Eco-justice levels the ethical playing field between humans and the rest of creation. It transfers moral notions usually reserved for discussions of human social ethics—such as fairness, equity, and justice—and applies these to human behavior toward nature.[56] The moral equivalency of this perspective can be seen in its advocacy for radical action on the part of human society to reform its unjust and oppressive relationship with the rest of the created order.

Ecocentric deep ecology turns the discussion away from a human-centered focus and attempts to reconfigure the moral universe by focusing on the symbiotic interrelatedness of nature. Goodness is that which contributes to the flourishing of the ecosystem.[57] Humans fade into the background of this philosophical landscape as a thoroughly integral part of a much wider web of life and existence.

Meta-ethical value theory radicalizes the ecocentric viewpoint in that it affirms the primacy of symbiotic interrelatedness but uses a more microscopic lens in its approach to nature. Often referred to as an "ethic of place," it claims that the starting point for any genuine ecotheology must be one's local and immediate encounter with nature.[58]

---

55. Good examples of this model are David J. Bryant, "*Imago Dei,* Imagination, and Ecological Responsibility," *Theology Today* 57, no. 1 (April 2000): 35–50, and Judith N. Scoville, "Fitting Ethics to the Land: H. Richard Niebuhr's Ethic of Responsibility and Ecotheology," *Journal of Religious Ethics* 30, no. 2 (Summer 2002): 207–229.

56. Larry Rasmussen has done the most work in this category with books such as *Earth Community, Earth Ethics* (Maryknoll, NY: Orbis Books, 1996) and articles such as, "Is Eco-Justice Central to Christian Faith?" *Union Seminary Quarterly Review* 54, no. 3–4 (2000): 107–124. Other examples include John B. Cobb Jr., *Sustainability: Economics, Ecology, and Justice* (Maryknoll, NY: Orbis Books, 1992) and Rosemary Radford Ruether, *Gaia and God: An Ecofeminist Theology of Earth Healing* (San Francisco, CA: Harper Collins, 1992).

57. Examples of this perspective include the theology of Thomas Berry and his disciples. Thomas Berry, *The Dream of the Earth* (San Francisco, CA: Sierra Club Books, 2006). Another good example is Jan Deckers, "Christianity and Ecological Ethics: The Significance of Process Thought and a Pan-experientialist Critique of Strong Anthropocentrism," *Ecotheology* 9, no. 3 (2004): 359–387.

58. Excellent examples of this type of ecotheology are Kirkpatrick Sale, *Dwellers in the Land: The Bioregional Vision* (San Francisco, CA: Sierra Club Books, 1985) and Douglas Burton-Christie, "The Spirit of Place: The Columbia River Watershed Letter and the Meaning of Community," *Horizons* 30, no. 1 (Winter 2003): 7–24.

Models of Christian Ecotheology

	Traditional Anthropo-centrism	Stewardship Anthropo-centrism	Eco-Justice	Eco-centric Deep Ecology	Meta-ethical Value of Place
Locus of Value	Human life has intrinsic value; nature has extrinsic value.	All creation has some intrinsic value; humans possess ultimate intrinsic value.	All creation has equal intrinsic value; there are no privileged species.	All creation as a constantly changing process has equal intrinsic value; differentiation and individuation are illusory.	The idea of intrinsic value only makes sense in a local, immediate context.
Ethical Relationship	Entirely one sided	Humans have greatest value although some reciprocity is implied.	Equality implied by the negation of privilege	Interdependence and reciprocity are central.	Restoration and reparation of sundered relationships
Human Mission	Humans should wisely use nature to achieve their goals.	Humans should manage the complex human/natural relationship so that all thrive.	Humans should overturn and radically reform their destructive and oppressive structures.	Humans need to rediscover their place within the symbiotic relationships of nature.	Humans need to encounter nature immediately both within themselves and in their ecological setting.
God	Feudal Lord	Benevolent CEO	Liberator	Panentheism	Animating Spirit
Jesus/Christ	Obedient Son of the feudal lord who sacrifices himself for all people	Agent or representative of the benevolent CEO who is sent as a teacher and exemplar	Agent or representative of the liberating God who fights oppressions and suffers the consequences	All humans are sons and daughters of God.	Spirit Guide
Sacrament	Nature is a mere instrument.	Nature is a valued instrument.	Nature reveals God's liberatory identity.	Nature is sacrament as nature reveals God.	Nature is sacrament as nature is animated by Spirit.
Church	Institution—Bride of Christ	People of God—Pilgrim People	Church of the Poor—Community of the Oppressed	Community of Creation	Communion with local ecosystem

This rather strict categorization of Christian ecotheology does not make clear the extent to which some ecotheologians have shifted freely between perspectives, and how most of them have done so unconsciously. Many authors have worked with multiple images of God, who could be a crusading liberator in one context and a few pages later be portrayed in very sterile, abstract, and transcendent terms as the animating principle undergirding the process of universal becoming. On the one hand, this fluidity of categories certainly leads to creativity and avoids the pitfall of theoretical notions becoming ossified or conceptually trapped.

However, these various theological models do not necessarily coexist peacefully, and some actually contradict the basic tenets of others. To talk in one context about God as a benevolent CEO who will ultimately guide humanity to eco-utopia does not always mesh well with the image of the church as a community of the oppressed in the next. Theoretical inconsistencies have the potential to lead to creative new insights, which is especially true when the authors are aware of them. However, more often, theoretical inconsistencies yield nonsensical theologies and lead to confusion, so it is important to have a clear map of the theoretical landscape.

Each of the ecotheological categories assumes a certain kind of natural order, which in turn presumes a place for human life in the cosmos.[59] The question is whether to endorse this vision and whether humans would even recognize themselves through this theoretical lens. Is there a privileged, special, or even identifiably distinct place for human existence in a realized ecotheological utopia? Is human dignity recognizably and qualitatively different from the dignity of other creatures, or is the difference only one of kind and not character? Does ecotheology demand a radical reconfiguration of the entire corpus of traditional Christian theology, or can remnants of that tradition inform and guide the way into an eco-friendly future?

One of the major unintended consequences emerging from humanity's awakening to its own toxic impact on the environment has been a thoroughgoing rethinking of philosophical anthropology. The longstanding notion that humans are qualitatively distinct from, and superior to, other creatures has been fundamentally challenged by an awareness of humanity's environmental sins, as well as a deepening scientific understanding of humans and their relationship to the vast web of life on Earth. More and more, it is becoming clear that only a deep ecological consciousness can rein in this destructive technological

---

59. These categories have been gleaned from various sources in ecotheology and from conversations with others working in environmental theology. Significant insight into these categories came from conversations with my colleague Kay Read, who has visually mapped human attitudes toward the natural world and come up with her own scheme of eight categories. Also, recognition is due to Willis Jenkins of Yale University since during his talk at the Annual Meeting of the Society of Christian Ethics in January of 2009 the inspiration and outline for these categories finally congealed.

trajectory. The idea that humanity is essentially distinct from the rest of creation and can use and consume the whole of creation as it sees fit[60] seems to be giving way to recognition that humans are creation, and it is they.[61] Therefore, its use and consumption are no longer morally neutral, and an ethic of the subjectivity of creation is beginning to worm its way into the ethical consciousness of the major religions.

Conclusion

Traditional Western notions of human dignity, which undergird much of contemporary social and political theories about the value and status of the individual person, are being challenged by the development of certain cutting-edge technologies that stretch the boundaries of established concepts of humanity. Some of these technologies affect the way the human is conceived and raise questions about the repercussions these changes might have on notions of human rights in the near future. Advances in the high-tech industries of biotechnology, cybernetics, and environmental science pose threats to Western ideas about human dignity as well as offer opportunities to re-vision the human in novel and more inclusive ways. In the end, one can respond to these challenges by retreating to the safe confines of current conceptions of human dignity or by seeing them as an invitation to open dialogue with new technologies in order to discover weaknesses and inadequacies in the traditional philosophical anthropologies so they can be exposed, updated, and corrected. Only then can these important concepts once again play their prophetic and humanizing role in society.

This is not the first time in history that ideas of human dignity have been challenged. Historical periods of disease, pestilence, famine, and natural disaster have all raised questions about the notion that humans possess a unique status, granted to them in the moral universe by a loving and powerful God. Social institutions like slavery and hierarchical social systems like royalty likewise compromised the belief in human dignity among recent ancestors. Certainly the Enlightenment stands out as one of the many historical moments when political, economic, and philosophical ideas about the individual had a profound impact on how Western culture understood the human and the way each individual ought to relate to the common good. The scientific discoveries of this

---

60. "There is a growing awareness of the sublime dignity of human persons, who stand above all things and whose rights and duties are universal and inviolable." *Gaudium et spes*, no. 27.

61. "People will recognize the inherent value of creation and the dignity of all living beings as creatures of God." Catholic Bishops of the Pacific Northwest and Canada, "The Columbia River Watershed," p. 14, *http://www.thewscc.org/images/stories/Resources/Statements/colrvr-e.pdf.*

same period, especially Galileo's rejection of a geocentric view of the universe, rocked Western notions of human exceptionalism and the widespread belief that the Earth was God's lonely little laboratory.

In the present moment, marked by a fascination with technological prowess, humanity faces a challenge similar to those encountered in other periods of human history. Because of rapidly advancing technology and its effect on humans and all other living creatures on the planet, traditional conceptions of human nature are no longer adequate and require reformation. Human dignity as an ethical formulation has been a reliable and inspirational tool for philosophers, religious leaders, policy makers, educators, and average citizens from a wide variety of cultures throughout the ages. It is an ethic worth preserving, but it cannot be preserved in amber. Like all other traditional philosophical and religious ideas, it will become dusty and useless if it is locked away like a museum piece. Human dignity theorists have to be willing to enter these dangerous dialogues and allow these precious ethical gems to be dynamically restored in the process.

Case Study

Designer Babies: The Fertility Institutes

A newlywed couple, madly in love, decides to conceive a child, but instead of turning out the lights and leaping into bed, they drive to the nearest fertility clinic for a genetic consultation. At the clinic, they are examined and tested. Eggs and sperm are taken from the prospective parents, who are then given a long form with a menu of checkboxes and asked to choose the various features they would like their child to have. Sound like a joke or a deleted scene from a sci-fi movie? Well this futuristic scenario is much closer than most people imagine. As Dr. Mark Hughes, the Director of the Genesis Genetics Institute, a large fertility laboratory in Detroit, and a pioneer of preimplantation genetic diagnosis (PGD), claims, "It's technically feasible and it can be done."[62]

Dr. Hughes goes on to say that no legitimate lab would offer such services because the scientific community would immediately ostracize it. However, assurances such as these offer cold comfort in a context in which one clinic, the Fertility Institutes in Los Angeles, has already flirted with offering its clients the ability to choose more than just the gender of their children.

(continued)

---

62. Gautam Naik, "A Baby, Please, Blond Freckles—Hold the Colic," *Wall Street Journal* (February 12, 2009), *http://www.online.wsj.com/article/SB123439771603075099.html.*

Case Study

Dr. Jeffrey Steinberg, a leading figure in the field of *in vitro* fertilization, runs the clinic. He is convinced that "we not bury our heads in the sand and pretend these advances are not happening."[63] Dr. Steinberg and his colleagues claim that they can predict certain characteristics, such as eye color, hair color, and complexion, with 80 percent accuracy. They also feel certain that this is just the tip of the iceberg and have plans to implement every conceivable customization as these become available through the advances of genetic science.[64]

> The Institute cannot change the DNA of the donating couple—if neither the mother nor the father has genes for green eyes, for example, then the Institute cannot give them a baby with green eyes. Yet within the constraints inherent in the DNA of the donating couple, The Fertility Institute is willing to screen embryos for these traits. The Fertility Institute wants to offer several other customizations, and many more are sure to be released in the coming years as the science behind screening for them is developed.[65]

In most contemporary technological societies, certain kinds of genetic selections are not only permissible but also desirable and beneficial in many instances. So, for instance, very few people have reservations about genetic screening for diseases and deformities before the implantation process; they want to ensure that the children born are not destined to lead lives of misery due to handicapping conditions that were easily preventable. Although more controversial than screening for disease and deformity, screening for gender has become customary in most countries, using the same PGD process in which a three-day-old embryo, consisting of about six cells, is tested in a lab.[66] Only embryos free of disease and of the desired gender—if the parents have also chosen to select for gender—are then implanted in the womb.

> Take the case of Cindy and John Whitley. Their first child died at the age of 9 months from a deadly genetic disorder called spinal muscular atrophy. Genetic analysis uncovered that the Whitleys statistically had a 1 in 4 chance of creating a child with spinal muscular atrophy each time they conceived. Unwilling to risk having another child with

(continued)

---

63. "'Designer Babies' Ethical?" *CBS News* (March 3, 2009), *http://www.cbsnews.com/stories/2009/03/03/earlyshow/health/main4840346.shtml*

64. Keith Kleiner, "Designer Babies: Ready or Not Here They Come," *Singularity Hub* (February 25, 2009), *http://www.singularityhub.com/2009/02/25/designer-babies-like-it-or-not-here-they-come/*.

65. Ibid.

66. Naik.

Case Study

the deadly disorder, the Whitleys used PGD to conceive three children, all healthy.[67]

However, the science of PGD, like all other sciences, is in a constant state of discovery, and the potential services it offers to couples seeking assistance continues to expand. Embryo screening has recently been used to create "savior siblings"—healthy spare embryos left over from the screening process that can be harvested to treat serious illness in the implanted embryo. It has also been used to weed out embryos carrying markers for diseases, such as breast cancer or other diseases that might not strike a person until much later in life. There are also rumblings that the technology has been used in cases of so-called "negative screening" in which, for instance, a child born to deaf parents is selected to be deaf him or herself.[68]

This science also raises the specter of eugenics and the development of a "master race." Even scientists who favor this kind of genetic choice recognize that only select individuals who live in highly developed technological cultures will have access to these types of procedures. Due to the costs and to the fact that, in most cases, these procedures will be deemed "elective" and, therefore, not covered by insurance or national health plans, only the relatively wealthy will be able to modify their offspring. Many ask whether this kind of genetic selection based on economic standing sets up a situation in which the process of natural selection will be replaced by a class-based evolution of the human species, in which members of a certain elite class will be able to generate offspring who are "superior" competitors and who represent a genetic "master race."[69]

A recent poll conducted by the New York School of Medicine demonstrates some degree of support for the notion of designing a better child. A majority of 999 people who sought genetic counseling said they supported genetic screening for eliminating disease, mental retardation, and blindness. Once again, such opinions tend to be relatively noncontroversial in American culture. However, the same survey revealed that 10 percent of the respondents supported genetic screening for both athletic ability and height and that 13 percent would use the procedure to achieve superior intelligence.[70]

Given the current state of genetic science, successful and consistent characteristic enhancement is very difficult to achieve. Even the simplest

(continued)

---

67. Ibid.

68. Ibid.

69. Matt Collins, "The Need to Regulate 'Designer Babies,'" *Scientific American* (May 4, 2009), *http://www.scientificamerican.com/article.cfm?id=regulate-designer-babies.*

70. Ibid.

Case Study *(continued)*

traits such as hair and eye color appear to be the product of multiple genetic and environmental factors, and knowledge of what these factors are and how they can be manipulated is incomplete, although increasing daily. More complex characteristics such as intelligence, athleticism, and happiness present enormous hurdles to geneticists attempting to identify the control mechanisms for these traits. Most of these characteristics require modification of the environment through development, rehearsal, and practice as children, adolescents, and adults in order to bear full fruit. Add to this complexity that there is no single cultural definition of "intelligence" let alone "happiness," and one begins to understand the difficulties associated with trying to genetically manipulate these characteristics at birth.

A few short months after announcing his clinic's ability and intention to offer hair, eye, and skin color as optional traits to their lab customers, Dr. Steinberg backed away from this commitment—after making "an 'internal, self-regulatory decision' to scrap the project because of 'public perception' and the 'apparent negative societal impacts involved.'"[71] However, most commentators agree that this change of heart on the part of one person at one clinic in Los Angeles will have no appreciable effect on the ever-increasing capacity to choose the traits of offspring.[72] Many are calling for government regulation; however, others contend that with the globalization of genetic sciences, these regulations will not be enforceable unless they can somehow be enacted internationally. Barring this unlikely eventuality, any country's national laws will have little or no effect on the inevitable march toward designer babies.

Questions

1. How does the choice of personal characteristics for one's children differ from choosing features for any other product?
2. Should parents have the right to purchase these traits from providers of fertility services as they purchase other consumer goods?
3. What does human dignity theory have to say about the increasing capacity to determine the characteristics of one's offspring?
4. In this case, the values of scientific advancement, the freedom to choose, and the dignity of the human are weighed against one another, sometimes in contentious ways. How might all of these values be preserved without sacrificing one or the others?

---

71. Collins, "The Need to Regulate 'Designer Babies.'"
72. Ibid.

Case Study

The People's Car[73]

Tata Motors of India was established in 1945 as a locomotive manufacturer and in 1954 branched out and began manufacturing commercial vehicles. It ended a fifteen-year collaboration with Daimler Benz of Germany in 2010, and now, at the end of the first decade of the twenty-first century, Tata Motors is one of the largest automobile manufacturers in India with annual revenues in excess of $14 billion. Today the company makes passenger cars as well as multi-utility, light, medium, and heavy commercial vehicles. The company exports its vehicles around the world and employs more than 1,400 engineers and scientists in six research and development centers in India, South Korea, Spain, and the United Kingdom.

In 2003, Tata Motors decided to design and manufacture the Nano, a tiny car costing around $2,500.[74] The company targeted the segment of the personal transportation market currently filled by motorbikes. The ideal consumer for the Nano would be individuals currently unable to afford a car and who use motorbikes as a form of family transportation. By 2009, the first Nanos began hitting Indian showrooms, and consumers immediately saw how this car offered all of the benefits of their automotive competitors, like Maruti and Suzuki, yet did so at an affordable price. The Nano was being touted as the car for the masses—at least that is what everyone at Tata assumed at first.

The automotive industry has been a major contributor to a number of airborne pollutants and has been identified as a significant factor in global climate change as well. Overall the transportation sector contributes about 24 percent to global carbon emissions. Cars and other light duty vehicles contribute about 10 percent to the global carbon emissions produced by carbon fuels, and in the car category, the small-car segment makes up the largest share of carbon emissions at 25 percent. Experts claim that this outsized contribution by the small-car segment is due to the fact that there are so many more of these vehicles on the road than of any other variety. The environment must also contend with the exponential growth in the number of vehicles of all kinds worldwide, from 50 million in 1950 to 580 million in 1997, a trend that seems unlikely to abate any time in the near future. If anything, the rate of vehicle production will likely increase as India and China add unprecedented numbers of new middle-class consumers every year. In fact, projections show that the number of vehicles on the road will triple between 2014 and 2050.

(continued)

---

73. This case study is based on a case study written by Shankar Narayanan, "Tato Nano: Environmental Concerns," which can be found at *www.caseplace.org*.

74. *http://tatanano.inservices.tatamotors.com/tatamotors/*.

Case Study   *(continued)*

When it was unveiled in 2008 at the Auto Expo in New Delhi, the Nano was marketed as the People's Car. In spite of its diminutive size, the vehicle is designed as a family car, with seating for four passengers and generous interior space. It is an all-aluminum construction, which makes it exceptionally light and the two-cylinder, fuel-injected engine and rear-wheel drive allow very good gas mileage. The Nano meets and exceeds all regulatory requirements in the markets where it is sold, which now includes most of the European Union. It has been touted as the product that will make car ownership an achievable goal for as many as 14 million Indian families, who currently cannot afford products from other manufacturers. The introduction of the Nano has lowered the cost of an entry-level car in India by 30 percent. Tata has broken through a major milestone in the mobility paradigm and is creating a whole new segment in the existing transportation market.

In addition to great gas mileage, solid safety, and low cost, the Nano also boasted having tailpipe emissions performance that exceeded all regulatory requirements of both India (Bharat III) and the European Union (Euro III). In fact, it had lower emissions than the motorbikes it was designed to replace. This combined with the lower fuel efficiency of most other cars meant that the Nano would provide low-cost transportation with a lower carbon footprint.[75]

However, in spite of all these positives, concerns emerged about the Nano's potential to degrade air quality and contribute to global climate change. The principal concern had to do with the potential popularity of an ultra-cheap car for the masses and how this would increase people's reliance on the automobile, rather than bicycles or mass transit, as their primary mode of transportation. J. D. Power Asia Pacific projected that the Nano will likely sell 100,000 units per year through 2013 and possibly double that number by 2014. An Indian rating agency claims that the Nano could increase overall automobile sales by 20 percent in its first year of production and has the potential of expanding the car market in India by 65 percent.

Additionally, some predict that the Nano will spur other manufacturers to slash prices on their vehicles and launch their own minicars, further exacerbating this trend toward greater reliance on cars. This expansion of the sheer volume of cars on the streets of India's crowded cities would intensify the already heavy congestion, which would, in turn, increase tailpipe

(continued)

---

75. The engine will require finer tuning in order to reach the highest and most strict emission standards of Euro IV. The company itself appears to be dedicated to being seen as an environmentally conscious manufacturer as can be seen at its website, *http://www.tatamotors.com/our_world/ we_care.php.*

Case Study   *(continued)*

emissions. Average speeds in major Indian cities such as Mumbai and Delhi have already fallen to 10–12 km/hr., and with the deluge of cars that the introduction of the Nano portends, this figure could easily drop to 5–10 km/hr. A study by the World Bank demonstrated that car emissions rise dramatically when average speeds fall below 40 km/hr. and spike even higher once speeds drop below 20 km/hr. Fuel consumption was four to six times as high at 5–10 km/hr. as it was at 40 km/hr., with corresponding tailpipe emissions. Tata based its emission claims for the Nano on ideal driving conditions, which assumed drivers would travel above 40 km/hr. Under actual conditions in the most crowded areas of India, the environmental impact of the Nano appears much bleaker.

Questions

1. Does the Tata Nano represent an egalitarian dream, as the company and its supporters claim, or an environmental nightmare, as environmentalists and others suggest? Explain.

2. In this case, two different principles of CST potentially clash. On the one hand, there is the egalitarian thrust of making a social good more accessible to a greater number of people who could not otherwise afford this product. On the other hand, this product could have a dramatically negative impact on the environment. How would you resolve this ethical dilemma?

3. If you were an executive with decision-making power at Tata, what would you recommend? How would you deal with these conflicting values?

4. If you were an Indian consumer with a small family that had to get around the busy and dangerous streets of Mumbai on a motorbike, what would your attitude be toward the Nano? Would you be tempted to buy one?

For Further Reading

Atkinson, Paul, Peter E. Glasner, and Margaret M. Lock. *Handbook of Genetics and Society: Mapping the New Genomic Era.* London: Routledge, 2013.

Cunha, Mario Viola de Azevedo. *New Technologies and Human Rights Challenges to Regulation.* Farnham, Surrey, England: Ashgate, 2013.

Head, Simon. *Mindless: Why Smarter Machines Are Making Dumber Humans.* New York: Basic Books, 2014.

Lanier, Jaron. *Who Owns the Future?* London: Allen Lane, 2013.

Scharff, Robert C., and Val Dusek. *Philosophy of Technology: The Technological Condition—An Anthology.* Hoboken, NJ: Wiley, 2013.

Weisbord, Marvin Ross. *Productive Workplaces: Dignity, Meaning, and Community in the 21st Century.* San Francisco, CA: Jossey-Bass, 2012.

Chapter 2

The Common Good and Corporate Governance

Thomas O'Brien

Introduction

The theme of human dignity highlights the value the Catholic Church places on individual human life, and after reviewing this highly developed moral principle one could be tempted to assume that all ethical dilemmas could be resolved simply by applying this powerful principle. However, the limits of the principle of human dignity come into focus when we begin to consider the good for communities, associations, and societies. What is good for a society does not always directly translate into an advantage for a particular individual in that society. Likewise, the option that would often produce the best result for a specific individual has the unintended effect of harming the greater good of the community. It is in response to the occasional incongruity between individual and group goods that the church adopted and developed the principle of the common good. As the text transitions from the theme of human dignity to the common good, it also transitions from a focus on the individual to one that is more broadly aimed at human communities and society as a whole.

It is difficult to speak of a "common good" today, especially in the context of large corporations operating within a global economy. The individualistic mindset that most people in Western cultures acquire from their social formation resists the notion of a good that is somehow shared. In addition, postmodern sensibilities predispose people to be suspicious of the idea that a good can be anything more than a perspective on reality that reflects the best interests of a certain elite group, often hiding behind the veil of the common good. Finally, the global economy and transnational business environments confront society with a logarithmically expanding number of competing notions of what constitutes the good, which, in turn, raises questions about the degree to which one can conceive of these goods as shared.

So why bother unearthing this philosophical corpse? What justifies this reconsideration of the common good? One answer lies in recent corporate scandals such as those at Enron, WorldCom, HealthSouth, and more recently Goldman Sachs, Lehman Brothers, CITI Bank, and Bank of America. Many observers of contemporary business practices are beginning to recognize that the blind pursuit of self-interest does not always yield the best results for anyone, let alone everyone. Is it possible that contemporary Western society is rediscovering that virtue is often its own reward and that the good of society requires a moral vision that can see beyond mere self-aggrandizement? Unfortunately, as corporations establish new policies based more solidly in ethical values, they often find that the embedded practices of corporate culture collide with and run contrary to these embryonic moral impulses.[1] While the narrow focus on self-interest and the interests of investors helps CEOs and other senior executives maximize their own returns, it can also lead to the diminishment of the good of human communities and their environment. All this has set the stage for a reconsideration of the common good.

The Common Good

Basic Assumptions

Some mistakenly equate the principle of the common good with the utilitarian ideal of "the greatest good for the greatest number." Others conflate the common good with the recent focus in business on *stakeholder value*, which broadens the traditional capitalist focus on the *maximization of shareholder value*. These theories are inadequate renditions of the common good primarily because they tend to work from individualistic assumptions about the human and society.[2] Most modern systems view persons as alienable from their social context. From this perspective, individuals are essentially monads, related only by mutual self-interest to a larger body through a social contract. For utilitarians, maximizing the good of an entire society is a massive project of aggregating all individual goods and weighing this sum against the

---

1. For a more detailed view of the cultural clash between standard liberal economic philosophy and broader notions of corporate culture derived from ethics theory, see John Dobson, "The Battle in Seattle: Reconciling Two World Views on Corporate Culture," *Business Ethics Quarterly* 11/3 (July 2001): 403–13.

2. The individualistic nature of utilitarianism is partially explained by the centrality of "happiness" as the locus of value for this system. While it is natural to speak about the "happiness" of individuals, it is plainly more difficult to conceive of the "happiness" of nonpersonal entities such as communities or society. Some versions of utilitarianism focus more on utility, usefulness, uselessness, and harm, rather than happiness and unhappiness, and these certainly can be applied in a way that resembles deliberations on the common good.

aggregate evils for any and all alternative courses of action. Similarly, maximizing stakeholder value for a business or community usually includes an equivalent aggregation of individual goods for those groups included in the stakeholder category. Utility and achievable ends comprise the sole focus of these systems. Questions of how to achieve those ends and for what purpose lie outside their area of concern.

The tradition of the common good, as expressed in the theories of major religious traditions, helps fill in gaps left by theories such as utilitarianism and stakeholder value. While the common good considers the good of the individual, for most religious traditions, it does so from a different vantage point. The common good tradition does not view the person as a lonely monad competing against other individuals but rather as essentially integrated into a network of social relationships. In other words, the human is primarily a social being. The conception of the person as an individual is secondary and is derived from a belief in the primordial interdependence of human existence. From this vantage point, the individual self is a manifestation of a process that includes all of one's past experiences and encompasses myriad social relationships. Humans are, first and foremost, social beings who belong, by necessity, within a larger social network. They cannot be properly understood except by some reference to their social relationships.

Much of the difference between the perspectives of modern ethical systems and the moral tradition of the common good can be traced back to their respective histories. In Western culture, the concept of the human as an individual came to full realization during the Enlightenment. The political and economic theories of John Locke (1632–1704) invested each individual with natural rights. These individuals freely entered into a social contract with one another, thus, forming the philosophical basis for the modern state.[3] The concept of right and wrong arising from these systems tends to focus on the good of individuals and the rights one holds in competition with other individuals.[4]

---

3. "To understand political power right, and derive it from its original, we must consider, what state all men are naturally in, and that is, a state of perfect freedom to order their actions, and dispose of their possessions and persons, as they think fit, within the bounds of the law of nature, without asking leave, or depending upon the will of any other man." John Locke, *The Second Treatise of Civil Government* 1690, Article II, Section 4, *http://www.constitution.org/jl/2ndtr02.htm.*

4. Although Enlightenment theories are clearly individualistic, Brian Stiltner argues convincingly that Locke's theories of the limited constitutional state and individual liberties were formulated within a theoretical context that also had the common good as one of its central concerns. For Locke, trust is essential to human existence because it constitutes the "bond" that makes society possible. Locke's defense of the right to private property begins with a recognition that in a state of nature all goods are held in common until individuals mix their labor with those goods, at which point those goods become the property of those individuals in whole or in part. The role of the state, therefore, is not so much a guarantor of individual property rights as these compete with the property rights of other individuals but more the guarantor of the common good through the recognition of the natural rights of individuals in the context of their obligations to society and their contractual obligations to the members of that society. Brian Stiltner, *Religion and the Common Good: Catholic Contributions to Building Community in a Liberal Society* (New York, NY: Rowman and Littlefield Publishers, Inc., 1999), 21, 25–6.

By contrast, most religious traditions have their origins in very different contexts than those that prevailed during and after the Enlightenment. Most religions arose out of small, tight-knit, premodern communities. Generally speaking, the conception of the human in these communities was not individualistic. The human is known and understood in the context of the community. The meaning of life is tied to one's relationship to the community and the role one plays in the life of that community.[5] Not surprisingly, therefore, the conception of right and wrong emerging from this context focuses more on the well-being of the whole group and less on the welfare of any one individual.

The individual person, in this context, is social by definition and is so in a profound way.[6] This conception of the individual differs radically from the view prevalent in contemporary North American societies. The "basketball star" example can help illustrate the differences between these viewpoints. Through an individualistic lens, one recognizes Lebron James as a talented and accomplished athlete. He and his accomplishments are normally viewed in isolation from the social, historical, economic, or relational context out of which, on closer examination, they obviously emerge. Most are convinced that the ticket, promotional, and advertising revenue his talent generates should belong to him and the owners of the team to which he belongs. For the modern North American, this is a very intuitive perspective. In fact, most do not see how it could be understood any other way.

However, the communitarian perspective of the common good recognizes James's accomplishments as also the achievement of an endless array of social support systems that made his individual triumphs possible. The support of family and friends, the instruction of teachers and coaches, the institutionalized sporting systems of the NBA, the money of the fans, the publicity of the media, the relative health of the economy, the relative freedom of the political system, and even the abundance of the fruits of the earth combine to form the foundation on which this superstar's career was built. Lebron James represents a singular athletic achievement that an incalculable number of people had some hand in making possible. This perspective takes nothing away from Lebron James and does not minimize his efforts; it merely gives credit where credit is due. It serves as a reminder that it took more than just the effort of an individual to create Lebron James the basketball superstar.

Every life is rife with these same sorts of social networks that have helped determine, not only what one has done, but also who one has become. These networks extend horizontally across contemporary personal, professional,

---

5. Aristotle, *Politics*, 1252b10–22; ed. Jonathan Barnes, *The Complete Works of Aristotle* (Princeton, NJ: Princeton University Press, 1984), 1987.

6. Aristotle, *Politics*, 1253a3–6; Ibid., 1988.

familial, governmental, corporate, national, and international relationships. They also stretch back in time to include all those generations upon which current social structures depend for their origin, maintenance, and advancement. Representative democracy has always been the form of government of the American republic, but Americans know their present political circumstance is the result of hard work, sacrifice, and long development by many preceding generations. Americans are no more individually entitled to democracy than Lebron James is individually entitled to professional basketball and all of those social and economic factors that go into making him a multimillionaire. These relationships form a part of the complex social milieu that shapes the essence of who one is; without them, one would have become someone different.

The same relational principles hold true in association with economic and business relationships. For instance, in corporate culture the myth of the self-made businessperson is a powerful motivational force.[7] Many claim it as part of their own success story, while most others aspire to incorporate aspects of it into their business persona.[8] Nevertheless, from the communitarian perspective of the common good, this myth of the self-made businessperson fundamentally distorts reality. Individual success and failure always occur within the context of a multitude of supportive or obstructive relationships with other people and social institutions. No one, regardless of the degree of his or her relative success, comes anywhere near the ideal of being self-made.[9] Success in a business context is always essentially a corporate achievement.

Fully grasping the meaning of the common good, however, entails going beyond the simple illustrations outlined previously. Although pointing out the interconnected social network that undergirds all individual achievement can prove helpful, it normally does not suffice in and of itself to convey what the common good might mean to twenty-first century readers. What has been described so far is often referred to as *the commons*; understanding why the good of the commons, or the common good, carries so much moral weight in religious ethics requires further exploration.

---

7. Belief in the self-made businessperson has strong roots in American mythology. For instance, the most successful fiction writer of the nineteenth century was Horatio Alger who told simple rags-to-riches tales in order to inspire inner-city youth to take advantage of America's social mobility. Works such as *Strive and Succeed: The Progress of Walter Conrad* typify Alger's work.

8. Real-life legends such as Andrew Carnegie, who climbed out of the slums of Pittsburgh to become the wealthiest businessperson of his day, lend credence to the belief that all Americans can succeed in business. Anomalies in Carnegie's life that explain his unprecedented success were often overlooked in order to portray his story as somehow archetypical.

9. Contemporary books such as *Giants of Enterprise: Seven Business Innovators and the Empires They Built* by Harvard Business School historian Richard S. Tedlow continue the mythmaking, regaling the reader with glowing success stories of the likes of Sam Walton, Thomas Watson, and Charles Revson.

A Catholic Understanding of the Common Good

Catholic philosopher Jacques Maritain (1882–1973) claimed that one could discern the common good by examining the experience of the human in community. In this way, Maritain's interpretation of the common good is a type of natural law reasoning that begins with a philosophical anthropology—a consideration of what it means to be human.[10] According to Maritain, people first recognize their own dignity and rights by observing their inclinations to preserve themselves and defend their kin. This is followed by the realization that other people share in this dignity because all people are essentially the same. Thus, people come to understand that the right to life and other basic rights belong to all. People then recognize the inclination to improve themselves and maximize their own potential. Once again, by extension it becomes clear that living well with others means helping them achieve their own potential because this is a basic drive common to all. People then identify the need for institutions to help protect their rights, provide for basic needs, and support their personal and collective flourishing. Patterns of organization and authority then develop in order to achieve these goals. Individuals and groups have to negotiate and adjust their relationship to larger social structures. The demands they make on each other in society need to be mediated and adjudicated, resulting in judicial systems. Therefore, the common good is a sensibility that arises from the way individuals naturally experience themselves in the context of other people in a society, and "for the viability of society, and in order to protect the dignity of all, some individual claims are superseded by the claims of the community."[11]

Therefore, from this perspective, the moral importance of the common good hinges on its importance for people.[12] Most religious ethical systems understand the person in regard to both the individual and social dimensions. The principle of human dignity highlights the ethical importance of individual nature, while the common good emphasizes the moral essence of communal life. The common good sees individual human nature as fully actualized only in community; people become individuals only through the myriad interactions in community with other persons. Society gives individuals a context in which to exercise their humanity and be recognized as human by others. Isolated

---

10. Jacques Maritain, *The Person and the Common Good* (London: Geoffrey Bles, 1948).

11. Stiltner, *Religion and the Common Good*, 91.

12. William O'Neill, S.J., claims that the common good is the context within which a proper understanding of individual rights can emerge and be made effective. "The common good thus appears as the *telos* of our reasoned speech (the ideal of 'an inclusive and non-coercive discourse among free and equal partners') redeemed in the rhetoric of basic rights." William O'Neill, S.J., "The Ethics of Enchantment: Rights, Reason and the Common Good," eds. James Donahue and M. Theresa Moser, *Religion, Ethics and the Common Good* (Mystic, CT: Twenty-Third Publications, 1996), 71.

individuals lack a humanizing context and, therefore, cannot experience themselves as persons. Thus, preserving a human community that facilitates human actualization comprises a fundamental moral duty. It is a moral failure on the part of a society that does not strive to establish conditions within the community that contribute to the flourishing of all members.

The principle of the common good rests on the assumption that the flourishing of the community also enhances the well-being of the individuals in that community: "When people act together for the sake of mutual benefits in which they all share, then they are acting both in others' interests (because others gain from their actions) and in their own (because they gain also)."[13] This assumption is the precise converse of the liberal assumption made first by moral theologian and economic theorist, Adam Smith (1723–1790). He believed that individual pursuit of self-interest would naturally lead to the greatest aggregate good for all in society. Because Smith's assumptions form the foundation of liberal capitalism and modern business philosophy, the common good may seem counterintuitive in capitalist contexts.[14] Nevertheless, the blind pursuit of self-interest in recent times by certain corporations and their well-compensated executives has led many to question the claim that self-interest inevitably leads to the good of all. Many have begun to reconsider other traditions that rely more on a collective vision of goodness, rather than on an individual one. The common good is one such vision.[15]

The Common Good and Private Goods

What is the relative value of individual, private goods in this broader context of the common good? Do private goods simply become absorbed as part of a

---

13. Bill Jordan, *The Common Good: Citizenship, Morality, and Self-Interest* (New York: Blackwell, 1989), 16.

14. "The Catholic doctrine of the common good is incompatible with unlimited free-market, or laissez-faire, capitalism, which insists that the distribution of wealth must occur entirely according to the dictates of market forces. This theory presupposes that the common good will take care of itself, being identified with the summation of vast numbers of individual consumer decisions in a fully competitive, and entirely free, market economy. Its central dogma (as expressed by Adam Smith, the founding father of capitalist theory, in his *The Wealth of Nations*, 1776) is the belief that each citizen, through seeking his own gain, would be 'led by an invisible hand to promote an end which was not part of his intention,' namely the prosperity of society. This does sometimes happen; but to say that it inevitably must happen, as if by a God-given natural law, is a view which can amount to idolatry, or a form of economic superstition." Catholic Bishops' Conference of England and Wales, *The Common Good and the Catholic Church's Social Teaching* (1996), no. 76, *www.cctwincities.org/document.doc?id=99*.

15. "The interdependence of persons on each other is a fact of human life. The prevailing ethos of Western culture, however, often leads us to forget how human well-being thoroughly depends on reciprocal cooperation with other people. The initiatives that engender both economic and cultural flourishing are social activities; they are embedded in networks of human interaction and interdependence." David Hollenbach, S.J., *The Common Good and Christian Ethics* (New York, NY: Cambridge University Press, 2002), 181–82.

collective good, or are they devalued to the point of nonexistence? From a classical Catholic point of view, the relationship between the common good and private good is analogous to the relationship between the whole and the component, or the body to its parts. A multitude of humans living together in a community bring into existence a new specific kind of being that is more than just an accumulation of persons. Similarly, the human body is more than merely the sum of its parts—the parts must relate in a specific way in order for the body to thrive. Although it has no substance of its own, society represents more than just a collection of individuals. It is essentially constituted by the relationships that exist; therefore, it is many substances interwoven into one body by the category of relation. Fundamentally, society is a web of relations between rational creatures unified into a system with a common social end.[16]

Although the common good includes all other goods of individuals and lesser associations, reducing the common good to a mere aggregation of all the private goods of its constitutive members is a mistake. This individualistic conception of the common good misconstrues and cheapens the qualitatively richer notion found in the writings of Aristotle (384–322 BCE) and medieval Catholic theologian Thomas Aquinas (1225–1274). They believed that the common good of society must be considered a qualitatively autonomous species of good that is both higher and richer in goodness than any other human good enjoyed by individuals or lesser associations. The more common a good is, the more perfect it is.[17] In fact, sometimes preserving or promoting the common good entails sacrificing private goods.[18] For instance, imposing a penalty on a criminal sacrifices a private good in order to restore public safety, a common good.[19]

Therefore, at the heart of the common good lies the principle that the whole is superior to the part.[20] It follows, then, that the good of the universe is of greater import than the relative goodness or evil of a particular thing; analogously, the good of a society is more important than the good of an individual.

> It is a greater perfection for something to be good in itself and the cause of goodness in others, than simply to be good in itself. Imperfect things tend towards their own good, namely the good of an individual; perfect

---

16. Jaime Vélez-Sáenz, *The Doctrine of the Common Good of Civil Society in the Works of Thomas Aquinas* (Notre Dame, IN: University of Notre Dame, Department of Philosophy, April 1951), 21.

17. M. S. Kempshall, *The Common Good in Late Medieval Political Thought* (New York, NY: Oxford University Press, 1999), 81–4.

18. "The common good of many is more Godlike than the good of an individual. Wherefore it is a virtuous action for a man to endanger even his own life, either for the spiritual or for the temporal common good of his country." Thomas Aquinas, *Summa Theologica,* Second Part of the Second Part, Question 31, Article 3, Reply to Objection 2.

19. Kempshall, *The Common Good in Late Medieval Political Thought,* 70.

20. Aristotle, *Politics,* 1253a 19–39; Barnes, 1988.

things tend toward the good of a species; more perfect things tend toward the good of a genus; the most perfect . . . secures the good of all being, the good of the universe"[21]

Therefore, any good of an individual that is a real good is rooted in the good of the community. Conversely, any common good that is a real good is at the same time the good of all individuals who share in that community. "The good shared with others is constitutive of the good of persons regarded one at a time; the good of persons regarded one at a time cannot exist without some measure of sharing in the common good."[22] Thus, the good of an isolated self is not a genuine good unto itself but an illusion because the isolated self is not sustainable or self-sufficient.

Ancient philosophers, such as Aristotle, believed that humans have a natural affinity for the common good, analogous to a part securing its own perfection in the whole and not solely for its own sake. Just as the good of the part has the good of the whole as its final cause, so every part of Creation loves its own good on account of the common good of the whole universe. A part loves the good of its whole not in order to direct the good of the whole toward itself but in order to direct itself toward the good of the whole. Using the basketball star illustration, the basketball community did not conform its rules and performance requirements to standards set by Lebron James in order that he could one day become a superstar. James has received the personal goods of fame, adulation, and wealth because he first directed his efforts toward the basketball community and conformed his performance to a model of perfection set by that community. In the political community, individuals love their own good as a result of loving the good of the community as the good on which their own good depends for its existence.[23] For instance, any virtue is an act of love for the good of another. At the same time, it is an act of love for oneself because it is also an act of love for the common good.[24] The more a virtue pertains to the good of a multitude, the greater it is.[25]

The total content of goods that a civil society can realize transcends in both degree and kind the goods private or domestic society can give the human: "A good society is one in which people share in a good quality of life, and value this association with each other as members of the same community. The value of shared association cannot be split into individual portions, any more than can

---

21. Kempshall, *The Common Good in Late Medieval Political Thought*, 84.

22. Hollenbach, *The Common Good and Christian Ethics*, 79.

23. Kempshall, *The Common Good in Late Medieval Political Thought*, 104.

24. "But that justice which directs man to the common good is a general virtue through its act of command: since it directs all the acts of the virtues to its own end, viz. the common good." Thomas Aquinas, *Summa Theologica*, First Part of the Second Part, Question 60, Article 3, Reply to Objection 2.

25. Aristotle, *Politics*, 1252a1–23; Barnes, 1986.

the value of a good party, a good meeting or a good religious ceremony."[26] The good of the whole society is, at the same time, a good for each individual because otherwise the common good would not be truly common.[27] The state or political community—*polis*—is the all-embracing and highest form of human association. Therefore, it represents the pinnacle of human achievement and embodies the greatest of the human goals. This good is both quantitatively and qualitatively more excellent than other goods of lower and partial communities or of individuals,[28] which explains why the common good has primacy over the private good of an individual.[29]

The Teleological Dimension of the Common Good

Not only is the common good a good shared by several beings, it also represents a "good" toward which a multitude is ordered. In this way, it has a *teleological* dimension. The common good is a final cause—a goal of perfection—toward which all of civil society is ordered.[30] For Aristotle, every human community tends toward an end that is its own goal—some good. Every community as a whole has an end, and this end is the "good life." No civil society fulfills its intended purpose unless it strives for the realization of a just and good life for all its citizens.

Therefore, the common good can mean two things:

1. The ordering of all the parts of the universe toward one another and toward the whole
2. The universal good that all things seek and in which all things participate and communicate

Likewise, the common good of the political community can have two meanings correlating to the two general meanings noted previously:

1. The result of individual virtuous activity as the common benefit that necessarily follows from individuals seeking their ultimate good of happiness and virtue

---

26. Jordan, 16.

27. "The common good preserves its formal difference (and primacy) in that it is a good for each individual without ceasing to be the very good which is simultaneously common to many, whereas the private good as such excludes any other; it is this individual's own good and for that reason is not good for another." Vélez-Sáenz, *The Doctrine of the Common Good of Civil Society in the Works of Thomas Aquinas*, 32.

28. Aristotle, *Politics*, 1279a23–39; Barnes, 2030.

29. Kempshall, *The Common Good in Late Medieval Political Thought*, 79.

30. Aristotle, *Nicomachean Ethics*, 1094a1; Barnes, 1729. Aristotle, *Politics*, 1252b28–1253c2; Barnes, 1987.

2. The unity of good in society that is distinct from a simple aggregate of individual goods

Therefore, the common good can be described as both the formal cause (the structural arrangement of individual goods) and the final cause (the goal toward which this arrangement is directed) of human society. In even simpler terms, the common good is both an ordered structure and a shared goal.[31]

Another way of looking at the two characteristics of the common good is to think of one as *descriptive* and the other as *prescriptive*. The descriptive aspect provides a way of viewing the world that often contrasts sharply with the individualistic perspectives to which North Americans have grown accustomed. It compels the viewer to see the social world, not as an aggregation of individual wants and needs, but as a complex web of mutual relationships that enables individuals to achieve far more than they would if left to their own devices. Because the descriptive common good affects the way one sees and understands the world, it offers a different set of lenses through which to view communal structures and social interactions. Grasping the common good more deeply allows one to know the world in a new and perfect way.

While the descriptive aspect of the common good raises awareness of the web of relationships that comprise and sustain the social world, the prescriptive aspect demands one act in a way that preserves this greater good even when confronted with competing individual goods. The prescriptive aspect is an ethic that requires individuals to foster this web of healthy, nurturing relationships, while resisting any temptation to pursue individual goods that might compromise or even undermine the good of the interrelated world. From this perspective, the common good offers a moral standard, against which the goods of any given society can be weighed.

Because the common good is the end toward which all other goods are ordered and to which they are subordinated, then a good for the community cannot be obtained through illicit or immoral means but only through morally licit means. If attained illicitly, then the good of the community, which above all else is a moral good, will suffer detriment to what is most essential to it. The moral goods of the community, such as justice, peace, and unity, can never be attained through immoral means and are always jeopardized by the use of such means.[32]

As mentioned in the Introduction of this book, the enslavement of a few to benefit the many is often used as an illustration of the moral equivocation at the heart of the utilitarian ideal. However, this kind of equivocation does not apply to utilitarianism's moral cousin, the common good, precisely because the achievement of the common good cannot be accomplished using immoral means. In other words, the achievement of the greatest good for all cannot be

---

31. Ibid., 97–100.

32. Vélez-Sáenz, *The Doctrine of the Common Good of Civil Society in the Works of Thomas Aquinas*, 85.

accomplished using the immoral means of enslaving a minority. Common good theorists would point out that the goodness achieved in such a circumstance would be fleeting at best and would very probably result in the breakdown of social norms that discourage and prevent the abuse and coercion of others that would in turn, undermine the common good.

Cooperation, Virtue, and Happiness

For Aristotle, a substance exists independently of any operation on it, meaning that it is not held together by the efforts of someone or something.[33] A society, on the other hand, is held together in a common life by a consensus, and this consensus is a kind of cooperation toward a common end. Cooperation, therefore, functions as the unifying force of a society, analogous, in many ways, to the unifying forces of quantum mechanics that hold the atomic structure together. An intensification of cooperation within a society constitutes an increase in the actuality of the society's very existence and, at the same time, a perfection of its ethical nature. Cooperation, therefore, is the key to both a society's goodness and strength. Aquinas referred to the ethical perfection arising from intense cooperation as peace. This scenario views unity and peace as identical. Both are characterized by a harmony of all wills and appetites in the love of common ends.[34]

The type of cooperation that binds a good society together requires all members of that society to live according to the virtues so that the common good can flourish fully. Living well means more than merely realizing one's full potential for one's own sake. Ultimately, it means living in order to achieve the good of the whole social order—and this entails living according to virtue. The common good is primarily the moral health of a society—the environment in which a person begins to develop an individual moral life and in which one person helps another to live well.

The common good is a vital depository to which all virtuous members contribute and from which all receive good in return. In the world of business, for example, applying the virtues of excellence and industry often leads to the creation of increasingly better products. In return everyone benefits from the good of greater use-value, which potentially leads to social progress. In this way, the common good serves as an interchange of aids, examples, and incentives to do what is good.[35] That this good is common means that all the component parts of

---

33. Aristotle, *Categories,* 2a15–4b19; Barnes, 4–8.

34. "But unity belongs to the idea of goodness, as Boethius proves (De Consol. iii, 11) from this, that, as all things desire good, so do they desire unity; without which they would cease to exist. For a thing so far exists as it is one. Whence we observe that things resist division, as far as they can; and the dissolution of a thing arises from defect therein. Therefore the intention of a ruler over a multitude is unity, or peace." Thomas Aquinas, *Summa Theologica,* First Part, Question 103, Article 3.

35. Vélez-Sáenz, *The Doctrine of the Common Good of Civil Society in the Works of Thomas Aquinas,* 38.

the community enjoy and share in it. Being the good of the whole, it is, thereby, effectively "common"—or at least communicable—to its parts. It follows that the one who pursues the common good simultaneously seeks one's own good. An ancient Roman proverb illustrates this point, claiming that it is better to live poor in a rich empire, than rich in a poor one.[36]

The common good is both a condition for and the result of the happiness that those persons who participate in the common good attain by living virtuously. Just as individuals need their body parts to work together in order to act, so only when united by the link of peace can the multitude be conducted to the virtuous operation that is happiness. Unity and peace do not formally constitute the happy life of the multitude but rather serve as a condition necessary for reaching it.[37] At the highest level of attainment in the happy life, the common good and the private good of the individual coincide, at least in a relative and imperfect way. On lower levels an incompatibility might truly exist between the two, but the primacy always belongs, and must always be accorded, to the common good.[38]

The goal of civil society from the perspective of the common good consists of helping humanity reach its highest good, which is simply living well. The individual avails oneself of society to compensate for any incapacity, either to achieve subsistence by oneself or to achieve an adequate level of flourishing to call one's life authentically human and transcend mere animal survival. Individuals need society for physical, moral, and intellectual development. Only there is a person's humanity fully actualized.[39] Harkening back to the basketball star illustration, the web of interrelationships that is society has served Lebron James well in his self-actualization as an athlete.

Some Problems and Reservations

So far, this chapter has focused on the real and potentially positive contributions to society that result from a commitment to the common good. However, a number of serious risks are associated with inadequate, inappropriate, distorted, or exaggerated applications of this communitarian focus. After all, both Aristotle and Aquinas assumed the institution of slavery was thoroughly legitimate,

---

36. Ibid., 63–64.

37. Ibid., 50–58.

38. "Actions are indeed concerned with particular matters: but those particular matters are referable to the common good, not as to a common genus or species, but as to a common final cause, according as the common good is said to be the common end." Thomas Aquinas, *Summa Theologica,* First Part of the Second Part, Question 90, Article 2, Reply to Objection 2.

39. Vélez-Sáenz, *The Doctrine of the Common Good of Civil Society in the Works of Thomas Aquinas,* 34–5.

fitting comfortably into their conceptions of the common good and a properly ordered social structure.[40] Therefore, a firm commitment to "the common good" raises questions about who is included in or, more importantly, excluded from, the definition of *common*. It also begs the question: "Whose definition of *good* holds privileged status in the conversation?" A reconsideration of the common good demands attending to these and other fundamental problems.

Three main problems plague attempts to realize the common good at local, national, and global levels. The first is the sheer complexity and scale of many business issues. Contemporary economic relations have become increasingly global, and individual decisions within this system result in outcomes that prove more and more difficult to predict. For instance, will a free-trade agreement actually achieve the common good for all in a developing economy—including the poor—by increasing the flow of goods and creating more jobs? Will trade restrictions achieve the common good by preventing enormous foreign companies from overwhelming their relatively tiny competitors and monopolizing these markets? How will these policies affect wages, social programs, the environment, and political relations? How will this affect the global common good? How can someone even grasp what the global common good is, let alone have some notion about how to foster this value? Should a business leader, then, support regional and global free trade or be more concerned with assisting local development efforts, even if these result in reduced profits for the company? Pursuing the common good in any given circumstance can be fraught with uncertainty because the common good—unlike utilitarianism—does not offer the illusion of certainty and precision associated with a calculable ethical formula.[41] Business decisions in a global economy are increasingly complex, and the common good, like most ethical values, can be a vague and imprecise guide.

The second problem faced by those trying to implement the precepts of the common good is the existence of scarcity in the global market and the routinely ruthless competition for finite resources that exists on all levels of the economy. Convincing all parties to foster the common good can be difficult—if not impossible—in a cut-throat business environment populated by executives who have been nurtured and schooled in the art of maximizing the bottom-line interests of the company. Getting executives to even recognize and take into account the interests of other parties often bears little fruit. Yet, persuading these

---

40. "Further, slavery among men is natural, for some are naturally slaves according to the Philosopher (Polit. i, 2). Now 'slavery belongs to the right of nations,' as Isidore states (Etym. v, 4)." Thomas Aquinas, *Summa Theologica*, Second Part of the Second Part, Question 57, Article 2, Objection 2.

41. As noted in the Introduction, many act utilitarians assume that one can base one's moral choices on a calculation that assigns numerical value to the outcomes of different alternatives one could choose in a particular case. Utilitarianism's detractors have pointed out countless times the precarious nature of somehow assigning a specific numerical value to different people's subjective experiences.

same individuals to consider a much broader horizon of economic interests represented by the common good usually requires a kind of conversion on their part.[42] However, business executives are not the only ones who have difficulties accepting the precepts of the common good. Even the poorest people in the most underdeveloped economies can experience the common good as counterintuitive and impractical in the context of scarce subsistence peasantry and the often dog-eat-dog atmosphere of informal markets. Competition and scarcity function at all levels of the economy to counteract and undermine the cooperative vision of the common good.

The final problem is the difficulty associated with identifying a single definition of the "common good" in the pluralistic context of the modern marketplace: "A danger exists within the common good tradition of seeking unity at the expense of diversity, solidarity at the expense of opposition, and community at the expense of individuality, all of which eventually undermine the common good."[43] Postmodernism, which reacts against the certainties of post-Enlightenment philosophies modeled on scientific theories and formulas, has raised legitimate questions about past assumptions of what all humans share in common. An awareness or suspicion has developed concerning those things that have been presented as good for society from a value-neutral vantage point, but which are, in fact, perspectives that normally represent the interests of a certain privileged group. This has resulted in a loss of confidence in the ability to articulate what a human is and how humans ought to relate to one another in community. "So not only do we not know what the human good is; there is no good of all human beings as such."[44]

In his book *The Common Good and Christian Ethics*, David Hollenbach addresses at length the issues raised by postmodernism and the existence of diverse and competing claims to the "good." He identifies three reasons people fear strong notions of the common good. First, they fear that the existence of strong competing ideas of the common good will result in intractable conflict and even violence, as one can witness today between Indian Muslims and Hindus. Second, others fear that powerful minorities holding a strong conception of the common good will oppress the majority of people who have different viewpoints, as happened on countless occasions in oppressive right-wing regimes in Latin America during the Cold War. Finally, some simply fear outright tyranny

---

42. A good resource that explores some success stories demonstrating this kind of conversion among top executives is John M. Hood, *The Heroic Enterprise: Business and the Common Good* (New York, NY: The Free Press, 1996).

43. Michael Naughton, H. Alford, and B. Brady, "The Common Good and the Purpose of the Firm," *Journal of Human Values* 1, no. 2 (1995): 233.

44. David Hollenbach, S.J., "The Common Good in the Postmodern Epoch: What Role for Theology?" eds. James Donahue and M. Theresa Moser, *Religion, Ethics and the Common Good* (Mystic, CT: Twenty-Third Publications, 1996), 5.

on the part of a powerful group that has a vision of the perfect society, as happened in Nazi Germany or fascist Italy.[45] In a society in which one group enjoys significant economic, political, or social privileges over other groups, often the dominant faction gets to define the "common good."[46]

In addition to the reticent attitude many have regarding the value of the common good, North American culture itself does not always provide the best context for ideas about the common good. First of all, one cannot simply presume that there is a good shared in common by all people or even by people who share similar economic, cultural, and social backgrounds. In a pluralistic context, in which multiple, well-defined, and occasionally antagonistic communities constitute the larger society, whose version of the common good should prevail? In addition, in a society that places so much value on individual liberty, a stress on the "common good" can be interpreted as an attempt to suppress or dilute that value by always subordinating the concern of the individual to those of the collective.[47]

North American culture is marked by its astounding variety and openness to diversity; therefore, it proves difficult to identify even those goods that are shared.[48] The pursuit of diversity and tolerance has displaced the pursuit of the common good as the reigning moral guideline for many in this society.[49] This has resulted in what Hollenbach terms "morality writ small," by which he means a nonjudgmental stance that pursues only modest virtues and ordinary duties. He believes this myopic, tolerant perspective dominates the American moral landscape, obscuring the loftier ethical goals of the common good that include social justice and equality.[50]

Despite the reservations and problems lurking beneath the otherwise placid waters of the common good, it can still be an essential component in a holistic business ethic. However, a careless and uncritical pursuit of the common good has the potential to produce results that are anything but good. In the end, pursuing the common good in contemporary North America demands massive and exhaustive consensus building among all constituents in society. Without such an all-inclusive consultative process, the "common good" is likely to devolve into the tyranny of the majority—or merely oppressive rule by the powerful.

---

45. Hollenbach, *The Common Good and Christian Ethics*, 14.

46. For a more extended discussion of the issues associated with the common good in a pluralistic context, see Martin E. Marty, *The One and the Many: America's Struggle for the Common Good* (Cambridge, MA: Harvard University Press, 1997), 62.

47. Ibid., 79.

48. Hollenbach, *The Common Good and Christian Ethics*, 21.

49. Ibid., 24.

50. Ibid., 30.

Conclusion

A number of important insights from the common good tradition can inform a business ethic for the twenty-first century. The first has to do with the very nature of the common good insofar as it "is a realization of the human capacity for intrinsically valuable relationships, not only a fulfillment of the needs and deficiencies of individuals."[51] The common good fulfills needs that individuals cannot fulfill on their own, and businesses are public institutions that, when ordered toward the common good, have the potential to represent much more to their employees and the community than simply a place to collect a paycheck. In other words, the common good challenges the modern business enterprise to realize noninstrumental values that humans can only attain together—goods that come into existence only in the presence of reciprocal solidarity and that cannot be enjoyed privately (e.g., justice).

A second insight involves the practicality of the common good precepts, which have been empirically tested and confirmed by game theorists. Contrary to capitalist intuitions, games devised to examine whether self-interest or cooperation actually produce the greatest good have consistently generated results that contradict the dictum that self-interested choices are beneficial—even for the individual.[52] Experiments that give points to participants based on their relative cooperation or competitive advantage consistently come out in favor of cooperative behavior.[53]

One such game is the Prisoners' Dilemma. Two criminals accused of a crime in which they both participated are arrested and brought to jail. Each prisoner is held in isolation from the other with no opportunity for consultation. The prisoners have two choices: (1) they can act on pure self-interest, in which case each prisoner will attempt to maximize his own advantage by implicating the other and exonerating himself; or (2) they can cooperate and act in accord with their mutual common good, and both could deny the charges levied against them. These two choices yield three possible outcomes: (1) both prisoners betray each other, in which case they both receive a two-year sentence; (2) one betrays the

---

51. Ibid., 81.

52. Details on a number of these experiments can be found in Leif Leivin, *Self-Interest and Public Interest in Western Politics* (New York, NY: Oxford University Press, 1991).

53. One such experiment placed two participants in a situation in which they could choose to either cooperate or be self-interested. If they both chose to cooperate, each would get one point. If they both chose to be self-interested, they would get 0 points each. If one chose to be self-interested and the other chose to cooperate, then the self-interested one would receive 2 points and the cooperative one would receive 0. The game would be played for 100 rounds and final scores were tallied for each participant. Participants who chose earlier and more often to be cooperative had the most points by a large margin. Those who chose to be self-interested early and more often were all grouped at the bottom of the final results.

other while the other remains silent, in which case the first is exonerated while the second receives a three-year sentence; or (3) both prisoners remain silent, in which case they both receive a one-year sentence.

In the long run, the Prisoner's Dilemma suggests that decisions based solely on self-interest do not always lead to the greater good of the participants when played out in experimental simulations and in real life. The sheriff in the prisoner's dilemma is expecting the prisoners to rely on this egoistic logic and is betting that the prisoners will choose the self-interested alternative, which will not result in the greater good of the prisoners. Egoistic choices, in fact do tend to undermine their overall good and lead to a less-than-optimum outcome for both prisoners. However, if the prisoners cooperate, the outcome for both is a higher utility value.

Examples of this preference for cooperative rather than competitive mindset abound in the business world. Cigarette advertising provides one example of the Prisoner's Dilemma. Cigarette manufacturers agreed to strict regulations on the advertisement of their products because it was the cooperative option that would reduce advertising costs across the industry. Before this legislation, cigarette companies were destined to counterbalance the costly advertising campaigns of their competitors with their own equally costly campaign or suffer the consequence of lost market share. The government regulation introduced a cooperative option like the Prisoner's Dilemma option #3 in which all parties cooperate and remain silent. Under this option, cigarette-company profits increased as advertising budgets plummeted.[54] These kinds of results should inspire all participants in the business world to more seriously consider, for practical reasons, the cooperative moral vision of the common good.

Another insight has to do with how individuals relate in community to the corporation. If it is true that individuality is determined in part by one's place in the community, then belonging to a certain type of community provides both an individual and a collective identity. It follows then that the moral character of the community or corporation—the principles it instills, the values it enforces, and the behavior it upholds—carries enormous ethical weight. This holds true for both internal relationships between corporate owners, managers, and employees, as well as for external relationships with government bodies, the community, and the environment. Laws and policies should fulfill the requirements of the common good in order to establish a working environment with a strong sense of collective identity. From the perspective of the common good, corporations need to pay more attention to the moral

---

54. Gidean Doran. "Adminstrativie Regulation of an Industry: The Cigaretter Case," *Public Administration Review* 39, no. 2 (1979): 163–170.

aspects of their corporate culture. In fact, the moral aspects should take precedence over all other considerations when a corporation is seeking to reform its culture.

Additionally, key individuals working for the company need to uphold the primacy of moral considerations when forming a corporation around the priorities of the common good. Leadership roles within the corporation should be defined first by their moral attributes, with the understanding that professional competence flows from the moral commitment to technical excellence. Presently, business roles are defined according to professional attributes that focus attention on things such as corporate survival, profitability, efficiency, productivity, marketing, finance, production, and human resources. Moral attributes that focus attention on things such as community, distribution, participation, contribution, justice, solidarity, courage, and moderation generally play a secondary role, if they play any role at all.[55] Perhaps one of the lessons learned from the most recent outbreak of corporate scandals will be an ancient one. The common good dictates that leadership should be, first of all, moral. Professional competence should flow naturally from a moral commitment to technical excellence.

Finally, the common good tradition stresses that individuals within society have both rights and responsibilities in relation to the larger body. Liberal political and economic traditions, founded on the philosophies of John Locke and Adam Smith, place greater stress on the rights individuals can claim from society. While individual rights remain crucial to a well-ordered society, society can also demand certain responsibilities from the individuals who reside within that body politic. The common good tradition has a broader understanding of responsibilities than the liberal traditions found in modern capitalist democracies. Every right an individual holds has a corresponding responsibility that needs to be exercised in order to maintain balance within the social milieu. In the business world, this aspect of the common good helps correct the distorted prioritization of profit maximization in every business decision. Although businesses have the right (and responsibility) to profit from their enterprise, they cannot achieve these profits at the expense of the common good. Businesses have a multitude of rights and responsibilities and the first of these is not always profit making. The good achieved for individuals must always be weighed against the good of the commons, or the common good.

---

55. Naughton, Alford, and Brady categorize these attributes into what they call fundamental desires (what I have termed *professional attributes*) and excellent desires (what I have termed *moral attributes*): 209–14.

Case Study

Executive Pay and Economic Crisis

For several years following the spring of 2008, U.S. banking and finance experienced its deepest crisis since the Great Depression of the 1930s. In the first few months of that catastrophic crash, the largest financial institutions, which had defrauded investors out of billions of dollars, were kept afloat by taxpayers, who funded an $800-billion slush fund that loaned enormous sums to insolvent insurance companies and teetering banks. Meanwhile, executives and administrative employees of these financial institutions were taking home disproportionate shares of the profits, even after the market had gone bad and these institutions were at risk of failing.

Bear Stearns, for instance, paid out $11.4 billion in compensation and employee benefits in the three years leading up to the crisis, while its shareholders only received on the order of $1.4 billion in J. P. Morgan Chase stock when the company was sold. The executives of Lehman Brothers received $21.6 billion in the same three-year period, and their shareholders were left with nothing when the company went bankrupt. During this same period, Merrill Lynch paid executives more than $45 billion, while its shareholders had to settle for stock in Bank of America that was worth less than a fifth of the original offer value. In 2007 alone, Citigroup paid out $34.4 billion in compensation and yet a few years later the company was valued at about half this figure. The most egregious case of all was the insurance giant AIG, which paid executives $165 million in bonuses in March 2009 as part of a larger $450 million package, in spite of the fact that the company had lost $61.7 billion in 2008 and had been bailed out by taxpayers to the tune of $170 billion.[56] Meanwhile, the pay of the average worker in the United States remained stagnant and the minimum wage eroded.

Long before the economic crash in 2008–09, executive pay was outsized in the United States, both in comparison to historical standards and to the norm in other contemporary capitalist countries. In 1980, the average CEO of a *Fortune* 500 company in the United States made 42 times the income of the average worker, which was in proportion to the ratio going back many decades to World War II. By the end of the 1980s, though, that ratio had jumped to 85 times,[57] and by the year 2000, it had ballooned to 525 times. An examination of data across cultures reveals a similar disparity. For instance, in Canada the contemporary ratio of executive compensation to

(continued)

---

56. "Attacking the Corporate Gravy Train," *Economist* 391, no. 8633 (May 30, 2009): 71–73.

57. John A. Byrne, "The Flap Over Executive Pay," *BusinessWeek*, no. 3212 (1991): 90–96.

Case Study

(continued)

average worker pay is 20 to 1, and in Japan, it is 11 to 1. Overall, CEOs in the United States make three times as much as their peers in other countries around the world.[58]

Many theories purport to explain these disparities in CEO compensation. One such explanation, the marginal revenue-production theory, claims CEOs in a competitive labor market who produce increased revenue for a company ought to be compensated according to the increased value they brought to the enterprise. If they do not receive compensation in line with their value, other companies will recognize the opportunity and offer these leaders a more lucrative deal. All of the companies referenced lost enormous revenue during the same period in which executive pay increased logarithmically. According to the theory of marginal revenue production, then, executive pay should have plummeted along with the bottom line.[59] However, in reality, executive pay seems to defy all laws of gravity.

Another theory used to explain the unusual and suspicious pay disparities in American corporations is known as tournament theory. This theory conceives of the various national CEO labor markets as different levels of a single-elimination tournament. The smaller global markets are likened to bush-league tournaments in which prizes are less lucrative because the competitors have less talent and the stakes are correspondingly lower. The American CEO labor market, by comparison, is the most elite and competitive tournament in the global capitalist arena and attracts the most select talent. Therefore, along with the highest stakes come the highest compensation and the most lucrative returns.[60]

Once again, there is little direct correlation between the theory and the actual practice of CEO compensation. If the tournament theory accurately described real practice, then CEO compensation in the various national economies would at least roughly correspond to the size and influence of that economy within the larger global marketplace. While American CEOs are the highest paid by far and the US economy is the largest on the planet, compensation in the second-largest economy,

(continued)

---

58. Economic Policy Institute, *State of Working America 2004/2005* (Ithaca, NY: Cornell University Press).

59. Derek Bok, *The Cost of Talent: How Executives and Professionals Are Paid and How It Affects America* (New York, NY: The Free Press, 1993).

60. David B. Wilkins and G. Mitu Gulati, "Reconceiving the Tournament of Lawyers: Tracking, Seeding, and Information Control in the Internal Labor Markets of Elite Law Firms," *Virginia Law Review* 84, no. 8, Symposium: The Law and Economics of Lawyering (November 1998): 1581–1681.

Case Study   *(continued)*

Japan, remains relatively low. In fact, CEO pay scales in places other than the United States do not seem to correlate to the relative size and influence of the national economy.

Other theories that try to explain and justify the unprecedented expansion in CEO pay in market terms, such as the opportunity-cost theory, suffer a similar fate. From the perspective of neoclassical market theory, increased access to financial markets in the United States has driven down the barriers to entry in many industries, which has, in turn, increased competition for talent. This increased competition for executive talent is often cited as the key catalyst for the current disparity in executive pay. However, this factor, when taken alone and compared historically and across national boundaries, does not seem to determine executive pay in any consistent pattern that would suggest this is somehow a causative factor.

While neoclassical capitalist economic theorists have attempted to validate the expansion of executive compensation, others have sought explanations outside the realms of market theories. Many have pointed out that executives from one company normally sit on the board of directors of other companies, which results in a closed system of country-club pals making decisions about each other's compensation. It seems unsurprising, then, that this small, elite group of individuals struggles to be critical, demanding, and modest in its remunerative policies when it comes time to evaluate the performance and salaries of the CEO. In these kinds of closed social systems a sort of mutual-admiration society develops that logically feeds the expansion of executive pay in a way that becomes difficult to track and nearly impossible to hold accountable to stakeholders, especially when those stakeholders regularly hear about the necessity of ever-increasing executive pay scales due to the always-escalating competition for talented leaders.

Many have complained that enormous executive bonuses and pay packages are tantamount to stealing from stockholders and other employees of a company. The argument suggests that American companies actually have become less competitive in relation to their global peers due to the wasteful squandering of capital resources on individuals whose contribution does not match the value of their compensation.[61] All of these issues raise questions about whether these compensation practices serve the common good.

(continued)

---

61. "Featured graphic: Worldwide Differences in Executive Pay, Culture, Well-Being, and Economic Growth," *Environment & Planning A* 42, no. 2 (February 2010): 255–56

Case Study   *(continued)*

Questions

1. How does the expansion of executive pay in deteriorating economic times affect the common good?

2. What principles does the common good offer that might suggest a different approach to executive compensation?

3. How would executive compensation be administered if it were ordered toward achieving the common good?

4. If you owned a *Fortune* 500 company, what would be the most important qualifications for your executive positions? What qualities would you look for in job candidates for CEO?

Case Study

A. G. Parfett & Sons Ltd.: Employee Ownership[62]

Steve Parfett is the managing director of a wholesale cash-and-carry operation in Stockport, UK, that was founded by his parents, Alan and Pat, in 1980. Parfetts is an established and respected business that has grown from a single store in Stockport into a sizable national enterprise. The firm now has revenues of almost $400 million per year and employs nearly 600 people at six trading depots located around the country.

In most respects, the story of Parfetts is typical of a successful family business, launched and maintained through years of hard work and sacrifice, first by Alan and Pat and later by their son Steve, who took over the helm when his father turned sixty in 1989. However, a decade and a half later Steve was in his fifties and looking toward retirement, which raised questions about the future of the business.

The potential third generation for the business, the children of Steve and his siblings were young, inexperienced, undercapitalized, or still in school, and although they showed interest in the family firm, none demonstrated a strong vocation toward it. Even if one or more of the next generation had shown both interest and acumen, their transition to leadership positions

(continued)

62. Information for this case was gathered from A. G. Parfett & Sons website, *http://www.parfetts.co.uk/*, as well as a series of ten case studies authored by Andrew Bibby, "From Colleagues to Owners," *http://www.caseplace.org/d.asp?d=4643*.

Case Study   *(continued)*

would have involved a potentially challenging interim period during which the company would have had to rely on professional management or run the risk that Steve would never really get to retire properly. The family began to seek alternatives to their dilemma. "I called the members of my family together in late 2006, and said 'we don't have to risk precipitous decisions but we do need to think about this,'" Steve says. The family agreed, and Steve began researching the options available to them.

After looking into various conventional options, such as a management buy-out, management buy-in, business sale to a competitor, and purchase by an overseas investor, Steve ultimately relied on past experience to help him settle on the right course for Parfetts. Steve had started his business career as an intern with the John Lewis Partnership, which was an employee-owned business, and was impressed with this model. Along with his finance director, David Grimes, Steve attended an employee ownership conference in 2007, and both returned energized and with new ideas about how to help the company transition to a new model of ownership. In January 2008, the family decided that Parfetts would become employee-owned. In order to accomplish this transfer of ownership, 55 percent of the shares in the company were initially deposited into an employee benefit trust (EBT). A bank loan with a fifteen-year maturity funded the purchase and was secured using the business's freehold properties.

In order to avoid burdening their new employee-owned business with debt, the Parfett family agreed to a 20 percent discount on the full-market value price for the 55 percent shareholding. Steve admitted that this probably represented "a bigger discount from what a competitor might have offered." The plan was to sell the remaining 45 percent to the EBT over the course of the next eight years. The Parfett family also agreed to forego dividends during this interim period.

Steve claimed that the family "spent considerable time debating the different types of employee ownership, and a key consideration was whether to go for individual ownership of shares." Instead they settled on what was known as the John Lewis model, in which all shares would be held collectively for the benefit of all employees. Because the workforce at Parfetts included large numbers of shop floor workers without immediate access to business finance instruments, this model was deemed more appropriate and would cause fewer problems going forward. Steve claimed that, "in terms of explaining employee ownership to people, the more straightforward the better. The danger of direct shareholding is that there is always someone

(continued)

Case Study

who gets excluded. We want all to be in it together." This model of employee ownership pays all staff an annual partnership bonus rather than paying out the traditional share dividends.

Communicating the radical changes in the ownership model to the employees was the next task that Steve and the other members of the management team had to tackle. "We put aside a full fortnight, and the whole executive board went around the business, meeting staff in groups of about twenty. We wanted to get across our passion and enthusiasm. People needed to understand. This was absolutely crucial," Steve explained. They held dozens of meetings and hired the independent consulting firm Baxi Partnership's Baxendale to help with this enormous task. Parfetts eventually put in place a new representative structure to facilitate employee input on critical management decisions.

A series of branch councils (one for each depot) comprised of elected staff replaced the more top-down management style of the past. Each of the branch councils, in turn, nominated two members to the new company-wide council, which had the task of planning and overseeing the strategic management of the company. "The normal executive board will run the business, but will be answerable to employees. I think we're open-minded about the question of employee participation on the executive board, but we don't think this is appropriate just at the moment," Steve explained. The EBT had been set up initially with two employee representatives (one of them the current finance director), two family members, and an independent chairperson.

In recent times, the employee-owned business sector has been growing. Only a decade or two back, only a handful of employee-owned businesses existed, and these were seen as anomalies that swam in waters well away from the mainstream of capitalist markets. Today, as this case demonstrates, the employee-owned business model cannot be dismissed so readily. Many conventional businesses encourage employee stock ownership; however, an employee-ownership model like the one used by Parfett means something more than mere share ownership. It means a business functions primarily for the benefit of the workforce, because the employees are—individually or collectively—owners of the business. This emerging model of business ownership challenges the traditional proprietor or share-owner models that currently dominate the landscape, while raising practical as well as moral questions about the way societies understand ownership.

(continued)

Case Study *(continued)*

Questions

1. Using the common good as the standard, how does the employee-owned business model compare to other traditional models of capitalist ownership?
2. What benefits and risks do you see in the employee-ownership model in comparison to other traditional models of ownership?
3. If you owned a business, under what conditions might you consider shifting to the employee-ownership model?
4. Do you think employee-ownership might someday become popular, or even dominate in the capitalist marketplace? Why or why not?

For Further Reading

Ahmad, Jamilah, and David Crowther. *Education and Corporate Social Responsibility International Perspectives.* Bingley, UK: Emerald, 2013.

Crouch, Colin. *Making Capitalism Fit for Society.* Hoboken: Wiley, 2013.

Gröschl, Stefan. *Uncertainty, Diversity and the Common Good: Changing Norms and New Leadership Paradigms.* Farnham: Ashgate Publishing Ltd., 2013.

Okonkwo, Bartholomew. *Christian Ethics and Corporate Culture: A Critical View on Corporate Responsibilities.* Cham Switzerland: Springer, 2014.

Rowe, Jonathan, and Peter Barnes. *Our Common Wealth: The Hidden Economy That Makes Everything Else Work.* San Francisco: Berrett-Koehler, 2013.

Thompson, Mike, and David Bevan. *Wise Management in Organisational Complexity.* Houndmills, Basingstoke, Hampshire: Palgrave Macmillan, 2013.

Zamagni, Stefano, Luigino Bruni, and Antonella Ferrucci. *Handbook on the Economics of Reciprocity and Social Enterprise.* Northhampton, MA: Edward Elgar, 2013.

Chapter 3

Stewardship and the Educated Consumer

Elizabeth W. Collier

Introduction

The last chapter ended with a discussion of the ways in which Christians are inspired by their tradition to care for those resources they own in common with others in society. One essential element of a complete understanding of the common good is the notion that humans share many things in common and that a major contribution to the common good is to nurture and care for the commons—that part of the world that is not owned by individuals but is held in common to be used by everyone. Stewardship is the recurring theme in CST that speaks most clearly to how and why people should care for the commons. It is a theme focused on explaining human responsibility for shared social structures, communal environments, and the global ecosphere. This chapter is dedicated to the task of illuminating the often hidden world of the commons and explaining how humans need to care for their interconnected world in order to achieve the common good.

This chapter starts with a short quiz. Ready? Choose three things that you have eaten today and write them on three different areas of a piece of paper. Now try to answer the following questions about each item: Was it raised organically or conventionally? Was it flown in from another continent? Was it harvested last night and driven to a farmer's market this morning? Did taxpayers subsidize its production? If you consumed fish, where did it come from? Was it given growth hormones or antibiotics? What nutrients did the three foods give you? Were the workers who participated in the production of the food paid a fair wage?

Most people in the United States would have trouble answering these questions. Even those who try to be informed consumers can often only discover fragments of information about the food they consume. Moreover, many remain unaware of the impact that current large-scale food production processes and transportation to market have on them, their health, their communities, and the environment. This disconnect does not just occur with food production. The same issue arises with almost everything people purchase and use everyday—clothing, cell phones, water bottles, toothbrushes.

People rarely know the *who, what, where,* and *how* products are made and what the human and environmental costs are. Although a detailed explanation of the *why* for this is beyond the scope of this chapter, generally speaking the reasons relate to global supply chains, in which the harvesting or extraction of raw materials and subsequent steps of production and transportation for just one product involves many subcontractors and workers in multiple countries. Even retailers who order and sell products are often unaware of the steps required to bring the products to market.[1]

If the processes of moving goods to market are unknown, how can consumers make ethical purchase decisions and how can companies make ethical production decisions? A concept developed in CST that relates to these ethical determinations is stewardship. Christians believe that humans are called by God to be caretakers or stewards of *all* of creation, including each other, everything found in nature, and the goods people create. The Christian tradition teaches that the goods of the earth are meant to contribute to the flourishing of all people and communities. This chapter examines the biblical roots of the concept of stewardship and then introduces the theological developments of the concept in Catholic social thought. The case studies that conclude the chapter invite readers to consider e-waste and food production issues in light of the principle of stewardship.

Biblical[2] and Theological Roots of Stewardship

Old Testament

The Christian understanding of stewardship is rooted in the two creation stories in the book of Genesis. These stories illumine the beliefs of the early Israelites regarding the origins of the world and of humanity, as well as how humans relate to one another and to God.

The first creation story (Genesis 1:1–2:3) includes several elements that indicate what the human disposition toward the created world should be. First, as God calls forth a new part of creation each day, God reflects on what was

---

1. Listen to the *Planet Money T-Shirt* podcasts to better understand the challenges involved in being an informed consumer or even an informed producer, *http://www.npr.org/series/248799434/planet-moneys-t-shirt-project.*

2. The scripture passages cited in this section are examples. They do not exhaust the references that could be cited in relation to the various points.

created that day and considers each aspect of creation to be "good." On the first day, for instance, God creates the light:

> In the beginning, when God created the heavens and the earth—and the earth was without form or shape, with darkness over the abyss and a mighty wind sweeping over the waters—
> Then God said, Let there be light, and there was light. God saw that the light was good. (Genesis 1:1–4)

This mantra occurs at end of the descriptions of most of the days of creation: "God saw that it was good." From a biblical perspective, creation itself is deeply imbued with goodness that God sees and declares. This goodness is an intrinsic goodness that goes to the core of everything brought into existence. The *being* of creation is good in and of itself. The text in Genesis is understood by Christians to be revealing to humans that they should likewise see the created world in this light and act accordingly.

As the creation story continues, God eventually gives humans "dominion" over creation:

> Then God said: Let us make human beings in our image, after our likeness. Let them have dominion over the fish of the sea, the birds of the air, the tame animals, all the wild animals, and all the creatures that crawl on the earth.

> God created [hu]mankind in his image,
>   in the image of God he created them;
>   male and female he created them.

> God blessed them and God said to them: Be fertile and multiply; fill the earth and subdue it. Have dominion over [creation]. (Genesis 1:26–28)

Scripture scholars point out that the words describing human dominion, or God's command for humans to subdue the earth, relate to the work that humans would have had to do to create livable situations when nothing had yet been tamed. The passages are not meant to sanction domination, as many understand that term today. For instance, in Genesis humans are forbidden from killing animals for food—plant life would sustain humans.[3] Christians interpret Genesis's use of the terms *dominion* and *subduing* in light of belief that God is loving, relational, and dynamic; that God's creative acts are imbued with goodness; and that God created humankind with an orientation toward caretaking relationships.

---

3. See Richard J. Clifford, S.J., and Roland E. Murphy, O. Carm., "Genesis," in *The New Jerome Biblical Commentary*, eds. Raymond E. Brown, S.S., Joseph A. Fitzmyer, S.J., and Roland E. Murphy, O.Carm, (Englewood Cliffs, NJ: Prentice-Hall, Inc., 1990), 11.

In the Christian view, humans are both part of creation and co-creators who are called to relate to the rest of creation as the Creator God relates to humankind. God dwells at the center of the relationships among all of creation. This points to a foundational element of stewardship: all of creation is in relationship. The principle of stewardship calls on humans to support just relationships among all of creation.

The book of Leviticus adds some important elements to the concept of stewardship. In Genesis, Exodus, and Deuteronomy, God establishes the Sabbath. On the seventh day of each week, the Israelites, their slaves, their livestock, and the resident aliens (foreigners living in their midst) are *all* to rest (Exodus 20:8–11). Leviticus institutes a further type of "rest" in the form of sabbatical and jubilee years. In Leviticus 25:1–8, God instructs the Israelites to sow and prune their fields for six years but to leave them fallow during the seventh year to rest the land. This sabbatical year both recognizes the necessity of resting the land to ensure its continued productivity and asserts God's ultimate ownership over the land.[4]

In the fiftieth year, the community would celebrate a jubilee year: "You shall treat this fiftieth year as sacred. You shall proclaim liberty in the land for all its inhabitants. It shall be a jubilee for you, when each of you shall return to your own property, each of you to your own family" (Leviticus 25:10). If a family had lost its land to others as payment of debt or for other reasons, that land was to be returned to the original family. The land ultimately belongs to God, with each family having land for its use and sustenance. During the jubilee year, debts were to be forgiven and slaves were to be set free. This concept of jubilee fits into the general disposition that humans should have toward one another, the land, and possessions—ultimately everything belongs to God. Humans act as caretakers of what God has given and this caretaking (not sole proprietorship) is central to creating a community in which every person and family can flourish.

The exhortations to observe the Sabbath, sabbatical year, and jubilee year point to some of the values necessary for a community to flourish and to maintain its covenant with God. In the biblical text, God sets other mandates to encourage care for those marginalized by society. For instance, financially struggling community members were not to be charged interest (Exodus 22:25). Farmers were not to harvest their entire crop but were to leave some for the poor to harvest (Exodus 23:11). The community was to care for the marginalized. In Scripture, the widow, the orphan, and the alien[5] are usually the most marginalized because these people did not have a senior male advocate in the patriarchal socioeconomic or political structures (Exodus 22: 21–24, Leviticus 19:34, Deuteronomy 10:17–18; 26). God hears the cries of

---

4. Bruce M. Metzger and Roland E. Murphy, eds., *The New Oxford Annotated Bible with the Apocryphal/Deuterocanonical Books*, New Revised Standard Version (New York, NY: 1991), 157.

5. The word *alien* is the term used to describe someone who was not born to one of the families in the clan or the "people" of that area. They were "foreigners" to one degree or another.

these marginalized peoples, and the community has a responsibility to care for them (Deuteronomy 15:7–11).

Fred Kammer, a Jesuit, a lawyer, and a former head of Catholic Charities USA, has written about an important cycle that recurs in the Old Testament. Referred to as the Cycle of Baal,[6] it begins with the community honoring its covenant with God and working together for the flourishing of all in the community. At the cycle's start, the Israelites understand the importance of being a caretaker or steward. As time passes, some in the community prosper more than others. Those who choose to be stewards continue to share their bounty with the community so the less prosperous could meet their needs. Some, however, choose not to be stewards but see themselves as the rightful owners of their bounty, selling it for profit or storing it for their own use later in case of a drought or a less plentiful harvest. When the prosperous adopt an "ownership" disposition, others suffer.

The owners, rather than focusing on God and God's covenant with the community, take as their "end"[7] the accumulation of power or wealth. As a result, the community goes from a situation in which all members could meet their needs to one of social stratification, leaving some economically disadvantaged and marginalized. When the community does not respond, the poor cry out to God for help, and God hears their cries (Job 34:28, Psalm 34).

Throughout the Old Testament when the cries of the poor become loud, God sends a messenger to remind the Israelites of their covenant and their responsibilities toward the community. Often those in power do not want to hear what the messenger (or prophet) proclaims (Proverbs 21:13), so they kill the prophet. In time, the decisions of those in power enslave the whole community of Israel. Then the whole community cries out to God for deliverance and God frees them from the enslavement. The Israelites return to a community configuration that values human dignity, stewardship, care for the poor, and all that God's covenant entails. This cycle is repeated throughout the Hebrew Scriptures.

Kammer argues that this cycle underscores that a community can only flourish if the whole group practices a stewardship that addresses the needs of all: "In [this] process, the three fundamental insights of their early scriptures were reinforced: the goodness of creation, their stewardship over these gifts, and their identity as community in which God dwelled and all, especially the poor, were cared for."[8]

---

6. Fred Kammer, S.J., *Doing Faithjustice: An Introduction to Catholic Social Thought* (Mahwah, NJ: Paulist Press, 2004), 26–37.

7. An "end" is something set as an ultimate value in life, toward which all action is oriented. Kammer talks about this in terms of creating "gods" other than God. Something such as money or power or prestige becomes the goal in life, rather than being a steward and contributing to the community and the development of human dignity.

8. Kammer, *Doing FaithJustice*, 34.

New Testament

The New Testament further develops the Hebrew Scriptures' understanding of caretaking and stewardship. It often refers to Jesus as "teacher," and many stories relate to or mention his teaching in synagogues. The understanding of the writer of the Gospel of Luke, for instance, is that Jesus has authority when discussing God and God's plan for humanity. Luke understands Jesus' teaching as a continuation of the truths in the Hebrew Scriptures.[9]

The concept of the jubilee in particular proves central to the portrayal of Jesus' ministry. In the Gospel of Luke, for instance, Jesus begins his public ministry in Galilee, preaching in the synagogue on the Sabbath. He reads from the prophet Isaiah:

> "The Spirit of the Lord is upon me,
>   because he has anointed me
>   to bring good glad tidings to the poor.
> He has sent me to proclaim liberty to captives
>   and recovery of sight to the blind,
>   to let the oppressed go free,
> and to proclaim a year acceptable to the Lord."
>
> Rolling up the scroll, he handed it back to the attendant and sat down, and the eyes of all in the synagogue looked intently at him. He said to them, "Today this scripture passage is fulfilled in your hearing." (4:18–21)

By showing Jesus reading from the ancient Jewish scrolls and preaching in the synagogue, Luke situates Jesus within the context of God's promises in the Old Testament and shows the continuation of the theme of the jubilee.[10] Jesus' ministry often discusses the themes of "restoration, beginning, faith in the sovereignty of God and conviction that the structures of social and economic life must reflect God's reign."[11] Kammer explains that Luke's presentation of Jesus "projects that whole matrix of meanings: the goodness and right order of creation; how Yahweh meant us to live together in covenant community sharing the goods of creation; and the privileged place of the *anawim* (those marginalized in society) at the heart of faithful living."[12]

Scholars often cite Matthew 25:31–46 when discussing the values that should order life. While the passage above from Luke describes initial days of

---

9. Robert J. Karris, O.F.M., "The Gospel According to Luke," in *The New Jerome Biblical Commentary*, 689. Jesus was raised in an observant Jewish family and would have been familiar with the Hebrew Scriptures.

10. Ibid., 689.

11. Ibid., 690.

12. Kammer, *Doing FaithJustice*, 47.

Jesus' public ministry, Matthew 25:31–46 can be viewed as its "grand finale."[13] Jesus tells the story of what may be the "end of times," or what some might call Judgment Day. People are separated into two groups, one on the right hand of the Son of Man, and one on the left. To those on the right, Jesus says that they are blessed and will inherit the kingdom prepared for them:

> "'For I was hungry and you gave me food, I was thirsty and you gave me drink, a stranger and you welcomed me, naked and you clothed me, ill and you cared of me, in prison and you visited me.' Then the righteous will answer him and say, 'Lord, when did we see you hungry and feed you, or thirsty and give you drink? When did we see you a stranger and welcome you, or naked and clothe you? When did we see you ill or in prison, and visit you?' And the king will say to them in reply, 'Amen, I say to you, whatever you did for one of these least brothers of mine, you did for me.' Then he will say to those on his left, 'Depart from me, you accursed, into the eternal fire prepared for the devil and his angels. For I was hungry and you gave me no food, I was thirsty and you gave me no drink, a stranger and you gave me no welcome, naked and you gave me clothing, ill and in prison, and you did not care for me.' Then they will answer and say, 'Lord, when did we see you hungry or thirsty or a stranger or naked or ill or in prison, and not minister to your needs?' He will answer them, 'Amen, I say to you, what you did not do for one of these least ones, you did not do for me.' And these will go off to eternal punishment, but the righteous into eternal life." (Matthew 25:35–46)

This passage highlights the belief that care of those in need is central to attaining salvation. This is consistent with the Cycle of Baal that Kammer describes: if the community does not help its neediest members, the entire community eventually becomes enslaved and needy. It also points to the necessity of the jubilee year, which allows for a restoration every generation. In the between times, if needs arise, individuals and the community have a responsibility to mind the gap.

In *Toward a Christian Economic Ethic*, Daniel Finn and Prentiss Pemberton argue that the responses to Jesus' commands about using material goods and property fall into two main categories. The "foregoers" are those who "renounce nearly all economic possessions and resources."[14] Jesus chose this lifestyle and commanded a similar lifestyle to many of his disciples. Pemberton and Finn call the second group "stewards," noting that "[Jesus] recognized another, broader, less austere economic ethic for those disciples not called to become foregoers.

---

13. Benedict T. Viviano, O.P., "The Gospel According to Matthew," in *The New Jerome Biblical Commentary*, 669.

14. Prentiss Pemberton and Daniel Finn, *Toward a Christian Economic Ethic*, 31.

This other public economic ethic was more readily universalizable and was required of all disciples."[15]

They cite Zacchaeus as an example of a steward. According to Luke 19:1–10, when Zacchaeus, a rich, chief tax collector, heard that Jesus was passing through the area, he climbed a tree in order to get a look at him. Jesus saw him and announced that he would be staying at Zacchaeus's house that night. Others were unhappy with Jesus' choice to stay at the home of a "sinner." They despised tax collectors, viewing them as collaborating with the Romans in their domination of the Jews. Zacchaeus says, "Behold, half of my possessions, Lord, I shall give to the poor, and if I have extorted anything from anyone, I shall repay it four times over" (Luke 19:8). Jesus does not tell Zacchaeus to give more or even the "right" amount; instead, he states that salvation has now come to his home. The message is that people determine their responsibility first by understanding their accountability to others, and second by deciding what to do based on one's available resources.[16]

Pemberton and Finn point out that Jesus calls not only the wealthy to stewardship but also people with few means.[17] In the parable of the talents (Matthew 25:14–30), in which the master of the household gives three servants money before he leaves for a journey, the person given the least amount of money was held accountable for not being a steward of even what little he had been given. He did not invest the money but hid it in the ground. Some interpret this parable from an economic perspective, but others discuss it in the context of one's ultimate disposition toward anything that one has access to. In the biblical text, God gives each person talents to use for the good of the community. Jesus tells the servant who buried the treasure, "For to everyone who has, more will be given and he will grow rich; but from the one who has not, even what he has will be taken away" (Matthew 25:29). The overarching point is that Jesus calls each person to be a steward. This entails determining what one needs for basic survival and what one can share with others. The story contains a warning of what happens when one does not demonstrate good stewardship: "And throw this useless servant into the darkness outside, where there will be wailing and grinding of teeth" (Matthew 25:30).

The parable of the widow and her offering to the temple fits into the foregoer category described by Pemberton and Finn.

> Many rich people put in large sums. A poor widow also came and put in two small coins worth a few cents. Calling his disciples to himself, he said to them, "Amen, I say to you, this poor widow put in more than all the other contributors to the treasury. For they have all contributed from their surplus wealth, but she, from her poverty, has contributed all she had, her whole livelihood." (Mark 12:41–44)

---

15. Ibid.
16. Ibid., 33.
17. Ibid., 35–36.

This story highlights that not everyone is called to the same approach to life. Individuals must determine whether they are called to be a foregoer or a steward. No matter one's original socioeconomic status, those seeking to live according to the Gospels must discern God's call regarding one's possessions.

The key is one's disposition toward created goods and money, which has a strong biblical foundation. According to the Bible, God gives everything to humankind as a gift. Many passages tell of people understanding that their gifts or resources are meant for the community. For those who saw Jesus' return as imminent, foregoing material goods and setting out to spread the word of his return made sense. Others, who did not see Jesus' return as imminent, a group that grew over time, grappled with how to understand more practical day-to-day realities such as property, wealth, relationship with the state, and so forth. They knew from the covenant with the Israelites that everyone in the community should have a voice in determining what resources to make available to the needy in the community. They also believed that people are called by God to use their gifts for the sake of the community. As it says in Romans 12:4–8,

> For as in one body, we have many parts, and all the parts do not have the same function, so we, though many, are one body in Christ and individually parts of one another. Since we have gifts that differ according to the grace given to us, let us exercise them: if prophecy, in proportion to faith; if ministry, in ministering; if one is a teacher, in teaching; if one exhorts, in exhortation; if one contributes, in generosity; if one is over others, with diligence; if one does acts of mercy, with cheerfulness.

This and other passages indicate that the community flourishes through the gifts of its members when all contribute.

Historical Development of the Concept of Stewardship

Early Church

During the initial decades after Jesus' death, his followers passed on their experiences of him and some wrote letters to other communities about their understanding of Jesus' mission and of how they should live. They also had to work out their relationships with the religious and political authorities. Initially Jesus' followers understood themselves as part of Judaism, but over time they became known as Christians and a community distinct from Judaism.

During the early centuries of the church, Christians sought to understand how Jesus' teachings affected daily life, and they spread their faith and established communities in many different geographical locales and cultures. They looked to the Scriptures and Jesus' teachings for guidance on how to handle such things as the goods of the earth, financial resources, and possessions; and they recorded their insights in sermons and writings. The following excerpts from early Christian writings provide a glimpse into how the church developed the thought of the Old and New Testaments.

The Didache, which dates from the later half of the first century or the beginning of the second, contains the following exhortations:[18]

> Give to everybody who begs from you, without looking for any repayment, for the Father wants that we should share his gracious bounty to all men.
>
> Give without hesitation and without grumbling, and you will discover who He is that will requite you with generosity. Never turn away the needy; share all your possessions with your brother, and call nothing your own.

Clement of Rome, the third successor to Peter, wrote about social solidarity:

> In Christ Jesus, then, we must preserve this corporate body of ours in its entirety. Each must be subject to his neighbor, according to his special gifts. The strong are not to ignore the weak, and the weak should respect the strong. The rich must provide for the poor, and the poor should thank God for giving him someone to meet his needs.[19]

A first- or second-century text called the *Shepherd of Hermas* comments:

> Live in peace with one another, care for one another, help one another. Do not enjoy God's creatures excessively and all by yourselves, but give a share also to those who are in need.
>
> Do good, and from the fruit of your labors, which is God's gift to you, give to all those in need without distinction, not debating to whom you will and to whom you will not give. Give to all, since it is God's will that we give to all from his bounties.[20]

Clement of Alexandria was an important intellectual figure in the third century. Although born in Athens, Greece, he was interested in the intellectual development of the Christian tradition and found a teacher and an intellectual community in Alexandria, Egypt.[21] He addresses a well-known text called *Who Is the Rich Man That Shall Be Saved?* to an audience consisting of intellectuals and wealthy people used to a lavish lifestyle.[22]

---

18. Peter C. Phan, *Social Thought: Message of the Fathers of the Church*, Vol. 20, (Wilmington, DE: Michael Glazier, Inc., 1984), 44–46.

19. Ibid., 46–47.

20. Ibid., 51–55.

21. Justo L. Gonzalez, *The Story of Christianity: Volume 1, The Early Church to the Dawn of the Reformation* (San Francisco, CA: HarperSanFrancisco, 1984), 71.

22. Phan, *Social Thought: Message of the Fathers of the Church*, 64.

Generally speaking, riches that are not under complete control are the citadel of evil. Those casting their eyes covetously on them will never enter the kingdom of heaven, because they allow themselves to be contaminated by the things of this world and are living proudly in luxury. Those concerned for their salvation should take this as their first principle, that, although the whole creation is ours to use, it is made for the sake of self-sufficiency, which anyone can obtain with a few things.[23]

These excerpts demonstrate a consistent thread in early Christian social thought: God created the goods of the earth and desired that humans take care of them and share them. In particular, the wealthy are to share with the poor, because the poor have no other means by which to attain what they need, and covetousness can lead to the suffering of others.

Another theme that developed in the early centuries of the church focuses on the unique gifts of each person. God created the world in such a way that people have access to different resources and have their own particular gifts. All of these are destined for the wider community if used rightly. This social destination of talents is integral to living in right relationship with communities functioning as God intended.

Medieval Period: Aquinas

One of the Catholic Church's most important theologians was Thomas Aquinas (1225–1274), a Dominican priest. A prolific writer, Aquinas left a systematic foundation for understanding God, the world, and how humans should relate to both. In his *Summa Theologica*, Aquinas discusses a broad array of issues related to God, creation, human existence, and the relationship between all of these and daily existence. His work takes the form of asking questions and then giving answers and objections, so people clearly understand why only one answer is correct.

Two parts of Aquinas's thought prove particularly relevant to stewardship: the purpose of creation and, within that context, the purpose of property. Aquinas places his theories within the larger framework of the natural law. The Catholic tradition believes that God created the world within the context of a certain eternal or divine order. The divine order within which something was created relates to the *nature* of that created entity, which then relates to how it functions properly in relationship with the rest of creation.

Although humans do not fully understand the overarching, eternal law, they can understand the nature of something and how to properly relate to it through reason. This is the "natural law." Through reason, humans can understand the

---

23. Ibid, 65–66.

order and nature of creation. Richard Gula explains: "This sense of 'reason' includes observation and research, intuition, affection, common sense, and an aesthetic sense in an effort to know human reality in all its aspects. In short, whatever resources we can use to understand the meaning of being human will be appropriate for a natural law approach."[24]

Aquinas focuses on the natural law in the *Summa* I–II, qq. 90–97.[25] It is set within the context of *exitus et reditus*, which means that all things come from God and all things return to God.[26] God has made all of creation with a certain purpose and order. Consistency with that order and purpose is the essence of the created entity's participation in the natural law. Ultimately everything will return to God. This maintains the emphasis of the Scripture and tradition preceding Aquinas. A person might possess something, but he or she is not the ultimate destination for that good. It is destined for the common good, and ultimately, God. What Aquinas specifically contributes is the insight that everything that has been created has a specific purpose within the natural law, and humans can use reason to understand the right stewardship of goods and property.

In the *Summa* II–II q. 66, Aquinas discusses the possession of external goods, arguing for the legitimacy of private property for three reasons: people take better care of things that belong to them personally; human affairs overall are better organized if people take responsibility for them; and clear ownership to property leads to fewer disputes. Aquinas explains that all of this comes about due to human law but has the value of and does not contradict the natural law. In addition to these arguments, though, Aquinas contends that humans need to share—clear ownership does not mean sole use of a good.[27]

Aquinas further explains the distinction between ownership and use of something in the case of necessity: "In cases of necessity everything is common property and thus it is not a sin for someone to take the property of another that has become common property through necessity."[28] For example, someone unable to feed his or her family might steal food and, due to the circumstance, not commit a sin. Aquinas would assert that in these circumstances it is not a sin to steal food because the purpose of food, within the context of divine law and natural law, consists of satisfying human needs. The one who possesses the

---

24. Richard M. Gula, S.S., *Reason Informed by Faith: Foundations of Catholic Morality* (Mahwah, NJ: Paulist Press, 1989), 224.

25. Aquinas, Thomas, O.P., *Summa Theologica*, I–II 90–97, *http://dhspriory.org/thomas/summa/FS.html#TOC09*.

26. Gula, *Reason Informed by Faith: Foundations of Catholic Morality*, 224.

27. *St. Thomas Aquinas on Politics and Ethics*, trans. and ed. Paul E. Sigmund (New York: WW Norton & Company, 1988), 72.

28. Ibid.

needed item can decide how to use it for the good of others. At the same time, if that person does not share and that good is truly necessary, then the individual in need "may legitimately supply his need from the property of someone else, whether openly or secretly."[29]

Aquinas challenges Christians to consider how personal possessions might serve others. One relevant example might be transportation. For example, a college student who lives off-campus has to figure out how to get to and from school, how to get groceries, and so forth. Some areas have good public transportation and some do not. Public transportation often takes longer than driving oneself and bad weather can add a complication. Sometimes one person in a group of friends has a car, though. That person probably pays for the car, insurance, gas, regular maintenance, and parking.

Aquinas would argue that on the one hand, privately owning a car is appropriate because it falls within established social conventions and satisfies his three reasons. However, the car owner is supposed to have the internal disposition of a *caretaker*. The car owner can use the car for the purposes consistent with ownership. Additionally though, the car owner must consider the ways in which the car can serve a wider social good than just what the owner needs. What is the social destination of a car? The owner needs to determine realistic parameters for sharing the car. Maybe this means that even though it requires leaving 30 minutes earlier than necessary, two friends who do not have cars can be picked up a few days a week. Maybe someone can be brought along to the grocery store once a week. In this context, the car owner has to make a choice to use the car for others. In another instance, a friend may have a genuine emergency that requires the owner to cancel other plans in order to drive the friend to wherever the emergency demands. The extent of necessity determines the extent of the obligation in order to fulfill the nature of the good and the obligations of stewardship.

Developments in Catholic Social Teaching

Late Nineteenth and Early Twentieth Century

Although significant events in Christian history and many important developments in the political, economic, and social spheres took place in the centuries following Aquinas, the nineteenth century saw the most significant explicit reflections on social issues and the development of the Catholic Church's official social teaching.[30]

---

29. Ibid., 73.

30. As mentioned previously the officially promulgated documents of the Catholic Church on social, political, and economic issues are often referred to as Catholic social teaching.

This section summarizes key points from three documents in order to show the development of the concept of stewardship from the late nineteenth century through the latter part of the twentieth century. It begins with *Rerum novarum* (On the Condition of Labor, 1891), commonly understood to be the first "official" document of the social encyclical tradition, addressing issues related to the Industrial Revolution. The chapter then discusses Pope Paul VI's encyclical *Populorum progressio* (The Development of Peoples, 1967), written shortly after the Second Vatican Council (1962-1965), a time when the church was grappling with increased communication, technology, the beginnings of globalization, issues with formerly colonized countries, and what some called "development" in places such as Latin America. Finally, the chapter looks at John Paul II's *Centesimus annus* (One Hundred Years after *Rerum novarum*, 1991). John Paul II's long papacy coincided with a period of significant development and expansion of globalization, a portion of the cold war era, a period of increased development worldwide, and the growing realization that Earth's resources are exhaustible.

Rerum novarum (On the Condition of Labor)

The encyclical *Rerum novarum*, promulgated by Pope Leo XIII in 1891, addresses the relationship between the laborer, his or her labor, and remuneration, the possibility of obtaining private property, and the rights and duties of the wealthy and the poor. The concept of stewardship is key to understanding the intersection of these issues.

> Moreover, the earth, even though apportioned among private owners, ceases not thereby to minister to the needs of all, inasmuch as there is not one who does not sustain life from what the land produces. Those who do not possess the soil contribute their labor; hence, it may truly be said that all human subsistence is derived either from labor on one's own land, or from some toil, some calling, which is paid for either in the produce of the land itself, or in that which is exchanged for what the land brings forth. (*RN*, no. 8)

Later in the same document, Leo XIII bolsters his argument about what is necessary for a working person. The head of household must be able to provide for the needs of the family, such as property for the present and for the future—to pass down as an inheritance to the children. Even more, though, the family serves as the basic unit of human community and "precedes" the state. This means that although humans set up various civil societies with rules and regulations for living in relative peace and order, none of these can justly keep people from fulfilling basic needs. Society cannot place constraints on individuals and families that disallow private property or effectively remove it from the realm of possibility.[31]

RN then explains how employers and managers should understand the work of their laborers and compensation:

> The following duties bind the wealthy owner and the employer: not to look upon their work people as their bondsmen, but to respect in every man his dignity as a person ennobled by Christian character. They are reminded that, according to natural reason and Christian philosophy, working for gain is creditable, not shameful, to a man, since it enables him to earn an honorable livelihood; but to misuse men as though they were things in the pursuit of gain, or to value them solely for their physical powers—that is truly shameful and inhuman. (*RN*, no. 21)

RN cautions employers not to require more from their workers than realistically possible, to pay people what is just and due to them, and not to take advantage of the duress of the poor and gain from their unfortunate circumstances.[32] *RN* then quotes Aquinas and discusses money in the context that Aquinas discussed property—one has a right to wealth, but the right *use* of wealth may require sharing it.

> To sum up, then, what has been said: Whoever has received from the divine bounty a large share of temporal blessings, whether they be external and material, or gifts of the mind, has received them for the purpose of using them for the perfecting of his own nature, and, at the same time, that he may employ them, as the steward of God's providence, for the benefit of others. (*RN*, no. 22)

RN explains that the twin sins of greed and "thirst for possessions" lead people away from this teaching. The Pope explains that people overcome by greed and the desire for possessions can end up miserable in the midst of their abundance. They can even make bad decisions and ultimately squander all that they have and all that they could have passed on to their heirs. *RN* revisits the practice of the early Christian communities of sharing goods so everyone had their needs met. This sharing especially impacts those in the community who

---

31. Another example of this relates to immigration. Catholic social teaching asserts that every human has a right to seek and find employment in his/her country of origin. However, if such employment does not exist, people have a right to migrate to another country to seek it. Although countries have the right to regulate their borders, this right to seek employment and meet one's needs precedes the existence of the state. Countries may not regulate their borders in such a way as to exclude those seeking work if the purpose in regulation is to maintain a high standard of living.

32. The duties of the workers are enumerated as well but will not be dealt with in this chapter.

have more or access to more. The document warns that the state cannot favor the rich over the poor—all people are equal and this equality precedes the state. The state must protect the common good, of which the poor are an equal and important part.

When *Rerum novarum* was promulgated in 1891, the Roman Catholic Church in the United States was growing rapidly due to the large numbers of immigrants from Catholic countries. In the nineteenth century, US Catholics understood stewardship as including prayer, fasting, and almsgiving, with a significant emphasis on the almsgiving. From the perspective of their faith, Catholics believed that when they helped "the poor" they gave an outward sign of their inward faith and that their salvation depended on these good works.[33] Given the socioeconomic status of most immigrants and the extensive network of Catholic institutions built to help those who needed money, resources, health care, assimilation, and so forth, US Catholics found plenty of opportunities to give.

At the turn of the twentieth century, though, the term *stewardship* became synonymous with money and the handling of personal financial resources.[34] Catholics established themselves in the political and economic life of the United States, the Catholic Church spread west, and more members moved out of the immigrant class and climbed the economic ladder. As Catholics had more, the Church and laity had to grapple with age-old questions: How much should one give to others? What constitutes surplus income? Is one's motive for giving important? Should the rich receive honors for donating large amounts of money?[35]

Although the terms *stewardship* and *steward* cropped up in conversations and writings, the terms did not often appear in official church teaching. *Rerum novarum* does not use them, and neither does *Quadragesimo anno* (The Reconstruction of the Social Order, 1931), Pope Pius XI's social encyclical. An important document promulgated by the US bishops in 1919, "The Bishops' Program for Social Reconstruction," mentions it only once: "The capitalist must likewise get a new viewpoint. He needs to learn the long-forgotten truth that wealth is stewardship, that profit-making is not the basic justification of business enterprise, and that there are such things as fair profits, fair interest and fair prices."[36] Although the term is not often used, *the concept of stewardship* appears in many places and connects to the concepts of human dignity, the

---

33. Mary J. Oates, "Interpreting the Stewardship Mandate: A Historical Exploration of the American Catholic Experience," *New Theology Review*, 4, no. 9 (1996): 11.

34. Ibid., 13.

35. Ibid., 13–17.

36. Administrative Committee of the National Catholic War Council, "The Bishops' Program for Social Reconstruction," February 1919, *http://www.stthomas.edu/cathstudies/cst/aboutus/bishopsprogram.html.*

common good, the preferential option for the poor, and other issues related to justice. In the second half of the twentieth century, the Church's recognition of the interrelatedness of these concepts increased and the understanding of stewardship in official writings expanded.

Populorum progressio (The Development of Peoples)

Giovanni Battista Montini was one of Pope John XXIII's closest confidants. They worked together closely throughout John XXIII's pontificate, which focused almost exclusively on calling, preparing for, and presiding over the Second Vatican Council (1962–1965).[37] Both men had similar ideas about what the hierarchy of the church needed to address in the institutional Catholic Church and the social sphere in light of global events.[38] Pope John XXIII died after the first session of the council, and Montini was elected pope, taking the name Paul VI.

Montini had extensive exposure to CST as a child. Early in his priesthood and while serving as archbishop of Milan, he showed great interest in working with the poor. As archbishop, he traveled to many impoverished areas and studied how different economic decisions affected the poor.[39] These experiences and the vision he shared with John XXIII form the backdrop for *Populorum progressio* (*PP*) a document he wrote after becoming pope.

Populorum progressio, promulgated in 1967, focused on economic justice. The topic of development became an important issue in the 1960s. Some areas of the world had been integrally involved in the Industrial Revolution, increased trade and interdependence, as well as technological advances. In these areas, primarily the United States, Western Europe, and Japan, standards of living had significantly increased. Other areas of the world had not seen such development and remained mired in difficult circumstances, in part because of colonialism and its aftermath. Other factors included internal conflict in nations experiencing military dictatorships, where insurgents supported by either the United States or the Soviet Union fought with various groups. Many had questions about how to view development. The difficulties of those in the undeveloped parts of the world were complicated by the historical, political, economic, and social forces at play.

---

37. Vatican II was an ecumenical council, a meeting of the world's Catholic bishops. Pope John XXIII called for Vatican II in 1959 in order to allow the church to "open the windows and let in some fresh air" and to respond to changes to contemporary realities. For more about Vatican II, see *What Happened at Vatican II*, John W. O'Malley (Belknap Press of Harvard University Press, 2010).

38. Allan Figueroa Deck, S.J., "Commentary on *Populorum progressio* (On the Development of Peoples)," ed. Kenneth R. Himes, OFM, *Modern Catholic Social Teaching: Commentaries and Interpretations* (Washington, DC: Georgetown University Press, 2005), 295.

39. Ibid, 196.

The pope attempted to address the situation, working with Catholic thinkers of the time in the process of writing *Populorum progressio*.[40] Paul VI wanted to offer a vision of development that involved more than simply economic development.

> The development We speak of here cannot be restricted to economic growth alone. To be authentic, it must be well rounded; it must foster the development of each [person] and of the whole [person]. As an eminent specialist on this question has rightly said: "We cannot allow economics to be separated from human realities, nor development from the civilization in which it takes place. What counts for us is [the human person]—each individual [person], each human group, and humanity as a whole." (*PP*, no. 14)

Paul VI explains the individual and communal dimensions of this development. Each individual must develop a vocation, which implies stewardship and participation in the community. God gives each person talents and passions whose ultimate destination are the community and God: "At birth a human possesses certain aptitudes and abilities in germinal form, and these qualities are to be cultivated so that they may bear fruit" (*PP*, no. 15) The development of one's qualities and contributions has God the Creator as their ultimate destination, or *telos*. This holds true for all human activity and is ultimately how one experiences and embodies self-fulfillment.

Because the individual is always in relationship with others, the fulfillment of the individual integrally relates to the fulfillment of the community and society.

> Each [person] is also a member of society; hence [he/she] belongs to the community of [humanity]. It is not just certain individuals but all [peoples] who are called to further the development of human society as a whole. . . . We are the heirs of earlier generations, and we reap benefits from the efforts of our contemporaries; we are under obligation to all [people]. Therefore we cannot disregard the welfare of those who will come after us to increase the human family. The reality of human solidarity brings us not only benefits but also obligations. (*PP*, no. 17)

The pope also discusses how the pursuit of possessions should not be the goal of individuals or nations. Although he does not use the words *steward* and

---

40. According to Deck in "Commentary on *Populorum progressio* (On the Development of Peoples)," many people with interests in CST, economics, Christian humanism—some of whom had also been involved in the writing or thinking behind Vatican II documents—from the United States, Great Britain, and France, all had a hand in the development of *PP*. Ibid., 296–7.

stewardship in this document, that is what he is talking about. When members of the community see themselves as owners—as opposed to stewards—of possessions that ultimately have a social destination, the result is social stratification within the community. Pursuing material goods as an ultimate end, or *telos*, prevents one from being fully human and hinders the fulfillment of both the individual and the larger community: "Avarice, in individuals and in nations, is the most obvious form of stultified moral development."[41] Paul VI draws on the creation stories and early Christian figures when he says: "it follows that every [person] has the right to glean what he needs from the earth."[42] As a result of this truth, "all other rights, whatever they may be, including the rights of property and free trade, are to be subordinated to this principle. They should in no way hinder it; in fact, they should actively facilitate its implementation. Redirecting these rights back to their original purpose must be regarded as an important and urgent social duty."[43]

Drew Christiansen, S.J., places these concepts from in *Populorum progressio* in the context of ecology, using the term *personal ecology* to describe the necessary elements for personal fulfillment (with God as *telos*): "basic needs, culture, education, esteem, participation in the common good, the spiritual life, growth in charity, and so on."[44] Christiansen uses the term *social ecology* to describe the existence of these elements and a sharing of advancements with other peoples to limit social imbalances and inequalities and ensure the possibility of human and societal fulfillment for all.[45] Stewardship and understanding the social destination of goods and advancements are crucial to the existence of such ecology.[46]

Sollicitudo rei socialis (On Social Concern)

John Paul II promulgated the encyclical *Sollicitudo rei socialis* (On Social Concern, 1987) to commemorate the twentieth anniversary of *Populorum progressio*. He begins by saying that "the social concern of the Church, directed towards an authentic development of [the person] and society which would respect and promote all the dimensions of the human person, has always expressed itself in the most varied ways" (no. 1).

---

41. Ibid., no. 19.

42. Ibid., no. 22.

43. Ibid.

44. Drew Christiansen, S.J., "Learn a Lesson from the Flowers," eds., Maura A. Ryan and Todd David Whitmore, *The Challenge of Global Stewardship: Roman Catholic Responses* (South Bend, IN: University of Notre Dame Press, 1997), 24.

45. Ibid.

46. For a more extensive discussion of *PP*, see Deck in "Commentary on *Populorum progressio* (On the Development of Peoples)," and his selected bibliography, 313–314.

Sollicitudo rei socialis (SRS) includes the first mention in an encyclical of the environmental aspect of development: "Nor can the moral character of development exclude respect for the beings which constitute the natural world . . ." (no. 34). John Paul II identifies three considerations related to the environment:

> The first consideration is . . . that one cannot use with impunity the different categories of beings, whether living or inanimate . . . simply as one wishes, according to one's own economic needs. . . .
>
> The second consideration is based on the realization . . . that natural resources are limited; some are not, as it is said, renewable. . . .
>
> The third consideration refers directly to the consequences of a certain type of development on the quality of life in the industrialized zones. (*SRS*, no. 34)

In outlining his concerns about development in general and specifically its impact on the environment, the pope calls on all people to understand what is at stake.

> Thus one would hope that all those who . . . are responsible for ensuring a "more human life" for their fellow human beings . . . will become fully aware of the urgent need to change the spiritual attitudes which define each individual's relationship with self, with neighbor, with even the remotest human communities, and with nature itself; and all of this in view of higher values such as the common good. (*SRS*, no. 38)

John Paul II puts everyone into relationship with nature itself, a nod to the foundational Christian belief that God created the world with a particular order and ultimate destination. When humans go beyond an orientation of *creation as gift destined for all* and make the accumulation and ownership of goods the ultimate goal, they upset this order and ultimately create serious problems for individuals, societies, and creation itself.

Business Application

There are several different ways of applying the concept of stewardship within business. The first relates to each person individually and is vocation oriented. CST challenges all people to consider how they can be stewards of the gifts God has given to them. Protecting human dignity and achieving the common good requires the participation of everyone. Each individual must ask what gifts, talents, passions, or resources can be of service to others. Throughout one's life the needs of communities and each individual's talents and resources will change or develop, such that one's capacity to serve changes over time.

One's discernment about how to be a steward is often tied to professional aspirations. Some people have jobs in which they use their best talents doing work in which they serve others—jobs in which the workers feel they are responding to the call to be stewards. Others respond to the call to be stewards outside of the workplace. A marketing professional might donate time to help a nonprofit organization improve its presence in a community. A salesperson might help the staff of a nonprofit association hone their sales and fund-raising skills. An accountant might serve on a parish finance council or assist a small enterprise as a volunteer.

A second way individuals respond to the call to be stewards is through decision making related to economics. In capitalist societies, most individuals can affirm or reject values or practices through decisions about spending money or investing capital. Note that those with little income in such societies are often limited in their exercise of finance-related stewardship, especially if they live in areas with few retailers.

The choice to buy goods such as toothpaste, toilet paper, and other basic necessities in a particular store is, in a sense, a vote for that store. In a capitalist system, the decisions made by consumers are intended to serve as checks and balances. If a company offers a good product at a good price, then consumers will reward that company with their business. However, the reverse is also true.

A person trying to respond to CST's call to be a steward might ask some of the following questions when discerning how to spend money: Am I able to purchase goods or services at a retailer that pays its workers a just wage? Am I able to support local and family-owned retailers? Am I willing to pay a higher price in order to avoid companies with unfair labor practices? Am I willing to research companies' business practices and factor the information into purchasing decisions? Good stewardship of one's purchasing power requires one to learn about how companies do business and to think critically in order to arrive at the best responses.

People can also exercise stewardship of their financial resources through choices about investments. Those with large capital investments or in a position to organize investors into voting blocs can pressure companies at stockholder meetings to contribute to the achievement of the common good. For example, the website of the Interfaith Committee for Corporate Responsibility lists shareholder resolutions it supports.[47] Its initiatives relate to everything from a company's impact in the environment, lobbying activities, CEO compensation and corporate governance, to human rights and tobacco marketing in developing countries.

Individuals can also exercise stewardship when opting to invest in a 401(k) or 403(b). On the one hand, the purpose of an investment portfolio is to

---

47. *http://www.iccr.org/shareholder/trucost/index.php.*

capitalize on profitable companies enough throughout one's career to be able to retire with sufficient resources. The maximization of the investment is important, especially for people who don't want to be in a position of relying on social safety nets at their retirement. On the other hand, investments serve to support companies. Investing in a company is a way of voting for it with one's dollars. Responding to CST's call to be a steward involves making informed choices about the companies one invests in.

CST's call to stewardship is meant for business leaders as well as individual consumers. For instance, if a business's production processes require water and produces waste such as a gas emission, the call to stewardship challenges its leaders to consider the environmental impacts and to mitigate any that are negative. This might require the business to spend money in order to minimize or eliminate the pollutants or clean the water and return it to its source. It might also require the business to adopt policies far more stringent than the law requires, especially if doing business in countries without pollution controls. The negative impact of businesses on the environment, especially large multinational corporations and the military industrial complex, is confronting humanity in life-altering ways, so responding to the call to stewardship in this particular area is of paramount importance.

The challenge of stewardship affects businesses as employers as well. Responding to the call to stewardship requires businesses to consider their use of human resources. How are employees compensated? How are work hours and employment opportunities and benefits allocated? What is the ratio between CEO or upper-level management pay and other pay scales within the company? Do the employees of a company have a disproportionate impact on the means-tested benefits due to low wages or poor benefits options from their employer?

As stated previously, the concept of stewardship challenges every aspect of business. How can a business enterprise be a steward of each and every thing that it has access to? These questions are asked in light of all things humans have at their disposal as understood by Christians as gifts from God and in the context of their honoring God's creation of the world and their ability to be co-creators.

Conclusion

The concept of stewardship is one of the central elements in the interconnected web of concepts that make up (CST). This chapter explores the theme of stewardship in the Hebrew Scriptures and how it related to the experience of the Hebrew people in ancient times. The New Testament shows how Jesus maintained the Jewish understanding of stewardship, and the early Christian writers worked out more specifically what the concept of stewardship meant to early Christian communities. From the medieval period forward, theologians and church officials have continued to develop the understanding of stewardship and apply it to the new circumstances. As this chapter shows, stewardship is fundamentally about one's disposition toward the created world and all created goods. CST calls people to act as caretakers and to understand that everything is a gift from God.

Case Study

E-Waste

For most segments of US society, mobile phones are now ubiquitous. Pre-school children can be more adept at using their parents' phones than their parents are! Not long ago, people had only landline phones and paid per-minute fees for long-distance calls. Now a person can take a self-portrait photo with a cell phone in one country and post it on Facebook via the phone's app, and a friend halfway around the world can view it on another cell phone a few seconds later and "like" it.

Mobile phone technology has made life around the world, for many, totally interconnected, more convenient, and in some instances, even safer. In the midst of the ubiquity of cell phones though, a rarely discussed issue lurks—what happens to the cell phone once someone has upgraded? Because the latest and greatest cell phones are quickly surpassed by new models, many people opt for a new phone when their contract comes to an end. This leads to a glut of technology that has not exhausted its lifespan. Cell phones can be donated for use in nonprofit services, or they can be dropped off in a box marked for recycling at big-box chain stores. But what happens to most cell phones when the original buyers are finished with them? A report in the *New York Times* indicates that people in the United States replace their cell phones every twenty-two months, and they discarded 150 million phones in 2010.[48] The article explains that women and children in poor countries, where many of the phones are ultimately dumped, spend time picking through e-waste and burning it in order to collect the metals so they can sell them to a recycler. Most of the metals, such as lead, cadmium, and mercury, are toxic, so exposure to them endangers the health of those involved.[49] In 2008 CBS's *60 Minutes* program investigated what happened to e-waste products (cell phones, tablets, and laptop computers) brought to a

(continued)

---

48. Leyla Acaroglu, "Where Do Old Cell Phones Go To Die?" *New York Times*, May 4, 2013, *http://www.nytimes.com/2013/05/05/opinion/sunday/where-do-old-cellphones-go-to-die.html?_r=0.*

49. Ibid.

Case Study   *(continued)*

citywide recycling event in Denver, Colorado. They followed one container of computer monitors that was shipped to Hong Kong, in violation of US and Hong Kong laws. The monitors ended up in a small town in southern China where people take apart the e-waste and burn it. The town is almost uninhabitable due to poor air and water quality, and those who live there suffer the consequences of the highly toxic environment: high-lead blood level in 70 percent of children and six times higher-than-average rates of miscarriages.[50]

According to an article in *Fast Company*, 17,000 tons of e-waste is thrown away or recycled every day.[51] This article gives many different infographics on why and how e-waste can be recycled. It claims that in the United States, the United Kingdom, and Spain, about 15 percent of e-waste is recycled, which is a higher percentage than in other countries. The article argues that recycling is important because in every one million mobile phones, there are "9 kilograms of palladium, 24 kilograms of gold, 250 kilograms of silver, and 9,000 kilograms of copper."[52] The article goes on to argue that it's easier to recoup these metals than to mine new ones and this is an area of business that can be greatly expanded and create many jobs.[53]

Questions

1. What issues related to the concept of stewardship apply to the information in this case study? (Consider the individual, the community, and business in general.)

2. Identify business practices cited in the case study that create a challenge for those committed to stewardship.

3. How does the concept of stewardship challenge consumer behavior associated with cell phones?

4. What is the relationship between stewardship and a business solution to the problem of e-waste?

---

50. *60 Minutes*, "Following the Trail of Toxic E-Waste," August 27, 2009, *http://www.cbsnews. com/8301-18560_162-4579229.html*.

51. Ariel Schwartz, "Visualizing the World's E-Waste Problem," *Fast Company*, *http://www. fastcoexist.com/1681368/visualizing-the-worlds-e-waste-problem*.

52. Ibid.

53. Ibid.

Case Study

Do You Know What You Are Eating?

When walking into a typical chain grocery store in the United States, one encounters a dizzying array of choices year-round. Strawberries, asparagus, and corn on the cob are available in Chicago in January. Almost any imaginable type of cereal is sold, from bran sticks and dried fruit to Reese's peanut butter cup or Oreo flavors. Shoppers can find both fresh baked goods and processed products with long shelf lives. Steaks, pork loin, salmon, or king crab legs are available. The products come from all over the world.[54]

With the obesity epidemic and exploding numbers of people with type 2 diabetes, both of which are and will continue to put greater pressure and cost on our health-care system, there has been increased scrutiny of what's on those grocery store shelves and on the lack of knowledge that people have when it comes to what they eat, what a serving size is, and whether companies are or should be involved in the solution. Many people don't know how many calories should be consumed each day to maintain a healthy weight or what the maximum amount of sugar is that should be consumed in one day. The same is true for sodium.

Many blogs, websites, and grass-roots movements encourage people to educate themselves on their food choices. The purpose of these is not to keep consumers from enjoying a jelly doughnut or Cheetos, but to help them understand what they consume in the aggregate and how to make generally healthy choices. Many websites will advise sticking to the perimeter of any grocery store—that's where the fresh produce, meat, fish and seafood, and dairy sections are located. They will also tell you that when shopping in the middle aisles, choose only items that have ingredients that can be pronounced and identified and appear close in form and substance to their original source in nature.

One ingredient that receives a lot of attention by consumers, food producers, and powerful, multinational agribusiness companies is high-fructose corn syrup. USDA research estimates that per capita consumption of high-fructose corn syrup in 1970 was 0.3 pounds, per person, per year. In 1980 that rose to CMS 10.70: lb. per year. In 2012, it reached 27.1 lb. per year.[55] Iowa State

(continued)

(continued)

---

54. It should be noted that the USDA estimates that 23.5 million Americans live in food deserts—places where there is no access to affordable, healthy food. With a population of around 314 million, this represents about 13 percent of the population. *http://apps.ams.usda.gov/fooddeserts/foodDeserts.aspx.*

55. US Department of Agriculture, Economic Research Service, Table 52, *Sugars and Sweetners Outlook*, updated May, 28, 2013.

Case Study   *(continued)*

University Extension and Outreach research shows that a 2-liter bottle of soda contains more corn than an 18-ounce box of corn flakes—there are 15 ounces in the soda and 12.9 ounces in the cereal box.[56] The pancake syrup on store shelves is corn syrup with brown coloring added, unless pure maple syrup is specifically noted on the label. The cost difference is a good indicator of the ingredients. The jelly on a PBJ sandwich might have fruit as its first ingredient, or the first ingredient might be corn syrup. CapriSun offers two types of drinks: one type that contains fruit juice and another that has corn syrup instead of actual fruit juice. Corn syrup is used as a sweetener in many products on the interior of the grocery store because food producers add sweetener to almost everything, including applesauce and canned peaches, and because it is cheaper than actual sugar. One reason it is cheaper is that the US government heavily subsidizes corn growers, so they aren't subjected to the pricing pressuresof supply and demand in the same way that producers of nonsubsidized products are.

Many consumer grass-roots movements have forced food producers to stop using high-fructose corn syrup and return to the original recipes of products. A 2010 *New York Times* story explains how ConAgra eventually decided, due to consumer pressure, to take corn syrup out of it's Hunt's brand ketchup. The companies that make Gatorade, Pepsi, Wheat Thins, and Starbucks sandwiches have all made changes to their products due to consumer pressure.[57]

The companies that produce and sell high-fructose corn syrup argue that it is no worse for the human body than sugar, but it is so much cheaper. They also have made efforts to change the language they have to use in food labels, such as to drop *high fructose* from the description. Both sides arguing about the inclusion of corn syrup in foods cite various studies supporting their own positions. What is clear though, is that sweeteners, sugar or corn syrup, along with other unhealthy additions, such as artificial colors, very high sodium levels, etc., pervade processed foods. Even if people agree that more Americans should be educated about how to make healthy food choices, whose responsibility is that? How are people educated?

(continued)

---

56. *http://www.extension.iastate.edu/publications/pm2061.pdf.*

57. Melanie Warner, "For Corn Syrup, the Sweet Talk Gets Harder," *New York Times*, May 1, 2010, *http://www.nytimes.com/2010/05/02/business/02syrup.html?pagewanted=all&_r=0.*

Case Study   *(continued)*

Questions

1. How does the concept of a "social destination for goods" challenge large corporate food producers and the products they make?
2. What questions might a person focused on stewardship of farmland ask agribusiness operations?
3. How does the information in this case study challenge individual consumers intent on being good stewards of their grocery dollars?
4. Many people agree that more Americans should be educated about how to make healthy food choices. Whose responsibility is that? Using stewardship as a guide, how might people become more educated?

For Further Reading

Catechism of the Catholic Church, Part 3, Section 2, Article 7, "The Seventh Commandment: You Shall Not Steal," *http://www.vatican.va/archive/ccc_css/archive/catechism/p3s2c2a7.htm.*

Catholic Climate Covenant: *http://www.catholicclimatecovenant.org/.*

Christian Brothers Investment Services, Inc., *Becoming a Catholic Fiduciary, http://www.cbisonline.com/fiduciary/media/pdf/CathFiduciary_FULL.pdf,* found at *http://www.cbisonline.com/fiduciary/default.asp.*

Schaefer, James, and Tobias Winwright, *Environmental Justice and Climate Change: Assessing Pope Benedict XVI's Ecological Vision for the Catholic Church in the United States.* Lanham, MD: Lexington Books, 2013.

Chapter 4

In Search of a Capitalist Option for the Poor

Thomas O'Brien

Introduction

The last chapter explained the ways good stewardship was an essential principle for all aspects of a business enterprise. Stewardship is a theme that acknowledges and illuminates the interconnected nature of the modern global economy and the complex relationships that characterize this contemporary corporate climate. It's especially concerned for those elements of the market that are easily overlooked and frequently forgotten when important decisions are made. An ethic of stewardship claims that we need to be attentive to these neglected elements of the marketplace, such as the polluted environment, the exploited workers, and the blighted communities, precisely because these underappreciated aspects may be the key to achieving the common good. This focus on what has been overlooked is precisely the basic motivation behind the theme of this chapter, the preferential option for the poor.

At first glance, a concept titled "preferential option for the poor"[1] might appear to be an awkward fit for a discussion about capitalist corporations, which mainly focuses on wealth maximization within a system of intense competition. Corporations and capitalists are not judged on the basis of their largesse toward the economically marginalized; neither are they expected to improve the lot of the least well off. Therefore, it is fair to ask: what does an "option for the poor" have to do with the mission of modern capitalism?

---

1. See John Paul II, *Centesimus annus* (1991), nos. 11, 57, for a discussion and definition of this theme of Catholic social teaching from an official perspective, *http://www.vatican.va/holy_father/john_paul_ii/encyclicals/documents/hf_jp-ii_enc_01051991_centesimus-annus_en.html.*

This chapter addresses the question by first defining an option for the poor and briefly explaining its place in the history of Catholic social teaching (CST). Illustrations demonstrate how this concept compares to, and differs from, the more familiar concept of charity. Unlike some other themes in CST, the "preferential option for the poor" is a theological concept; therefore, references to Scripture and tradition provide a deeper understanding of this ideal.

This chapter also explores the apparent incongruity between Catholic and capitalist social theories.[2] It examines some recent developments in what is known as social business or social enterprise, which challenge and expand narrow, classical notions of laissez-faire capitalism precisely by turning to the poor in a way that closely mirrors what is called for in CST. These contemporary developments challenge the belief that the preferential option for the poor is inherently antagonistic to markets, competition, companies, and the law of supply and demand. These social enterprises suggest that capitalism has suffered from a myopic social vision that can be corrected by the application of a new kind of social lens that not only makes room for the poor, but also recognizes that the poor represent some of the best opportunities in the emerging global economic climate.

Preferential Option for the Poor: A Primer

When North American Catholics first encounter the concept of the preferential option for the poor, their initial instinct is often to ask how this differs from *caritas*, or charity. They say: "Didn't we learn about this in religious education or summer Bible camp when we were in grade school?" Most recall being told to be nice to the poor and give canned food at Thanksgiving or toys at Christmas. Some harbor romantic Dickensian images of Tiny Tim living in squalor and hobbling around with his makeshift crutch. Others hold darker conceptions of poverty that cast the poor into the role of social outcast, miscreant, or criminal. Nevertheless, whether the poor warm people's heart or deeply disturb their psyche, most understand that the Catholic Church wants them to be nice and give to the poor, especially during certain holidays. Disabusing people of such overly simplistic notions usually takes great effort, and in the end, many still walk away hearing, not what was said, but what they expected to hear about Christian concern for the poor.

The preferential option for the poor is not charity. It does not negate or contradict charity; it simply belongs to a different conceptual genus. These two concepts should be thought of as complementary within the larger framework of

---

2. See Pius XI, *Quadragesimo anno* (1931), nos. 102–110, for a more extended discussion of CST on the problems this perspective sees in the capitalist system, *http://www.vatican.va/holy_father/ pius_xi/encyclicals/documents/hf_p-xi_enc_19310515_quadragesimo-anno_en.html.*

Catholic morality. While charity is a close relative of *agape,* or love, the preferential option for the poor is in the same conceptual family as *aequitas,* or justice.[3] Like love, charity applies to smaller-scale, interpersonal settings, while the preferential option for the poor, like justice, tends to have a broader social focus.[4] A perspective informed exclusively by charity tends not to question or challenge the legitimacy of the social structures that have created conditions of privilege and poverty. It is generally uninterested in questions regarding what caused poverty in the first place and may even accept explanations that include some kind of characterization of the poor as lazy, stupid, or backward. By contrast, the preferential option for the poor focuses primarily on the structural causes of poverty, and it normally rejects biased rationalizations that tend to dehumanize the poor and marginalized.[5]

In practice, charity tends to be a temporary and limited redistribution of wealth from relatively privileged individuals to certain select groups of poor people. For this reason, it can be accompanied by attitudes of paternalism—in which social superiors share their superfluous wealth with social inferiors without questioning why or how these disparate social roles developed in the first place and whether they are legitimate from the perspective of someone who embraces the Christian message.

By contrast, the option for the poor tends to inculcate a different kind of practice, one that involves standing in the shoes of the poor, working and living with the poor, and forming equal peer-to-peer relationships that highlight the dignity of all parties.[6] CST understands such social inequalities as unnatural and, therefore, imposed against the will of God. For this reason, they are considered sinful, and Catholics are called on to rectify any circumstances of injustice.[7] From this perspective, charity may be necessary, but it is only a temporary first step. The genuine Christian mission, according to the option for the poor, involves undermining and eventually overturning these disordered hierarchical relationships so that humans can return to a primordial state of equality. Therefore, taking an option for the poor ultimately focuses on the achievement of justice, which undermines the distortions of privilege and power and restores right relationships between people.

Option for the poor also serves as a hermeneutic—a way of seeing and interpreting the world—that favors viewing and understanding the world from

---

3. John Paul II, *Centesimus annus,* no. 58.

4. John Paul II, *Sollicitudo rei socialis* (1987), no. 42, *http://www.vatican.va/holy_father/john_paul_ii/encyclicals/documents/hf_jp-ii_enc_30121987_sollicitudo-rei-socialis_en.html.*

5. John Paul II, *Centesimus annus,* no. 28.

6. US Catholic Bishops Conference, *Economic Justice for All* (1986), no. 16, *http://www.osjspm.org/economic_justice_for_all.aspx.*

7. Kevin E. McKenna, *A Concise Guide to Catholic Social Teaching* (Notre Dame, IN: Ave Maria Press, 2002), 72.

the perspective of the poor and oppressed. Some theologians, such as Fred Kammer, claim that the world looks very different from the point of view of the poor and marginalized than it does from positions of wealth and power.[8] This theology gives preference to the perspective of the poor because only from this point of view can the artificiality of hierarchical privilege be truly seen and understood as disordered and sinful.[9] CST sometimes refers to this preference for the grass roots as *subsidiarity*. The option for the poor, therefore, entails being with and standing alongside the poor and oppressed, which connects it to the key theme of *solidarity* in CST.

From a Christian theological perspective, not only humans take an option for the poor. God was the first to give special attention to the poor, and the Scriptures encourage one to view God's actions as a model for personal behavior. Both the Old and New Testaments exhort people to defend the poor and lift up the lowly.

Foundations in Scripture

Option for the poor, as a perspective within Christian theology, also includes a particular interpretation of Scripture. It is certainly not the only, or even the prevailing, interpretation of any given book or passage in the Bible. However, CST encourages reading Scriptures in the light of the experiences of the poor, recognizing that those experiences can shape the way the reader understands and appropriates the messages gleaned from these texts. The claim is that, at least in some instances, the scriptural text is best understood through the eyes of one who has suffered, or one who stands with and advocates for those who suffer, from poverty and marginalization.

This interpretation of the Bible grounds the concept of social equality in the theological insight that people are creatures of the Creator God[10]—possessing a special dignity and playing a unique role in the order of the universe (Genesis 1:26). In the first chapter of Genesis, the human is formed in the image of the Creator: "God created mankind in his image; / in the image of God he created them; / male and female he created them" (Genesis 1:27). The story asserts that creation was given over as a common heritage for all people to enjoy responsibly.[11] Nothing in the first chapter of Genesis suggests that some persons can or

---

8. Fred Kammer, S.J., *Doing Faithjustice: An Introduction to Catholic Social Thought* (New York, NY: Paulist Press, 1991), 447–49.

9. Pontifical Council for Justice and Peace, *Compendium of the Social Doctrine of the Church*, (Washington, DC: US Conference of Catholic Bishops, 2004), 449.

10. Ibid., 182.

11. Vatican Council II, *Gaudium et spes* (1965), no. 69, *http://www.vatican.va/archive/hist_councils/ii_vatican_council/documents/vat-ii_cons_19651207_gaudium-et-spes_en.html*.

should receive a greater or lesser share of the goods of creation. Therefore, this creation story is often referenced as a rationale for the concept of the universal destination of the goods of creation: "See, I give you every seed-bearing plant 1on all the earth and every tree that has seed-bearing fruit on it to be your food; and to all the wild animals, all the birds of the air, and all the living creatures that crawl on the earth, I give all the green plants for food" (Genesis 1:29–30). According to this interpretation, God formed humans without distinctions regarding ownership rights and dominion. The Genesis narrative when read from the perspective of the option for the poor implies that people are called to incorporate this equality into their social, political, and economic institutions.

The option for the poor can also inform how one understands God's actions in the book of Exodus. God takes an "option for the poor" by stepping in to deliver the Hebrew people from their enslavement in Egypt. The Exodus narrative recounts how the slaves suffer oppression at the hands of the Egyptian pharaoh and how God hears their cries of suffering, takes pity on their plight, and sends them a charismatic leader in the person of Moses. Moses then acts as God's agent, delivering God's messages to the pharaoh and ultimately leading the people out of bondage and into the Promised Land.

From the perspective of the option for the poor, the Exodus story upends the common expectation in the ancient world that God favors those who possess wealth and power because he has showered them with so much privilege and status. While in the ancient world the divine being was usually portrayed as the protector of privilege and power, the God of Moses takes an entirely different option and sides with the poor and dispossessed, subverting the plans of the pharaoh and the Egyptians.

After the people of God enter the Promised Land, they not only share a common heritage as creatures of a creative God and as benefactors of divine deliverance, but they also take on the status of subjects, with Joshua, Judges, and the books of Samuel casting God in the role of divine king. The Hebrew people form a confederacy of self-governing tribes that rely on God for sustenance and deliverance (Joshua and Judges). Eventually, God's chosen people are tempted to establish a human kingdom, convinced they cannot face challenges from foreign invaders without one. Through the prophet Samuel, God expresses great displeasure and warns the people that they will suffer oppression at the hands of their new human king (1 Samuel 8). The people ignore God's warnings and elect Saul as king. According to an interpretation of the Bible informed by the option for the poor, the subsequent history of the Kingdom of Israel, as told in the books of Samuel, Kings, and Chronicles, testifies to the rightness of God's original counsel against setting up an oppressive hierarchy in the midst of the people.

This way of reading the Bible is not limited to the Hebrew Scriptures, but extends to the Gospels. The option for the poor sees Jesus not only as God's agent but also as the actual Son of God. This makes him a unique kind of *imago dei* for his followers. Christianity holds that Jesus does not merely represent the divine, but is intimately united with God. Therefore, Jesus' behavior in the Christian Scriptures mirrors the behavior of God in the Hebrew Scriptures. From this hermeneutical perspective, Jesus is the providential Son of the Creator as he multiplies the loaves for the multitudes, demonstrating to the crowds the universal destination of the goods of creation (Matthew 14:13–21; Mark 6:31–44; Luke 9:10–17; John 6:5–15). He is the Son of the Deliverer as he performs healing miracles again and again, bringing outcasts back into communion with the people of God. He is the Son of the King as he fulfills the promises of the *Magnificat* (Luke 1:46–55) and lifts up the lowly, while casting the mighty from their high places. From the perspective of an option for the poor, Jesus is understood as uplifting and reinforcing the already well-established understanding that God takes the side of the poor in order to correct the disorder that humanity has wrought by privileging a few at the expense of the many.[12] God sides with the poorest in order to reestablish the intended primordial equality between all people.

Catholic vs. Capitalist Social Praxis

Understanding the comparative section of the chapter requires an awareness of a few critical caveats. First, general references to capitalist theory allude to the popular neoclassical[13] movement of the Chicago school of economics, which is founded on Milton Friedman's assertion that deregulated markets are the most productive and stable and that government intervention should only be utilized as a last resort.[14] Secondly, capitalism is a real and functioning economic system that governs most exchanges of goods and services around the world. The preferential option for the poor, on the other hand, is a guiding theory for many Catholics, and even some non-Catholic, nongovernmental organizations (NGOs) around the world. Therefore, comparing these two ways of viewing the organization of the economy will, at times, seem like comparing apples to oranges. Finally, the preferential option for the poor is an essentially religious concept that, in many ways, needs to be translated into a secular context for application in nonparochial settings. By contrast, capitalism long ago shed any

---

12. World Synod of Catholic Bishops, *Justice in the World* (1971), no. 5, *http://www.osjspm.org/justice_in_the_world.aspx*.

13. Yuval P. Yonary, *The Struggle Over the Soul of Economics* (Princeton, NJ: Princeton University Press, 1998), 29

14. Friedman's seminal work was an analysis of the history of the Great Depression, which he concluded was the result of failed government monetary policy. Milton Friedman, *Two Lucky People: Memoirs* (Chicago: University of Chicago Press, 1999), 253.

and all of its religious roots and, therefore, for the sake of this comparison, there will be an attempt to reinvest it with some of its religious underpinnings.[15]

Despite significant differences between these two distinct visions of economic society, both are idealistic conceptions that make utopian claims about the potential societal outcomes if and when either theory is thoroughly and rigorously applied.[16] Because of the inherent idealism at the root of both systems, it is important to evaluate how each understands economic, social, and political power and analyze the adequacy of that understanding in relation to the ways social systems actually work.

In unusual and even ironic ways, theoretical capitalism has a relatively impoverished and naïve conception of economic power and the problems associated with its unbalanced accumulation.[17] While it is true that self-interest may be a significant culprit behind the eagerness of capitalists to avoid conversations that focus on income disparity and uneven resource distribution, it is also true that capitalist theory has little to say about the accumulation of economic power by the elite and how this can easily distort the fundamental laws of the market.[18] Capitalism does have a well-developed critique of government power and its minimal and strictly limited role in a market economy. Nevertheless, aside from basic antitrust and taxation theories, capitalism has few conceptual resources to confront and prevent the emergence of dictatorial economic power.[19]

Capitalist theory, in fact, seems to hold positively naïve notions about the human condition and behavior within market structures.[20] The capitalist market ideology of the invisible hand seems to depend on the patently flawed notion that no one will accumulate excessive power, and that, even if individuals or companies do, they will miraculously behave themselves instead of using that power to gain further unfair advantage.[21] If individuals and corporations do misbehave,

---

15. For a more complete discussion, see Harvey S. James Jr. and Farhad Rassekh, "Smith, Friedman, and Self-Interest in Ethical Society," *Business Ethics Quarterly* 10, no. 3 (July 2000): 659–674.

16. For more on Friedman's utopian vision of free-market economies see William Greider, "Friedman's Cruel Legacy," *The Nation* (December 11, 2006), *http://www.thenation.com/doc/20061211/greider*.

17. For a more complete discussion of power distribution in global capitalism, see Marcus Taylor, "Rethinking the Global Production of Uneven Development," *Globalizations*, 4, no. 4 (December 2007): 529–542. See also, Jacinda Swanson, "Power and Resistance: Perpetuating and Challenging Capitalist Exploitation," *Contemporary Political Theory* 6, no. 1 (February 2007): 4–23.

18. Radu Vranceanu, "The Ethical Dimension of Economic Choices," *Business Ethics: A European Review* 14, no. 2 (April 2005): 94–95.

19. Denis G. Arnold, "Libertarian Theories of the Corporation and Global Capitalism," *The Journal of Business Ethics* 48, no. 2 (December 2003): 156.

20. For a more extended discussion of the impoverished libertarian capitalist ideas of power, see Robert J. Antonio, "Reason and History in Hayek," *Critical Review: An Interdisciplinary Journal of Politics and Society* 1, no. 1 (Spring 1987): 58–73.

21. More on the relative empty notion of the governing power of the invisible hand can be found in Richard Cornuelle, "The Power and Poverty of Libertarian Thought," *Critical Review: An Interdisciplinary Journal of Politics and Society* 6, no. 1 (Winter 1992): 1–10.

then ostensibly the markets will discipline their misbehavior through the loss of consumer support. However, this conception of markets disciplining themselves, born in the microeconomic setting of eighteenth-century, informal, merchantilistic markets, makes little sense in the context of massive, complex, twenty-first–century, global markets in which consumers in one part of the world have little or no access to or knowledge about the behavior of subcontracting producers on the other side of the globe.[22] The power of the consumer to be aware of or organize a boycott with other geographically distant consumers becomes exponentially more difficult given the complexity and distance of modern global markets.

By contrast, the principle of the preferential option for the poor has a more critical and developed notion of power that is deeply suspicious of the concentration of both political and economic power.[23] These suspicions are grounded in a thoroughgoing critique of hierarchy that draws some of its theoretical inspiration from an interpretation of the Bible. For instance, the critique of political hierarchical power draws justification from the power struggles at the heart of the book of Samuel. Two factions among the people of Israel vie over whether they should embrace the monarchical political structures of their rivals or continue to trust that God would send charismatic leaders to deliver them (1 Samuel 8). The monarchists win the battle in Samuel, but the subsequent narratives of Israel's monarchy tell the story of God's ongoing displeasure over Israel's displacement of God's egalitarian reign with human kings who then reigned, almost without exception, in corrupt, impious, and ruthless ways (see, for example, the stories of King Ahab; 1 Kings 16:28—22:40). According to the book of Kings, God eventually handed the kingdoms over to its enemies and brought an ignominious end to Israel's experiment in political hierarchy (2 Kings 25).

Economic inequality receives a similarly cold reception in this interpretation of Scriptures. Theologians espousing the preferential option for the poor regularly refer to the jubilee-year legislation in the book of Leviticus to indicate that egalitarianism was written into the structure of early Israelite society.[24] According to the text, every forty-nine years a jubilee year would be celebrated and all slaves would be freed, all debts forgiven, and all people would return to and settle their ancestral lands (Leviticus chapter 25). The law addressed the three principle ways in which someone living in that society could become

---

22. G. R. Bassiry and Marc Jones, "Adam Smith and the Ethics of Contemporary Capitalism," *Journal of Business Ethics* 12, no. 8 (August 1993): 624–5.

23. World Synod of Catholic Bishops, *Justice in the World*, no. 5.

24. Some examples include, Paul W. Hollenbach, "Liberating Jesus for Social Involvement," *Biblical Theology Bulletin* (October 15, 1985):151–157. See also Jacob Milgrom, "The Land Redeemer and the Jubilee," in *Fortunate the Eyes That See*, eds. Astrid B. Beck, Andrew H. Bartelt, Paul R. Raabe, and Chris A. Franke, (Grand Rapids, MI: Eerdmans Publishing Co., 1995), 66–69; and Robert Gnuse, "Jubilee Legislation in Leviticus: Israel's Vision of Social Reform," *Biblical Theology Bulletin* (April 15,1985): 43–48.

permanently dispossessed, or conversely, permanently privileged. By freeing slaves, forgiving debts, and reenfranchising the dispossessed, the law assured that no persistent class distinctions could take hold. The jubilee year is one among many scriptural foundations supporting the belief that God does not tolerate hierarchical class distinctions and actively intervenes to subvert them by taking the side of the poor whenever humans sinfully try to create and maintain them.

Although the Catholic preferential option for the poor has a well-developed understanding of power and is acutely aware of its potential for accumulation and abuse, there appears to be a disconnect between this theory and the leadership practices of many members of the Catholic Church's hierarchy.[25] While wielding masterful theoretical categories against the dangerous accumulation of political and economic power among secular authorities, many members of the hierarchy of the Roman Catholic Church seems oblivious that these very same critiques apply most readily to its own structures, born of a bygone, monarchical, and paternalistic era.[26] Until the Church addresses its own need to radically reform the way power is distributed and exercised in its own structures, many will find it difficult, if not impossible, to heed and take seriously its fine critiques against the accumulation of power in the political and economic realms.

A discussion of the accumulation, distribution, and exercise of power leads to the related issues of social structure. For capitalism, the question is, "In what sort of society does a laissez-faire economy thrive?" Neoclassical capitalist theory assumes that genuinely unencumbered markets, functioning purely under the guidance of fair competition and the laws of supply and demand, will result in a society organized according to some kind of meritocracy.[27] The markets will favor innovative, industrious risk takers and, conversely, will punish those who are lazy, stupid, and timid. A kind of social Darwinism determines the fittest competitor in the commercial ecosystem.[28] In this way, free-market social theory functions as a type of natural law, with *nature*, in this context, represented by the market itself.[29] Like other versions of the natural law, once the

25. For a more complete discussion of the issues surrounding the preferential option for the poor and how this should impact church structures, see Leonardo Boff, *Ecclesiogenesis: The Base Communities Reinvent the Church* (Maryknoll, NY: Orbis Books, 1986), especially chapter 5: "*Questio Disputata* I: Did the Historical Jesus Will Only One Institutional Form of the Church?"

26. A more detailed discussion of this tension can be found in Helen Ruth Ebaugh, "The Revitalization Movement in the Catholic Church: The Institutional Dilemma of Power," *Sociological Analysis* 52, no. 1 (1991): 1–12.

27. Arne Heise "The Political Economy of Meritocracy: A Post-Kaleckian, Post-Olsonian Approach to Unemployment and Income Inequality in Modern Varieties of Capitalism," *Review of Radical Political Economics* 40, no. 1 (January 1, 2008): 67.

28. George Mickhail and Arsen Ostrovsky, "MetaCapitalism: The dialectics of impoverishment," *Critical Perspectives on Accounting* 18, no. 6 (2007): 671.

29. Linda Kintz, "Finding the Strength to Surrender," *Theory, Culture & Society* 24, no. 4 (July 1, 2007): 111.

natural behavior has been identified—in this case, behavior that is competitive, innovative, and industrious—then it becomes morally incumbent on those who exist in the natural world, in this case virtually everyone, to abide by these norms or face the consequences: economic marginalization and poverty. In this system, actual poverty is not simply an economically tragic status, but it also represents a moral failure. Evil, therefore, comes in two forms: (1) on the systemic level, evil is any law, policy, regulation, tax, tariff, or other externality that interferes with the freedom of the market to deliver the highest quantity and quality goods and services at the lowest possible cost;[30] (2) on the personal level, evil is any kind of anticompetitive behavior or trait. In fact, any behavior that does not make one a more competent, agile, and ferocious competitor is morally suspect.[31]

On the surface, the logic of neoclassical capitalist social theory seems straightforward and unassailable. However, just beneath the rational veneer a number of fundamental problems fester. Neoclassical capitalism is adept at identifying external forces such as taxes and government regulations as problematic; yet, it has few resources to identify and analyze the enemies within its own ranks. Therefore, when companies use their wealth and power to manipulate and rig the markets, they frequently find that they are rewarded rather than punished for their misbehavior.[32] In the first few years of the twenty-first century, the energy giant Enron collapsed after a series of scandalous stories appeared in the press arguing the enormous profits reported by the company over the course of more than a decade were largely fictitious and resulted from their use of deceptive accounting techniques and lax regulation and oversight. In the Enron case, external actors such as the government and investigative journalism needed to step in to identify and properly address this corporate scandal. Examples from the corporate world such as Enron suggest that markets are sometimes slow and inefficient at policing themselves and that they rely more on external social institutions to do it for them than neoclassical capitalist theorists would like to admit.

Notions of equality and fairness in the neoclassical capitalist understanding of the economy rely, in part, on ideas drawn from opportunity egalitarianism, in order to distinguish this system from elitist conceptions of economic entitlement.[33]

---

30. For a defense of this position, see Raghuram G. Rajan and Luigi Zingales, "Making Capitalism Work for Everyone." *World Economics* 7, no. 1 (January 1, 2006): 1–10.

31. Other capitalist theorists are more circumspect, such as E. Woodrow Eckard Jr., "The Free Market Incentive: Self Interest vs Greed" *Business Economics* 15, no. 4 (September 1, 1980): 32; Ekard argues that Smith was not advocating greed, only that universal benevolence was unnecessary for the economy to function in a way that benefited most.

32. Jacqueline Savukinas, "The Collapse of Enron: Market Failure or Criminal Conspiracy?" (PhD dissertation, George Mason University, 2005).

33. One such call for opportunity egalitarianism in developed economies can be found in the following editorial in "Leaders: A Question of Justice? Poverty and Inequality," *The Economist* (March 13, 2004): 13.

Opportunity egalitarianism is the notion that every actor in a market economy ought to enter that system with access to all of the necessary opportunities in order to survive and even thrive in that system. Once one has entered the system on equal footing, one's relative success then depends on personal effort and ingenuity.

Opportunity egalitarianism is assumed, but never demonstrated, by neoclassical capitalist social theory, and in this case, the theory again demonstrates its shortcomings. It is clear to most observers that basic opportunities in the United States, such as education, health care, nutrition, and shelter, are not distributed on an egalitarian basis but are instead strongly influenced by an individual's financial status.[34] Once the opportunity-egalitarian foundations of neoclassical capitalist theory's conception of justice have been called into question, it becomes difficult to distinguish how capitalism is more just and, therefore, more desirable than any other competing economic system, at least regarding the important measure of equal access, participation, and opportunity.

Not surprisingly, the theory of the preferential option for the poor calls for entirely and diametrically different social structures than those proposed by neoclassical capitalism. Unlike the competitive social Darwinism of capitalist markets, the preferential option for the poor posits a cooperative vision of economic relations[35] based on a theology of divine creation. This theology asserts as its first principle that the goods of creation are the common inheritance of all humans. All other principles of ownership and distribution are subordinated to this foundation of the universal destination of the created order.[36] Therefore, while it is good and just that humans create private property by mixing their labor with capital, the private property they produce is always under a "social mortgage,"[37] that is, it is legitimately the property of the one who created it only insofar as others in society do not have a significantly greater need for those resources.[38] In this way, CST subordinates the right to

---

34. The following article makes a similar argument concerning the way Adam Smith believed there were poor distribution patterns in some free markets and this meant that demand would not always create its own supply, i.e., demand for good education in poor neighborhoods would not always result in good education systems for poor people. James E. Alvey, "Adam Smith's Three Strikes Against Commercial Society," *International Journal of Social Economics* 25, no. 9 (January 1, 1998): 1425–1441.

35. John XXIII, *Mater et magistra* (1961), nos. 89–90, 143, 211, 239. *http://www.vatican.va/holy_father/john_xxiii/encyclicals/documents/hf_j-xxiii_enc_15051961_mater_en.html.*

36. John XXIII, *Pacem in terris* (1963), nos. 132–145, *http://www.vatican.va/holy_father/john_xxiii/ encyclicals/documents/hf_j-xxiii_enc_11041963_pacem_en.html.*

37. John Paul II, *Sollicitudo rei socialis,* no. 42.

38. Paul VI, *Populorum progressio* (1967), no. 23, *http://www.vatican.va/holy_father/paul_vi/ encyclicals/ documents/hf_p-vi_enc_26031967_populorum_en.html.*

private property—an absolute right in neoclassical capitalist theory—to the common good and the universal destination of goods.[39]

As mentioned in the discussion of power, the preferential option for the poor resists the accumulation and institutionalization of all forms of social power. It rejects and actively seeks to undermine the creation and maintenance of hierarchical orders, which tend to undermine conceptions of equal human dignity as well as the absolute sovereignty of the divine. CST has consistently shown support for workers' unionization and associations.[40] These invest the poor and dispossessed with the power and means to raise themselves in the social order and confront the artificial and oppressive power of the economic hierarchy of capitalism, which always places the owners in a privileged position in relation to the workers.[41] In this way, the preferential option for the poor calls for more than opportunity egalitarianism and always tends toward strictly egalitarian social, economic, and political relationships.[42]

While it is difficult to argue against the egalitarian ideals of the preferential option for the poor, enormous practical obstacles stand in the way of achieving such a lofty ideal in the real world. The immediate and problematic obstacle is simply that the preferential option for the poor offers no theory about how a society establishes, transitions to, or maintains these strict egalitarian structures. This task would be easier if there were positive historical examples, but an honest reading of the historical record only highlights that efforts to impose strict egalitarianism have tended to spark violent conflict and have rarely resulted in a society that is any more equal or beneficial for the poor.[43] The history of utopian egalitarianism raises serious questions about whether these ideals can be implemented or whether this theory is so much pie-in-the-sky wishful thinking.[44]

---

39. John Paul II, *Laborem exercens* (1981), no. 14, *http://www.vatican.va/holy_father/john_paul_ ii/encyclicals/documents/hf_jp-ii_enc_14091981_laborem-exercens_en.html.* .

40. Support for labor unions can be seen in all of the Catholic Church's major social teaching documents dating back to Leo XIII, *Rerum novarum* (1891), no. 49, *http://www.vatican.va/holy_ father/leo_xiii/encyclicals/ documents/hf_l-xiii_enc_15051891_rerum-novarum_en.html.*

41. Ibid., no. 20.

42. Paul VI, *Octogesima adveniens* (1971), no. 22, *http://www.vatican.va/holy_father/paul_vi/ apost_letters/documents/hf_p-vi_apl_19710514_octogesima-adveniens_en.html.*

43. A number of utopian experiments come to mind immediately that illustrate their impracticality. Oneida, New York, was the site of one such Christian utopian socialist community of the nineteenth century. The Oneida Community lasted for almost forty years with varying degrees of success at implementing and sustaining egalitarian principles. Internecine battles over property and leadership eventually eroded the community.

44. Some would argue that it is unfair to judge the success of a movement based on its permanence because no society can claim permanence in the long run. In other words, all societies, utopian or otherwise, fail at some point regardless of their reigning ideology. Some would claim that the importance of utopian communities lies in their contribution to the collective moral imagination, that is, in their capacity to challenge the status quo and contribute to a vision of a more just world.

The Quest for a Capitalist Option for the Poor

Even this admittedly limited comparison makes it clear that the preferential option for the poor stands in stark contrast to neoclassical capitalism. Unlike most other ethical systems, CST is a worldview, much like capitalism itself. Unfortunately for Catholic social ethicists, these worldviews are largely incompatible. It seems then that the chapter really should end here. It began with the suspicion that these two were not going to get along well, and sure enough, has demonstrated just that. Capitalists and Catholic social theorists can continue to look for common ground and apply the preferential option for the poor in a business setting, but an honest assessment of their fundamental incompatibility would counsel against it.

In theory, capitalism and CST play so poorly with each other that keeping the two separated seems like the best option. Nevertheless, in practice, some activists and socially minded capitalists have experimented with creative hybrid organizational forms that hint at the almost unthinkable possibility that the best way to achieve an option for the poor might be through organizations that look much like capitalist businesses. These social-service/capitalist chimeras can potentially unite the concerns of both capitalism and the preferential option for the poor.

Some of these new hybrid organizations have recently emerged from what is variously referred to as the citizen, or NGO, movements that began appearing in the late 1960s. These organizations formed when it became clear that neither business nor government could or would solve many of the world's most intractable problems. At first, this movement produced organizations modeled on traditional nonprofit structures. Recently, however, it has experimented with structures that more closely mirror the familiar capitalist business model. These experiments challenge the notion that an option for the poor merits no consideration in a corporate boardroom or that efficiency, marketing, and advertising are always exploitative. They ask the question, "Can capitalism take an option for the poor?"

A close examination of the practices of nongovernmental, or citizen,[45] organizations serving the needs of poor and marginalized populations yields four distinct structural models: The most common model is the traditional charitable social service agency[46] that pursues an exclusively social mission, embraces a two-tiered management/direct-care organizational structure, and depends financially on fund-raising and donations. A second model, often labeled bottom of the

---

45. The term *citizen sector* is borrowed from David Bornstein, *How to Change the World: Social Entrepreneurs and the Power of New Ideas* (New York, NY: Oxford University Press, 2004), 4.

46. Walter W. Powell and Richard Steinberg, eds., *The Nonprofit Sector: A Research Handbook* (New Haven, CT: Yale University Press, 2006).

pyramid[47] (BoP), espouses a social mission and pursues profits in markets that treat the poor as consumers while otherwise embracing the organizational and cultural milieu of competitive capitalism. A third model is the traditional cooperative organization[48] that pursues a social mission on behalf of a particular constituency, embraces flat, participative structures, and relies financially on the sales of goods and services. The final model, the freshly minted "social business,"[49] pursues an exclusively social mission on behalf of the poorest but otherwise embraces the cultural milieu of competitive capitalism, financially sustaining itself through the sale of its goods and services. This section of the chapter explores each of these models for their potential both to take a preferential option for the poor and to embrace the efficiency and vibrancy of capitalism. What remains to be seen is whether there is such a thing as a capitalist option for the poor.[50]

Nonprofit NGOs

Probably the most familiar organizational structure of the four alternatives to standard free-market, profit-maximizing capitalism is the traditional nonprofit organization. Nonprofit organizations have explicit and exclusive social missions,[51] and many function on a transnational level without any government or corporate affiliations. Their causes often relate to the interests and needs of the poorest and most marginalized groups, but nonprofit organizations do not necessarily limit their focus on the lowest classes. The organizational structures of nonprofit organizations are normally bifurcated, with one group handling management tasks of administration, fund-raising, and government lobbying and a second focusing on direct-care tasks associated with service provision and advocacy. Often, but not always, these two divisions have little to do with each other, therefore, a middle-management structure may be added to facilitate communication between direct-care and administration. Nonprofit organizations not only do not make a profit, but also they most often do not engage in real-income–generating activities

---

47. C. K. Prahalad, *The Fortune at the Bottom of the Pyramid* (Upper Saddle River, NJ: Wharton School Publishing, 2006).48. Richard C. Williams, *The Cooperative Movement: Globalization from Below* (Burlington, VT: Ashgate Publishing Company, 2007).

48. Richard C. Williams, *The Cooperative Movement: Globalization from Below* (Burlington, VT: Ashgate Publishing Company, 2007)

49. Muhammad Yunus, *Creating a World without Poverty: Social Business and the Future of Capitalism* (New York, NY: PublicAffairs, 2007).

50. In this context, the term *capitalism* no longer refers to the theory and practice of the neoclassical variety but is used as a more nonideological, generic term meant to evoke the broader culture of worldwide market economies.

51. J. Gregory Dees, Jed Emerson, and Peter Economy, eds., *Enterprising Nonprofits: A Tool for Social Entrepreneurs* (New York, NY: John Wiley & Sons, Inc., 2001), 2. In their book, the editors reframe the definition of *entrepreneurship* for a nonprofit context in which success "is generally measured not by how much profit you make, but by how well you serve your social mission."

of any sort. Therefore, these organizations often rely heavily, or exclusively, on fund-raising, grants, and donations.

In recent years, a growing movement within the nonprofit sector has been advocating "social entrepreneurship,"[52] which takes many of its cues from the world of mainstream profit-maximizing capitalist business. This movement aims to make social enterprises more enterprising by using management tools borrowed from business. Social entrepreneurship places greater emphasis on helping organizations better define their missions, recognize new opportunities, mobilize resources, increase accountability, understand risk and risk management, innovate, plan for the future, and attract new "customers."[53] This movement had its roots among those who began to notice that the best nonprofit managers tended to be those who had transitioned from executive positions at profit-maximizing businesses and that the traditional countercultural organizer, more frequently than not, was no match in the CEO chair for someone with an MBA.

However, even after adjusting for the nonprofit sector's new openness to managerial insights from capitalist business, many of these social service agencies still make an ambivalent match in the search for a capitalist option for the poor. Most of these organizations are neither self-sustaining nor revenue-generating; they will always require a constant influx of fresh charitable gifts, which, in turn, will demand a bloated management structure to support massive fund-raising and donation collection. The devotion of so much effort, time, and personnel to tasks that have no real connection to the social mission of the organization is the true Achilles' heel of nonprofit organizations from the perspective of profit-maximizing business. However, if the traditional nonprofit organizations can break away from permanent dependence on a fund-raising model, they have the potential to be a match for a capitalist option for the poor.

Although nonprofit organizations normally serve social missions that encourage solidarity with the poor and vulnerable, they can also be a problematic match for a preferential option for the poor to the extent that some still focus on charitable giving[54] or providing free services.[55] This, in turn, often leaves the poor dependent on the organization, rather than able to gain human dignity through independence or interdependence. While charity and free services often prove necessary and frequently help create the preconditions for further progress toward holistic development, they do not represent unfiltered examples of what

---

52. Ibid., 13. They claim that, "social entrepreneurs are shifting the emphasis from charitable relief to new more systematic ways of improving social conditions." Their focus is on reducing dependence on charitable assistance by engaging people and giving them primary responsibility for improving their own lives.

53. Bornstein, *How to Change the World*, 62.

54. For instance, organizations such as Food for the Poor.

55. Here, one could include traditional homeless shelters and soup kitchens.

CST means by a preferential option for the poor. Not all nonprofit organizations function out of a traditional charity model, however, and many have transitioned to a mission that promotes genuine empowerment and independent development for the poor and vulnerable.

Bottom of the Pyramid

An alternative to the nonprofit organization has emerged from within profit-maximizing capitalism itself and is sometimes referred to as businesses at the bottom of the pyramid (BoP).[56] These businesses claim to serve both the traditional capitalist profit motive as well as a social mission aimed at improving the quality of life for the poorest people of the world.[57] The products and services of these BoP businesses relate closely to the interests and needs of the poorest and most vulnerable because their design has often been shaped by market research among these target populations. The structures of these BoP businesses are indistinguishable from the organizational patterns found in other profit-maximizing businesses. They may be sole proprietorships, limited liability companies, or large share-held corporations. The assumption is that these businesses will make a profit from selling goods and services to the poor, just like any other profit-maximizing entity would from selling its wares. The only difference is that BoP businesses normally are inspired by a social mission that helps shape and guide its product development, marketing, advertising, and employment patterns.

BoP businesses fit perfectly in mainstream, free-market, profit-maximizing capitalism, because they do not essentially contradict any of the central tenets of this system. BoP businesses are self-sustaining enterprises that claim profit making as one of their primary missions. They are also founded and established within a legal framework indistinguishable from the way any other business is recognized by national and international governing bodies.

However, the characteristics that make BoPs such a good match for free-market capitalism can also make them a problematic match to a preferential option for the poor. Any organization that takes an option other than an exclusive option for the poor runs the risk of taking an option against the poor. BoPs do have a social mission; however, that some of them also must serve the profit-maximization goals of their shareholders[58] places these companies in the position of being forced to act in ways that could contradict their

---

56. For a more extended discussion of BoP business theory, see Stuart L. Hart, *Capitalism at the Crossroads: Aligning Business, Earth and Humanity* (Upper Saddle River, NJ: Wharton School Publishing, 2007), 111–66.

57. Prahalad, *The Fortune at the Bottom of the Pyramid*, 10.

58. Lisa Harjula, "Tensions between Venture Capitalists' and Business-Social Entrepreneurs' Goals," *Greener Management International* 51 (Summer 2006): 79–80.

social mission.[59] As Muhammad Yunus points out in his book, *Creating a World without Poverty*, "In the real world, it will be very difficult to operate a business with the two conflicting goals of profit maximization and social benefits."[60] In a competitive investment environment such as the stock market, these publicly held companies could be gradually pressured into types of behavior that undermine the social goal and steer the company toward preferentially servicing profit maximization. Although these models of free-market enterprise frequently do make otherwise scarce goods and services accessible to the poorest and most vulnerable,[61] they do not always represent an altogether satisfying match for a capitalist preferential option for the poor. Nevertheless, from the perspective of the preferential option for the poor, BoPs represent a dramatic shift in the right direction within capitalism.

Cooperatives

The cooperative movement dates back to the middle of the nineteenth century and has existed since then as a viable alternative to the individualistic model of capitalist ownership. Cooperatives are employee- and/or consumer-owned organizations that exist for the benefit of an undercapitalized class of people, so that they can establish and operate businesses in order to provide fair remuneration, just wages, and affordable prices for their producers, employees, and customers. Credit unions are one ubiquitous example of cooperative financial institutions. Other well-known cooperative brands include Ace Hardware, CarpetOne, Florida's Natural, and Land O'Lakes.[62] These organizations pursue both commercial and social goals. Though not strictly nonprofit in nature, profits are normally reinvested into the operation or passed on to the producers, employees, and customers in the form of prices breaks and wage increases. Cooperatives are democratically organized and encourage, or even demand, the participation of the members in the decision-making processes. These jointly owned organizations normally participate in markets dominated by profit-maximizing, capitalist corporations and often compete directly with them.[63]

---

59. Renee Kuriyan, Isha Ray, and Kentaro Toyama, "Information and Communication Technologies for Development: The Bottom of the Pyramid Model in Practice," *Information Society* 24, no. 2 (April 2008): 103–4.

60. Yunus, *Creating a World without Poverty*, 33.

61. There are many excellent examples in Prahalad, *The Fortune at the Bottom of the Pyramid*, 113–245.

62. For more information on cooperatives visit the National Cooperative Business Association: *http://www.ncba.coop/abcoop_ab_brands.cfm*.

63. The character of this competition is not always friendly as can be seen in the frequent lawsuits that banks have brought against large credit unions, challenging their relatively open fields of membership.

Because cooperatives already coexist in the same social and financial space as profit-maximizing, capitalist businesses, it would appear, at least on the surface, that cooperatives represent a good match for free-market capitalism.[64] However, there is often significant friction between the two in both theory and actual practice.[65] The history of the cooperative movement is filled with instances in which their profit-making counterparts attempted to break them up or bring legal action against them.[66] Sometimes these frictions are motivated by simple competitive jealousy and at other times by the belief that their tax-exempt status gives cooperatives an unfair advantage in the marketplace. Sometimes cooperatives suffer from a type of participative governance that is not conducive to efficiency, and many cooperative boards have become bogged down and gone out of business because they could not agree on otherwise simple, fundamental issues.

In relation to the preferential option for the poor, cooperatives represent organizational structures that generally serve the needs of people disadvantaged by the practices of mainstream capitalist businesses. From this perspective, many things about cooperatives are appealing, such as their participative governance, democratic decision-making processes, and capacity to create bonds of solidarity between different social and economic classes. However, cooperatives are not necessarily geared toward the needs of the poorest and most vulnerable people in society. In fact, most North American cooperatives serve the concerns of working- and middle-class people and small-scale business owners. Nevertheless, one can find fine examples of cooperatives all over the developing world designed specifically to meet the needs of the poorest and most marginalized peoples.[67] Cooperatives, therefore, represent a promising model in spite of not always being deemed a perfect match for the high ideals of the preferential option for

---

64. For a good introduction to the history and current application of the cooperative ownership model within the global economy, see Richard C. Williams, *The Cooperative Movement* (Burlington, VT: Ashgate Publishing Company, 2007).

65. A number of good books chronicle the successes and challenges of the Mondragon worker-owned cooperatives in Basque country. One such book is George Cheney, *Values at Work: Employee Participation Meets Market Pressure at Mondragon* (Ithaca, NY: Cornell University Press, 2002).

66. Several excellent resources discuss the long and colorful history of cooperatives in the United States. Steven Leikin explores the ideological conflicts and harsh practical consequences of nineteenth-century American laborers pursuing "cooperation" as an alternative to "competition" in his book *The Practical Utopians: American Workers and the Cooperative Movement in the Gilded Age* (Detroit, MI: Wayne State University Press, 2004). For a bird's-eye view that traces the history and development of the international cooperative movement from its foundation, see Johnston Birchall, *International Co-Operative Movement* (Manchester, UK: Manchester University Press, 1997). For a more microscopic perspective on a particular time and place that examines labor union experimentation with cooperative ownership models, see Dana Frank, *Purchasing Power: Consumer Organizing, Gender, and the Seattle Labor Movement, 1919–1929* (New York, NY: Cambridge University Press, 1994).

67. Go to *http://www.ncba.coop/resources.cfm?rcatid=18* for links to dozens of cooperative organizations worldwide that address the most basic needs in Asia, Africa, and South America.

the poor. To the extent that cooperatives focus on creating bonds of solidarity and remain open to serving the needs of the poorest and most vulnerable, they can be outstanding examples of a capitalist option for the poor.

Social Businesses

The fourth and final model is currently under development. In fact, much of what can be said about this model is contingent because it is yet a nascent movement. Its founder and first implementer, Muhammad Yunus, refers to the model as social business. Simply stated, a social business is designed to produce socially desirable dividends rather than profits for investors.

> It sells products at prices that make it self-sustaining. The owners of the company can get back the amount they've invested in the company over a period of time, but no profit is paid to investors in the form of dividends. Instead, any profit made stays in the business—to finance expansion, to create new products or services, and to do more good for the world. [68]

Yunus equates current globalization to an unregulated 100-lane highway that can easily favor the huge and fast mega-corporation vehicles, while squashing and destroying smaller, slower movers. He claims entire sectors of the global economy ignore the needs of the majority of people in order to gain obscene profits in markets aimed at the wealthy. Yunus believes that free markets should be contexts in which inspiration, creative energy, efficiency, dynamism, and freedom can be exercised for the benefit of all, and he asserts that the current market system can be changed in order to meet this grand objective. [69]

The social business movement was launched when Yunus and other innovators in the 1970s began to experiment with microcredit. [70] A microcredit loan is one for a relatively tiny amount that helps the poorest people in a society to launch their own enterprises. This, in turn, empowers them with the means to pay back the loan, but more importantly, to live independently without relying on begging or charity: [71] "Through microcredit, donors can shed the old hand-out mentality and become true partners in progress with the people of the developing world." [72] Recognizing that they could not properly address poverty in many cases by merely

---

68. Muhammad Yunus, *Banker to the Poor: Micro-lending and the Battle against World Poverty* (New York, NY: PublicAffairs, 2003), xvi.

69. Ibid., 5–6.

70. Yunus, *Banker to the Poor*, 115–130.

71. For more information on microcredit, see Beatriz Armendáriz and Jonathan Morduch, *The Economics of Microfinance* (Cambridge, MA: The MIT Press, 2005).

72. Paul Smith and Eric Thurman, *A Billion Bootstraps: Microcredit, Barefoot Banking, and the Business Solution for Ending Poverty* (Chicago, IL: McGraw-Hill, 2007), 45.

loaning money, microcredit organizations eventually expanded by adding services for its customers in order to make sure the money they loaned was used in the most effective way and had the greatest impact. These included savings accounts, insurance policies, health services, literacy programs, and even some traditional charitable services. Over time, these services became businesses unto themselves, and the social business model was born.[73] In 2007, Yunus's Grameen Bank and the French company Danone Dairy created a social business partnership to develop, manufacture, and market a cheap yogurt product aimed at providing the poorest children of Bangladesh with a nutritious, cheap, and popular food source. So far, the venture has met with resounding success.[74]

Social businesses resemble other capitalist businesses in most ways. They are not charities, and unlike traditional nonprofit organizations, they aim to fully recover their costs through the sale of products and services. A social business is a nonloss, nondividend business, in which any surplus is reinvested in the business operations and can be "passed on to the target group of beneficiaries in such forms as lower prices, better service, and greater accessibility."[75] In fact, social businesses *should* make money in order to pay back their original investors and support the pursuit of their goals. For these reasons, few obstacles seem to stand in the way of the social business model receiving the blessing of capitalist theory.

Neoclassical theory, however, would have significant reservations about the centrality of the social mission in the social business model and its priority over the pursuit of profit. Most neoclassical-capitalist theorists would categorize these social missions as positive externalities, that is, the indirect effects of an economic transaction on the rest of the economy. One classic instance of a positive externality is the beekeeper that keeps the bees for their honey but whose bees also pollinate surrounding crops. In most cases, the value generated by the pollination was not directly intended by the beekeeper; however, it may ultimately be greater than that of the harvested honey. Some strict neoclassical-capitalist theorists might claim that the social mission of social businesses merely raises the pursuit of positive externalities to a primary, rather than secondary or tertiary, concern.

As this study has shown, the more difficult endorsement is the one from the preferential option for the poor. However, social businesses appear to face few obstacles as long as their central focus remains the social mission to the poorest and most marginalized peoples. Social businesses were originally conceived and continue to thrive in the context of solving the problems of the poorest. By definition, social businesses cannot pay out profits as dividends to investors; therefore, they can concentrate on the social mission without concerning themselves with distractions from outside forces. As self-sustaining organizations,

---

73. Ibid., 77–78.

74. Yunus, *Creating a World without Poverty*, 149–162.

75. Ibid., 24.

they serve as a model for their clients who are, in turn, encouraged to be independently interdependent. This spirit of interdependence fosters the recognition of human dignity and contributes to the common good. To the extent that the social business movement remains close to its founding spirit, it appears to be a very good fit for CST preferential option for the poor.

Conclusion

This chapter compared the worldviews of capitalism and the preferential option for the poor to find some common ground between these two seemingly incompatible systems. These two worldviews posit entirely different and even opposing conceptions of the political economy and what constitutes righteous and just behavior within the global marketplace. Nevertheless, four promising models of business organization—traditional nonprofit organizations, bottom-of-the-pyramid businesses, cooperatives, and social businesses—fulfill, at least in part, the requirements of both capitalist market theory and CST preferential option for the poor.

At first glance, Catholic and capitalist social theory and practice seem hopelessly at odds with each other. Catholic social practice and teaching has consistently condemned capitalism as an elitist, individualistic, materialistic, and reductionist ideology that undermines human dignity by exploiting and excluding the poor. Capitalist social thought and practice has retorted by claiming that the option for the poor is a socialistic, paternalistic, nostalgic, regressive, and plebian ideology that threatens human dignity by restricting economic initiative and human freedom. Until recently, Catholic business leaders felt forced to either choose between these two diametrically opposed conceptions of the marketplace or simply ignore one or the other—or both.

However, the recent dawn of alternative capitalist-business models in the citizen sector of society has led practitioners to explore organizational models that seem fundamentally compatible with both social theories. Through the development of these new corporate structures, practitioners are investigating a new social space that exists somewhere between the business and government sectors. Social enterprises seek profits but reinvest them in operations designed to create social value for the poor and vulnerable sectors of society and foster bonds of solidarity among their constituents. They compete with other companies to bring products and services of the highest value to people who have never had this kind of corporate attention. In so many words, they seek to lift up the lowly in small incremental ways, which closely mirrors the vision of the Kingdom of God in the Gospels and the preferential option for the poor in CST. Even with the emergence of these new models of capitalism from below, some may still experience the preferential option for the poor as paradoxical, but they can no longer dismiss it as mere poppycock.

Case Study

TOMS Shoes

The main page of *www.TOMSshoes.com* makes it clear that this is no run-of-the-mill online retail operation. Although there are shoes for sale in virtually any color, size, and style—and the buyer can easily browse, compare, purchase, and check out just like at any other online store—TOMS also offers experiences unlike almost any other for-profit retail operation. In addition to shopping, visitors can read about "Our Movement," in which they can see video of a "shoe drop" and read about the history of the company. Shoppers can "Get Involved" as interns or volunteers to help distribute shoes in the developing world. They can also join the "Community" of producers, consumers, and distributors of TOMS shoes in an ongoing dialogue about this unique company and its commitment to social entrepreneurship.

TOMS shoes was founded in May 2006 by world traveler and entrepreneur Blake Mycoskie.[76] He got the idea for the company while on vacation in Argentina,[77] where he noticed that many of the children in the poorer areas of the country had no shoes and, as a result, suffered from cuts, bruises, and infections.[78] Some of these shoeless children also could not attend school because of public hygiene policies, and many of the children suffered from podoconiosis, a disease transmitted through volcanic silica in the soil that penetrates the skin and makes its way into the lymphatic system. Over time, the lower legs swell and open sores and ulcers develop, leaving the feet open to infection.[79]

Mycoskie recognized the simple cure for all of these woes: a reliable source of free shoes. So when he returned to the United States, he brought with him 250 pairs of shoes made in the traditional canvas Argentine style known as *alpargata,* with the intention of manufacturing them for sale to American consumers.[80] He planned to use the proceeds to support the manufacture of additional shoes for distribution to poor children. Some local media coverage in Los Angeles brought in enough orders for him to return to Argentina with new shoes and three interns in tow. Through this original

(continued)

76. Case Western Reserve University, "TOMS Shoes: From Soul to Sole," Case Study, *http://worldbenefit.case.edu/innovation/bankInnovationView.cfm?idArchive=1153.*

77. Joanne Fritz, "5 Lessons in Corporate Social Responsibility from TOMS Shoes," About.com, *http://nonprofit.about.com/od/socialentrepreneurs/a/tomsshoescorporaterespons.htm.*

78. Case Western Reserve University.

79. Patrick Byers, "Help Provide Shoes to 30,000 Children in Ethiopia," *Responsible Marketing Blog, http://responsiblemarketing.com/blog/2008/12/05/help-provide-shoes-to-30000-children-in-ethiopia.*

80. Nathan Ketsdever, "Social Capitalist Profile: Blake Mycoskie of TOMS Shoes," *Compassion in Politics Blog, http://compassioninpolitics.wordpress.com/2009/04/14/social-capitalist-profile-blake-mycoskie-of-toms-shoes/.*

Case Study   *(continued)*

act of charity, the idea for TOMS shoes was hatched, and a one-for-one social business model became the guiding principle for the new company. For every pair of shoes sold by the online company, another pair would be given away free to a child in the developing world.

The company grew exponentially from its humble beginnings and by October 2010 it had given away more than 1,000,000 pairs of shoes. Mycoskie chose to meet this vital need using a for-profit model rather than the more familiar charitable organization because he was convinced that a for-profit business was a more sustainable entity than a charity.

> I think the term "social entrepreneur" is very relevant because I believe you can do well by doing good. TOMS is a for-profit business, and it's important that we have profit so we have sustainability. I've always said that with a charity, what happens when you have a time like right now, (when) economic times are tough and the donors maybe aren't there, the charity really suffers. But the nice thing about TOMS is it being a for-profit business, we're continuing to sell shoes so we can continue to give shoes.[81]

Mycoskie spends much of his time these days taking customer volunteers on what he calls "shoe drops," at which they literally greet the children and physically slide shoes onto their bare feet.

> I think the advantage of being a small business that's giving back in such a substantial way is that our customers really become our marketers. So when someone buys a pair of TOMS, they're not just buying a pair of shoes, they're kind of joining a movement. And they want to participate in that. And so when they wear their shoes, and someone says, "what are those?" they never say "TOMS." They tell the whole story. They say, 'When I bought this pair of shoes, a child got a pair.' And that's the best type of marketing you can have.[82]

Questions

1. What other products or services might lend themselves to Mycoskie's one-for-one model of social entrepreneurship?
2. In what ways has the philanthropic dimension of the business actually supported the expansion and profitability of the business?

(continued)

---

81. Sharon Cook, "These Shoes Help Others Get a Step Up," CNN.com (3/26/09), *http://www.cnn.com/2009/LIVING/homestyle/03/26/blake.mycoskie.toms.shoes/index.html#cnnSTCText.*

82. Ibid.

Case Study   *(continued)*

3. If you had a choice between purchasing products or services that were developed using either a social entrepreneurial model or a traditional for-profit model, which would you choose? Why?

4. Does the business model of TOMS Shoes constitute a preferential option for the poor or is it just another example of charity? Why or why not?

Case Study

Farmville

Anyone who uses the Internet social-networking site Facebook on a regular basis probably has played, or knows someone who has played, the addictive role-playing game Farmville. In Farmville, players are cast in the role of farmers and are given some basic resources (the cyber equivalent of 40 acres and a mule). They spend their time on their virtual plot of land, sowing, plowing, harvesting, buying, and selling various crops and tending their sheep, cows, pigs, chickens, and other sundry beasts. As players grow and maintain their new virtual agribusiness enterprise, they meet other farmers and become each other's neighbors and friends. Players are also regularly awarded with endless honors and ranks as they continue to pursue their dreams of pastoral utopia.[83]

As players advance and decide to add to the farm or purchase special crops, they can gain access to special features by investing real money in the process rather than relying on the virtual coins produced by the sale of crops, fruit, and other produce on the farm. When farmers buy "Sweet Seeds for Haiti" to plant on their farms, half of those proceeds are donated to two nonprofit development organizations: fonkoze.org and fatem.org. Both organizations are involved in microfinance and grass-roots development projects in the poorest nation in the Western Hemisphere, Haiti. Demonstrating the power of the Internet, Facebook, the gaming community, and the social entrepreneurial business model Zynga, the company that created the game, raised more than $580,000 in the first six weeks after launching Farmville.[84]

(continued)

---

83. Much of the information in this case study comes from personal experience playing the game.

84. See *http://www.zynga.com*.

Case Study

(continued)

The money that virtual farmers "donate" goes toward a variety of critical development projects, such as the school-meal program in Mirebalais that helps feed undernourished students. The funds also support a revolving-loan program for mothers under the age of 15 to help them start and sustain small businesses, which, in turn, feed their families and ensure they can finish school and receive basic health care. The creators of Farmville call their new model "social gaming," because the game itself becomes a vehicle through which Facebook members meet and interact with one another. In the words of founder and CEO Mark Pincus, "We want Zynga to be a way that people connect with each other through games and fun, a way that is so meaningful to them and becomes such a daily behavior that they can't imagine what life was like before."[85]

However, the term *social gaming* also applies to the way Farmville leverages the popularity and self-motivational elements of online gaming to achieve more than merely a good profit. For each dollar spent on certain items in Farmville, Zynga donates 50 cents to Fatem and Fonkoze, which is similar to the one-for-one concept pioneered by Mycoskie at TOMS Shoes. With more than 500 million estimated users on Facebook as of 2013, it is easy to see how Zynga can both make a profit and make a difference:[86] "We are thrilled to be able to offer our players the opportunity to be part of change in a way that can represent positive contributions to human capacity."[87]

Questions

1. Identify other ways that companies such as Zynga might use gaming, social networking, or other Internet resources to fulfill a social mission for their profitable company.
2. Do you think the philanthropic dimension of Farmville actually supports the expansion and profitability of the game? Why or why not?
3. You have almost infinite choices with regard to online gaming opportunities. Are you now more likely to seek out games that fulfill a social mission? Why or why not?
4. Does the business model of Zynga constitute a preferential option for the poor or is it just another example of charity? Why or why not?

85. Ibid.

86. Dean Takahashi, "Zynga Raises More Venture Capital for Social Gaming Expansion," *VentureBeat* (November 17, 2009), *http://venturebeat.com/2009/11/17/zynga-raises-more-venture-capital-for-social-gaming-expansion/*.

87. Mark Pincus, *http://www.zynga.com*.

For Further Reading

Dorr, Donal, *Option for the Poor and for the Earth: Catholic Social Teaching.* Maryknoll, NY: Orbis Books, 2012.

Eberly, Don E. *The Rise of Global Civil Society: Building Communities and Nations from the Bottom Up.* New York: Encounter Books, 2008.

Groody, Daniel G., and Gustavo Gutiérrez. *The Preferential Option for the Poor beyond Theology.* Notre Dame, IN: University of Notre Dame Press, 2013.

Grusky, David B., and Szonja Szelényi. *The Inequality Reader: Contemporary and Foundational Readings in Race, Class, and Gender.* Boulder, CO: Westview Press, 2011.

Michelini, Laura. *Social Innovation and New Business Models Creating Shared Value in Low-Income Markets.* Berlin: Springer, 2012.

Osburg, Thomas, and René Schmidpeter. *Social Innovation Solutions for a Sustainable Future.* Berlin: Springer, 2013.

Prahalad, C. K. *The Fortune at the Bottom of the Pyramid.* Upper Saddle River, NJ: Wharton School Publishing, 2005.

Rieger, Joerg. *Opting for the Margins: Postmodernity and Liberation in Christian Theology.* New York Oxford University Press, 2003.

Samli, A. Coskun. *Globalization from the Bottom Up: A Blueprint for Modern Capitalism.* New York: Springer, 2008.

Chapter 5

And Justice for All, Not Just the 1 Percent

Patrick Flanagan

Introduction

The last chapter ended with case studies that analyzed the place of social businesses in the emerging global corporate landscape. It was argued that this could, in some circumstances, be related to the principle of the preferential option for the poor in CST. The focus on the poor and marginalized as producers and consumers in social businesses is very different from the way in which the mainstream corporate world views these sectors. The instinct to include those who are normally excluded, to seek opportunities to serve those with limited opportunities, and to restructure the business enterprise in order to serve more than just the needs of an investor class are the same ones that inform the broad ethical principle of justice. This chapter begins by reviewing the economic crash of 2008 through the lens of movements reacting to the mistakes of financial executives who had pursued their own benefit to the detriment of everyone else.

In December 2010, a groundswell of grassroots public activity known as the Occupy Movement sprouted in many parts of the world. People took to the streets and logged online to protest disproportionate social and economic policies and practices that seemed to favor a select portion of the population. While protests in each locale had their particular focus, all decried the unjust socioeconomic and political structures that kept people impoverished and removed them from critical conversations about finance and the economy. In their rallying cries, their speeches, and slogans—the most popular being "We are the 99%" and "'99%' pay for the mistakes of the '1%'"—they demanded justice.[1]

Demonstrations, protests, and, at times, violent revolutions became a reality in the Occupy Movements of northern Africa and the Middle East. The Arab Spring, as it has come to be identified, brought a new hope to oppressed people. Citizens in the Arab world gradually came to experience freedom in a previously unknown way and to appreciate the possibility of a more just society. That motivated men and women to transform unjust socioeconomic and political structures.

The Occupy Movement put an end to "business as usual." Ordinary citizens staged massive assemblies and strategically employed social media, despite government efforts to censor or shut down popular websites such as Facebook, YouTube, and Twitter.[2] In some nation-states, these public expressions of dissatisfaction helped topple or seriously challenge long-reigning oppressive powers, such as that of Ben Ali, who would be deposed as president of Tunisia because of the efforts of the Occupy Movement.

People protested against nations in which leadership had been historically confined to a select group of families and their constituencies, namely those whom they identify as the 1 percent who seemingly controlled most, if not all, of the finances, resources (oil, for example), legal structures, and military personnel. The protesters understood that the power of the monopolies was often perpetuated by corrupt use of government power to ensure totalitarian rule and, in some instances, was compounded by leaders of other countries tolerating human rights violations.

The demonstrations in Tunisia, Egypt, and Libya piqued the interest of Americans who shared similar concerns and motivated them to initiate similar campaigns for economic justice.[3] In September 2011, the Occupy Movement took root on American soil. Some described it as the "springtime of global growth gone local"; others, such as Tennessee activist Van Jones, acknowledged its relationship to the Arab Spring by calling it the "US Autumn."[4] Philosopher

---

1. Michele Hardesty, "Signs and Banners of Occupy Wall Street," *Critical Quarterly* 54, no. 2 (2012): 23–27.

2. Kevin M. DeLuca, Sean Lawson, and Ye Sun, "Occupy Wall Street on the Public Screens of Social Media: The Many Framings of the Birth of a Protest Movement," *Communication, Culture & Critique* 5, no. 4 (2012): 483–509.

3. For more on the Arab Spring and justice, see Tom Chesshyre, *A Tourist in the Arab Spring.* (Guilford, CT: The Globe Pequot Press Inc., 2013); Lin Noueihed and Alex Warren, *The Battle for the Arab Spring: Revolution, Counter-Revolution, and the Making of a New Era* (New Haven, CT: Yale Books, 2012); Joel Peters, *The European Union and the Arab Spring: Promoting Democracy and Human Rights in the Middle East* (Lanham, MD: Lexington Books, 2012); Nasser Wedday and Sohra Ahmari, eds. *Arab Spring Dreams: The Next Generation Speaks Out for Freedom and Justice from North Africa to Iran* (New York: Palgrave Macmillan, 2012).

4. Michael Scherer, "The Return of the Rabble Rouser," *Time* 21 (November 21, 2011): 44–47.

Cornel West identified it as the "democratic awakening" that heightened "political consciousness."[5]

As people assembled in public spaces, most notably New York City's Zuccotti Park, the cries demanding economic and social justice echoed those made thousands of miles away in Cairo's Tahrir Square. The public demanded answers and action from government leaders, and consumers called for greater accountability and increased transparency in economic decision making. Occupiers demanded more participative horizontal structures and public policies that encouraged participation in economic decision-making processes. The "Protester," *Time* magazine's person of the year for 2011, sought answers from Wall Street for the economic recession beginning in 2007.[6] People demanded accountability and responsibility from multinational corporations and banks in the aftermath of the financial collapse. The Occupy Movement leaders emphasized that global economic power was controlled by the wealthiest 1 percent of the population and questioned why.[7] They asked hard questions about economic imbalances and looked for avenues to secure greater economic justice in the marketplace for the 99 percent without global economic power. Occupiers sought sustainable monetary, fiscal, and social policies that considered all economic players.

Defining Justice

The *Catechism of the Catholic Church* (*CCC*) and *The Compendium of the Social Doctrine of the Church* in 2005 both offer insight into justice. The *CCC* teaches that,

> *Justice* is the moral virtue that consists in the constant and firm will to give their due to God and neighbor. Justice toward God is called the "virtue of religion." Justice toward men disposes one to respect the rights of each and to establish in human relationships the harmony that promotes equity with regard to persons and to the common good. (No. 1807)

---

5. Cornel West, "We Are in a Magnificent Moment of Democratic Awakening," *http://www.democracynow.org/2011/10/24/dr_cornel_west_we_are_in*.

6. Kurt Andersen, "The Protester," *Time* 178 (December 14, 2011): 26–60.

7. Josh Bivens and Lawrence Mishel, "Occupy Wall Streeters Are Right About Skewed Economic Rewards in the United States," Economic Policy Institute, October 26, 2011, *http://www.unibaker.com/occ_wallstreet_44_OWS_rightaboutskewedeconomicrewards_Economic_Policy_Inst.php*. Noam Chomsky, *Occupy*. (Minneapolis: Consortium Book Sales & Distribution, 2012). Sarah Van Gelder, *This Changes Everything: Occupy Wall Street and the 99% Movement* (San Francisco: Berrett-Koehler Publishers, 2011).

Justice, according to the *CCC*, is essentially both horizontal *and* vertical. The responsibilities to God and those to neighbor *cannot* be divorced.

People are schooled in the virtue of justice and, over time, move from external prompting to an internal commitment to speak and act justly. Initially, children learn right from wrong from parents and other authority figures, but as people mature, they are able to discern values and virtues that promote justice and act accordingly without external pressure. As they participate in the corporate world and contribute to the economy, many people experience a dissonance between the corporate-world transgressions and what was passed down as "right" or "just" in formative years. Some even find the issue of right and wrong in the marketplace confusing. Keenly aware that justice had been compromised on so many levels in so many areas of the marketplace, Arab Spring and Occupy Movement protesters were indefatigable in their efforts to expose injustice and strategize for a more promising future, particularly in the economic sphere of life.

The Occupy Movement was a response to two notable financial scandals: the Madoff affair and the subprime mortgage lending crisis. Both cases involve far-ranging economic injustices. Bernard Madoff's Ponzi scheme, which bilked investors out of approximately $65 billion, went undetected for years and affected more than 4,000 people across the continental United States, Europe, Asia, and Latin America.

Concurrent with the Madoff Ponzi scheme was the popular sale of mortgages during the housing bubble that fueled interest, speculation, and demand in realestate properties.[8] Although selling mortgages is appropriate banking activity, some financial institutions engaged in unjust practices. Lending agencies such as Countrywide Financial and Washington Mutual sold subprime mortgages to people without the means to repay the loans. This predatory lending, as it has been termed, led to widespread delinquencies, subsequent foreclosures, and eventually the bursting of the housing bubble.[9]

These two examples demonstrate individual and corporate wrongdoing.[10] In choosing wrong actions, all those complicit suspended justice and contributed

---

8. Marc Jarsulic, *Anatomy of a Financial Crisis: A Real Estate Bubble, Runaway Credit Markets, and Regulatory Failure* (New York: Palgrave Macmillan, 2010). Major Coleman IV, Michael LaCour-Little, and Kerry D. Vandell, "Subprime Lending and the Housing Bubble: Tail Wags Dog?" *Journal of Housing Economics* 17, no. 4 (2008): 272–290.

9. Joseph Fried, *Who Really Drove the Economy Into the Ditch* (New York: Algora Publishing, 2012).

10. Some recently scholarly treatments of justice that analyze the financial crisis in light of the Occupy Movement can be found at Gerald J. Beyer, "Solidarity and Occupy Wall Street: A Tale of Two Movements," *Political Theology* 13, no. 1 (2011): 5–13. William A. Gamson and Micah L. Sifry, "The Occupy Movement: An Introduction," *The Sociological Quarterly* 54, no. 2 (2013): 159–163; Zhang Xinning, "On the First Anniversary of Occupy Wall Street Movement: Gains, Losses and Perspectives," *International Critical Thought* 3, no. 1 (2013): 133–138.

to the economic recession that began in the United States in 2008.[11] Since then other nations have suffered economic downturns for related reasons.

Justice was tested even further during this painful time of economic recession. With the fiscal health of the world's markets in the midst of what has been termed the harshest economic recession in modern times, consumers and employees were confused as to why corporate executives were compensated at mammoth levels.[12] Justice demanded a different course of action, and the Occupy Movement sought to see to realize it.

Justice is the right course of action or speech, but how is a right course of action distinguished from its opposite? Who determines right and wrong?[13] Is it possible that some people involved in Bernie Madoff's scheme or subprime lending believed their actions were right? Concretely, doing justice—the right thing—can take on different expressions. Is there a universal definition? The occupiers had a common idea of justice. For instance, in New York City, the General Assembly of the Occupy Wall Street Movement approved a "Declaration of the Occupation of New York City," which outlines the wrongs of corporations in concert, at times, with government consent.[14] There is a further concern raised by the detractors of justice though. If it is good to seek justice, why do so many people seem to ignore or compromise this value in their lives and communities? It is to questions such as these that the discussion now turns.

Historical Appreciations of Justice

Justice has taken many different expressions throughout history. In search of a definition of *justice*, people have expressed and meted out the meaning in various, sometimes conflicting, ways; and arriving at a common appreciation of justice proves a difficult task. Nevertheless, even the most contentious debates about a definition of *justice* can be reframed to identify common ground. For instance, the overarching concern of the Occupy Movement, reflective of its definition of

---

11. Deepak Lal, "The Great Crash of 2008: Causes and Consequences," *Cato Journal* 30 (2010): 265–278; Victor Lewis, et al.: "Was the 2008 Financial Crisis Caused by a Lack of Corporate Ethics?" *Global Journal of Business Research* 4, no. 2 (2010): 77–84. Yochanan Shachmurove, "Economic Crises: Past, Present and Future," *International Journal of Business* 15, no. 4 (2010): 363–375.

12. Thomas Donaldson, "Executive Compensation," *The International Encyclopedia of Ethics* (2013). Camelia M. Kuhnen and Alexandra Niessen. "Public opinion and executive compensation," *Management Science* 58, no. 7 (2012): 1249–1272. Kevin Murphy, "Executive Compensation: Where We Are, and How We Got There," *Handbook of the Economics of Finance* (Elsevier Science North Holland, 2012).

13. Michael Sandel, *Justice: What's the Right Thing to Do?* (New York: Farrar, Straus, and Giroux, 2010).

14. "Declaration of the Occupation of New York City," *http://www.nycga.net/resources/documents/declaration/*.

justice, is the injustice created by imbalance in economic order. Occupiers claim that the present economic organization favors the few over the many. How precisely that imbalance should be righted, however, can result in competing claims, and clearly the "in-fighting" among the Occupiers exemplifies this tension.[15]

Students in my classes also can serve as an example of the diverse appreciations of justice. Whenever I teach about the topic, I ask students to write down the meaning of *justice*. More often than not, they indicate that it is about harmonious relationships and good order, being fair or equitable, having just desserts or satisfaction, or even as something natural to a person. Each definition offers a perspective on justice. From there, we attempt to move toward common ground; consensus generally follows. When I then ask about who makes those definitions, the students generally respond with silence. Once in a while a student will suggest "the law" or "the government." I refer them to the aforementioned Occupy Movement and suggest that even legal authorities can get it wrong and allow economic and social injustice to flourish.

So, how then does one adequately define *justice* in such a way that it might merit the assent of all, or most of the people living in a society? Revisiting philosophical and theological foundations provides insightful answers to these issues. Some argue that justice can only be genuinely understood by an experience of its opposite. This stems from the idea that everyone has an innate sense of justice and that times of challenge activate it. Thomas Aquinas (1225–1274) identifies this sense as *synderesis*, a person's "moral sonar" to know right from wrong.[16] According to Aquinas, this natural human capacity or disposition always points in the direction of truth and justice.[17] By contrast, injustice is, at best, a hedging of the truth and at worst, an outright violation of it. Injustice serves individual needs at the cost of another. It does not seek what is fair, good, and right for the community but subordinates justice for personal gain or to advance a particular narrative.

This orientation or "compass of justice" always seeks "right order," as Plato defined *justice*. In Plato's *Republic*, Socrates teaches that justice is evident when the person and the city-state are "well-ordered."[18] In the city-state, each of the three classes of people—artisans (farmers, weavers, etc.), guardians (auxiliaries

---

15. David Hollenbach, *Claims in Conflict: Retrieving and Renewing the Catholic Human Rights Tradition* (Mahwah, NJ: Paulist Press, 1979).

16. Thomas Aquinas, *Summa Theologica*, I, Q. 79, a. 12, *http://www.newadvent.org/summa/1079.htm.*

17. Anthony Celano, "The Relation of Prudence and Synderesis to Happiness in the Medieval Commentaries on Aristotle's Ethics," ed. Jon Miller, *The Reception of Aristotle's Ethics* (Cambridge: Cambridge University Press, 2012), 125–144. Angela McKay, "Synderesis, law, and virtue." *The Normativity of the Natural* (Cham: Switzerland: Springer, 2009), 33–44. Robert J. Smith, *Conscience and Catholicism: The Nature and Function of Conscience in Contemporary Roman Catholic Moral Theology* (Lanham, MD: University Press of America, 1998). S. J. Reedy and Brian Michael, "The Faith That Does Prudence: Contemporary Catholic Social Ethics and the Appropriation of the Ethics of Aquinas." *Lumen et Vita* 2.1 (2012).

18. Allan Bloom, trans., *The Republic of Plato*, 2nd ed. (New York: Basic Books, 1991).

and soldiers), and rulers (complete guardians)—have certain powers and functions. Artisans must produce and be industrious; auxiliaries must carry out the rulers' directives; and guardians must rule. Plato sees individuals as having a soul with a tripartite structure analogous to the structure of the city-state. The appetitive part of the human soul hungers after possessions—especially money; the spirited, courageous part seeks honor and expresses emotion; the rational part engages in wise deliberation and pursues the truth.[19] Justice, for Plato, is realized when individuals contribute to society according to their class and when the individual's interior aspects are harmonized:

> Justice . . . isn't concerned with someone's doing his own externally, but with what is inside him, with what is truly himself and his own. One who is just does not allow any part of himself to do the work of another part or allow the various classes within him to meddle with each other. He regulates well what is really his own and rules himself. He puts himself in order, is his own friend, and harmonizes the three parts of himself. . . . He binds together those parts and any others there may be in between, and from having been many things he becomes entirely one, moderate and harmonious.[20]

If each class of people fulfilled its designated role, justice would prevail in the state. The same holds true for the individual person. If one keeps reason, spirit, and desire in check, justice will reign. For Plato, justice is a template for an ideally ordered society as well as an integrated person. Justice establishes responsibilities so that all might have an opportunity to flourish.

Aristotle's definition of *justice*, found in Book 5 of his *Nicomachean Ethics,*[21] relies on the concept of virtue. Defined as that which leads a person to the good life, a virtue is the golden mean between the extremes of excess and deficiency. The virtue of justice, for example, defines a center point between selfishness and selflessness. Aristotle conceived of virtue not as a static entity but as something dynamic that the human as well as the city-state could develop through practice and testing. Justice, like its associative cardinal virtues of temperance, prudence, and fortitude, can be practiced, perfected, developed, and eventually embedded in one's character.

Religious traditions enumerate the virtues in different ways. Christianity lists seven virtues and divides them into two categories: theological and cardinal. Given by God and aided by God's grace, the theological virtues of faith, hope,

---

19. Ibid., 441e–442d.

20. Bloom, *The Republic of Plato*, 443c–e.

21. Robert C. Bartlett and Susan D. Collins, trans., *Aristotle's Nicomachean Ethics* (Chicago: The University of Chicago Press, 2011).

and charity help a person grow closer to God. The other four, called cardinal virtues from the Latin *cardo* meaning "hinge," are justice, fortitude, courage, and temperance. They are sometimes referred to as hinge virtues, because from them all other virtues, such as patience, honor, loyalty, and cleanliness, hang.

For Aquinas, the virtue of justice is a function of the will: "a constant and perpetual will to render to everyone his [sic] due."[22] He connects prudence with the intellect and fortitude and temperance with the regulation of the passions and appetites, but justice is always directed toward other persons. It is never self-serving or ignorant of the needs of others and is always concerned that one's neighbors have their rightful due. Ensuring justice requires an ongoing examination and perfection of the will through reason and faith.

According to Aquinas, charity plays an integral role in perfecting the will and assists justice in regulating common life.[23] While charity engenders mercy in a person, it can also lead to such a profound sense of empathy toward one's neighbors as to distract from meting out justice.[24] Aquinas qualifies the relationship between justice and mercy by noting that justice without mercy is oppression and mercy without justice is pity.

Any philosophical consideration of justice within the last century includes a consideration of Harvard philosophy professor John Rawls who understood *justice* as *fairness*. His pivotal text *A Theory of Justice* defines *justice* as involving an *impartial* distribution of goods.[25] Rawls built his argument on what he termed a "veil of ignorance": members of a given society would propose a theory of justice in which people would flourish, while "being blind" to all the variables that comprise peoples' sociopolitical lives.[26] This "veil of ignorance," Rawls believes, eliminates any personal claims and would lead to jettisoning any utilitarian theory of justice, partially out of fear that one's own good might be left out for the good of another. From behind this "veil of ignorance," Rawls suggests that any self-interested, rational person would propose two principles of justice: the "principle of equal liberty," giving every person equal access to the entire array of rights a society offers and the "difference principle," whereby socioeconomic inequalities would favor the least advantaged.[27]

---

22. Thomas Aquinas, II:II, 58.1.

23. Thomas Aquinas, I–II, q. 62, a. 3; II–II, q. 23, a. 1.

24. Thomas Aquinas, II.II, 29.3.

25. John Rawls, rev. ed., *A Theory of Justice* (Harvard: President and Fellows of Harvard College, 1999).

26. T. Pogge, *John Rawls: His Life and Theory of Justice* (New York: Oxford University Press, 2007). Olatunji A. Oyeshile, "A Critique of the Maximin Principle in Rawls' Theory of Justice," *Humanity & Social Sciences Journal* 3 (1): 65–69, 2008.

27. Catherine Audard, *John Rawls* (Michigan: Acumen, 2008). John Rawls, *Justice as Fairness: A Restatement*, ed. Erin Kelly (Harvard: President and Fellows of Harvard College, 2001). Paul Voice, *Rawls Explained: From Fairness to Utopia* (Chicago: Open Court Publishing Company, 2011).

Rawls's understanding of justice complements those of Plato, Aristotle, and Aquinas. Like the statue of *Lady Justice*, the blindfolded figure holding the scales of justice found outside many courthouses and civic buildings, Rawls asserts that justice is or should be "blind." The scales of justice represent the desire for fairness and truth amidst competing claims. From this perspective, personal investment and egoism ought to be jettisoned

This review of philosophical underpinnings offers an appreciation of what justice means as well as a sense of the possible relevance and application of these ideas in contemporary economics. In their definition of justice as a virtue, Aristotle and Thomas Aquinas offer encouragement and hope. These two thinkers do not view justice as static and concrete but as dynamic, ongoing, and in process. The dynamic nature of justice brings hope that, even in times of crisis or desperation, new understandings of justice will reveal themselves and serve to correct a wayward society. Aristotle and Aquinas also believed that people can become more just through education and testing. Therefore, even those who act unjustly or lack awareness of justice can learn to see with new eyes and mend their ways.

In order to appreciate more fully Aristotle and Thomas Aquinas's understanding of justice, the figure of a triangle might explain the obligations that flow from justice. The top of the triangle represents the state while both bottom angles represent either individuals or groups of people. The justice the state owes to the public, called distributive or legal justice, flows from the top. This often consists of those things the state provides its citizenry, such as public service, protection, health, welfare, and education. The state justly provides its citizens with these services and rights as part of the social contract.

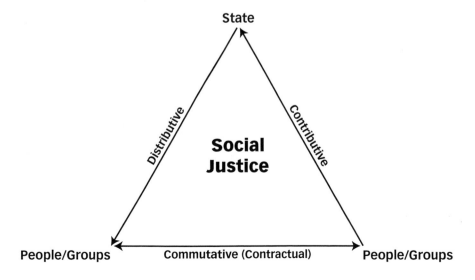

Proceeding in reverse, the justice that flows from the public to the state is referred to as contributive justice. While distributive justice addresses the issue of what the state owes its citizens, contributive justice answers the question, "What do citizens owe the state?" This encompasses such things as taxes, abiding by laws, and jury duty.

The base of the triangle illustrates commutative or contractual justice, which exists between individuals or groups of people. Some examples include mutual respect and the freedom to pursue individual goals unhindered by others attempting to fulfill their own goals. Various laws and regulations protect individuals, businesses, and groups from interference originating from others in society who either oppose or neglect them.

The instructive value of the triangle lies in comparing different kinds of triangles. One kind of triangle, not unlike an isosceles one in which only two sides are equal, might favor the state by drawing the angle at the top much broader than the others. In this scenario, the laws of the nation highlight and prioritize the relationship of individuals and groups to the state, while minimizing other relationships and distancing citizens and groups from one another. Another demonstrates how justice can be distorted when one sector of society is given priority over another. The type of triangle that best represents a state of true justice is the equilateral triangle. When all angles and sides are the same, a state of equilibrium, or social justice, prevails.

Another type of justice, called retributive, restorative, or reparative justice, seeks to ensure the ideal construction of justice and remedy any violations of it. This broad category includes the familiar heading of "criminal justice," which metes out punishments to those who have been proven to trespass justice. After a period of incarceration, the offender returns to society and is responsible to the demands of justice in society. This type of justice might also well include physical or emotional care or monetary award for the victims. Ideally, justice reaches its fullness when both the perpetrator and victim have an opportunity to be reconciled in some sort of meaningful way.

Biblical Roots of Justice

The concept of justice appears throughout the Bible, starting with the creation stories in Genesis and running all the way through the stories of hopeful restoration in the book of Revelation, the last book of the New Testament. Christians believe these sacred texts chronicle a love story between God and God's people. Justice serves as a tangible expression of that unconditional love and reveals a God who is the archetype of justice. The book of Psalms acknowledges this: "You are righteous, LORD, / and just are your judgments / You have given your testimonies in righteousness / and in surpassing faithfulness. . . . Your justice is forever right, / your law true" (119:137–138,142).[28]

The Bible shows God demonstrating divine love by both promoting and defending justice and presents God as attentive and consistently just, prompting the people to respond with justice even when challenged by oppressive leadership or unjust situations. God manifests love and justice and expects humans to respond by expressing their love of God, self, and neighbor by acting justly.

Justice, in this view, is fidelity to the demands of relationship between God and humanity or among the human community itself. Texts throughout the Hebrew Scriptures, express the human hope for a just relationship between God and humanity. The prophet Micah captures God's expectation well: "You have been told, O mortal, what is good, / and what the LORD requires of you: / Only to do justice and to love goodness, / and to walk humbly with your God" (6:8). The author of Proverbs acknowledges that those who practice justice and mercy will "find life and honor" (21:21). The Psalmist weighs in: "Blessed are those who do what is right, / who deeds are always just" (106:3). The Scriptures relate how God proposes justice as a constitutive element of the relationship between humanity and God as well as how humanity incorporates these demands of relationship or, in some instances, does not.

Mishpat

The Hebrew Scriptures use two words to connote justice: *mishpat* and *sedaqah*. The Hebrew word *mishpat* appears more than 200 times in the Hebrew Scriptures and refers to treating all people equally, whether this involves care, protection, or punishment. Justice as *mishpat* does not discriminate because of race, color, creed, origin, or orientation. *Mishpat* has several similarities to Rawl's appreciation of justice. However, it differs from Rawl's understanding of justice because inherent to *mishpat* is the idea that each person is an image of God, or *imago dei*.

Mishpat both acknowledges and extends human dignity. It is not only fairness in punishment of wrongdoing, but also in the extension of care and protection of *all* people. *Mishpat* entails giving a people what is their just due or, better yet, that to which they are rightly entitled. The Old Testament employs the word *mishpat* when speaking of groups of people on the fringes of society and often out of reach of justice. *Mishpat* reveals the nature of God as the just one:

> The LORD your God . . . who executes justice [*mishpat*] for the orphan and the widow, and loves the resident alien, giving them food and clothing. (Deuteronomy 10:17–18)

---

28. Other passages that illustrate God as the just one can be found here: 2 Chronicles 12:6; Nehemiah 9:8; Psalms 7:9; 11:7; 33:5, 37–38; 99:4; 103:17; 116:5; Isaiah 30:18; 61:8; Jeremiah 9:24.

And again,

> [The LORD who executes] justice [*mishpat*] for the oppressed, / who gives food to the hungry. / The LORD sets prisoners free; / the LORD gives sight to the blind. / The Lord who raises up those who are bowed down; / the LORD loves the righteous. / The LORD protects the resident alien, / comes to the aid of the orphan and the widow, / but thwarts the ways of the wicked. (Psalm 146:7–9)

The letter of James in the New Testament captures the essence of God's *mishpat* in a first-century Palestinian context when it asserts that the "religion that is pure and undefiled before God and the Father is this: to care for orphans and widows in their affliction and to keep oneself unstained by the world" (James 1:27). This type of religion was evident during the time of Jesus and after his death and Resurrection as the disciples attended to the marginalized and sought to dismantle oppressive societal structures that oppressed the poor (Matthew 9:35–38; Acts 3–4; 5:12–16).

Scripture identifies those precious to God's heart as the *anawim*, the most abandoned and powerless of society: widows, orphans, and resident aliens. In contemporary parlance, this group would consist of the "last, lost, and the least," such as the underemployed, migrant workers, single parents, refugees, and the elderly. Nicholas Wolterstorff expands this list of "bottom ones, the low ones, the lowly" to include "the impoverished" in what he calls the "quartet of the vulnerable."[29] Drawing on the understanding of justice as *mishpat*, one can measure the justness of a society, an organization, or the marketplace by how it promotes or neglects these often-marginalized groups of people.

The Bible asserts that God's love is limitless and especially bestowed on those whom society might discard as useless or relegate to the margins. God is a "father to the fatherless, defender of widows" (Psalm 68:6). Rawls's understanding of justice as blind, then, does *not* coalesce with the biblical concept of *mishpat*. Scripture scholar John Donahue observes:

> Biblical justice is not "blind," nor totally impartial. It is partial to those most affected by evil and oppression—symbolized in the Old Testament by four groups of widows, orphans, the poor, and strangers in the land, and embodied in the New Testament by Jesus' mission to those on the social and religious margins of society.[30]

---

29. Nicholas Wolterstorff, *Justice: Rights and Wrongs* (Princeton, NJ: Princeton University, 2010), 75–79.

30. John R. Donahue, "Biblical Perspectives on Justice," in *The Faith That Does Justice* (New York: Paulist Press, 1977), 76.

The Bible recommends justice modeled on the universal love of God as a basis for all relationships.

On the other hand, God's action is unrelenting toward those who choose infidelity, who are not faithful to the demands of justice. The Bible contains many examples of this relationship between justice and fidelity. In the second creation story in Genesis, Adam and Eve chose obedience to a serpent over faithfulness to God and were banished from the garden. In a subsequent story, God consigned Cain to a life of vagrancy for killing his brother, Abel as Cain had broken God's command against murder. Later in Genesis, Noah builds an ark at God's command and allows only the just aboard. Those on the ark survive the great flood. In Genesis 19, God destroys the cities of Sodom and Gomorrah for their lack of faithfulness, and in the book of Exodus, the Egyptians and their sympathizers endure a deluge of plagues and the eventual death of their firstborn because they lacked faith in the power of the God of their Hebrew slaves.

When God's justice was taken for granted, abused, or questioned, God sent prophets to remind people of God's love for them and call them back to right relationship. For instance, the prophet Isaiah charged the people to live in justice: "Learn to do good. Make justice your aim: redress the wronged, hear the orphan's plea, defend the widow" (10:1-3). Isaiah, like so many of the other prophets, fearlessly took the leaders of the people to task: "Those . . . robbing my people's poor of justice, / making widows their plunder, and orphans their prey!" (Isaiah 10:1-2) And then adding the taking to task part: "What will you do on the day of punishment[?]" (Isaiah 10:3) In the Gospel of Matthew, Jesus rebuked the injustice of the Pharisees—men who were specifically tasked with ensuring justice: "Woe to you, scribes and Pharisees, you hypocrites. You pay tithes of mint and dill and cummin, and have neglected the weightier things of the law: judgment and mercy and fidelity" (Matthew 23:23).

Sedaqah

While *mishpat* extends the range of human concern, *sedaqah* has to do with being just or righteous in relationships with God, self, and others. Striving for right relationships in family or society appears in biblical narratives. The 1971 World Synod of Bishops wrote,

> According to the Christian message our relationship to our neighbor is bound up with our relationship to God; our response to the love of God, saving us through Christ, is shown to be effective in his love and service of people. Christian love of neighbor and justice cannot be separated. For love implies an absolute demand for justice, namely a recognition of the dignity and rights of one's neighbor. Justice attains its inner fullness only in love. Because every person is truly a visible image of the invisible God

and a sibling of Christ, the Christian finds in every person God himself and God's absolute demand for justice and love.[31]

Sedaqah, then, can be appreciated as antecedent to *mishpat*. In fact, if the equity and fairness specific to *sedaqah* characterized human relations, then *mishpat's* force of justice would be unnecessary.

Sedaqah in the marketplace would eliminate the need for the corrective action of *mishpat* for it serves as an a priori condition for justice. The lack of *sedaqah* often necessitates *mishpat*. Social justice thrives when these two types of justice govern human relations.

Christians believe that Jesus illustrates what justice is and encourages people to live up to its demands. The Gospels recount the stories about the life and teachings of Jesus that emphasize the importance of justice. In Matthew's Gospel (6:33), Jesus directs his disciples to "seek first the kingdom [of God] and his righteousness." In Luke's Gospel (4:16–19), he fleshes out the meaning of God's justice:

> [Jesus] came to Nazareth, where he had grown up, and went according to his custom into the synagogue on the sabbath day. He stood up to read and was handed a scroll of the prophet Isaiah. He unrolled the scroll and found the passage where it was written:
>
> "The Spirit of the Lord is upon me,
>   because he has anointed me
>   to bring good glad tidings to the poor.
> He has sent me to proclaim liberty to captives
>   and recovery of sight to the blind,
>   to let the oppressed go free,
> and to proclaim a year acceptable to the Lord."

Motivated by this divine love for those who have experienced injustice, Jesus reminds the people that as often as they cared for the hungry, thirsty, poor, sick, imprisoned, or naked, they did it for him (Matthew 25:31–46). Jesus identifies with the lowly ones, those marginalized by injustice.

Jesus also takes on religious leaders who have behaved hypocritically and violated justice. In the Gospel of Matthew (22:22), Jesus castigates the Sadducees and Pharisees. Similarly, in Luke 11:42, "Woe to you Pharisees! You pay tithes of mint and of rue and of every garden herb, but you pay no attention to judgment and to love for God. These you should should have done, without overlooking the others." Injustice does not simply "occur" by happenstance; it is perpetuated by people like the religious leaders of Jesus' time.

---

31. World Synod of Bishops, *Justicia in Mundo* (1971), no. 34.

Roman Catholic Social Teaching

The theme of justice permeates Judeo-Christian Scriptures, and given its root-edness in sacred Scripture, CST also reflects this emphasis. CST addresses the socioeconomic and political life of society and takes as its starting point the reality of the day. Justice winds through modern CST. The documents—from Leo XIII's groundbreaking encyclical *Rerum novarum* (On the Condition of Labor, 1891) to Benedict XVI's *Caritas in veritate* (Charity in Truth, 2009)—consistently empha-size the virtue of justice as the benchmark for human relations and socioeconomic political structures. The documents, each written at a critical juncture in history, offer insights into how to resolve unjust economic and social realities.

Catholic social teaching takes inductive or "bottom-up" analysis to political, social, and economic issues. The movement toward these three issues is distinctive from the deductive or "top-down" approach the Catholic Church uses to evalu-ate biological, medical, and sexual situations. Using a methodological practice of "see, judge, act," CST seeks to "see" by uncovering challenges or disruptive forces that threaten or weaken human dignity and the common good.[32] CST "judges" situations in light of principles drawn from Scripture and the Catholic Church's tradition, such as life and dignity of the human; call to family, community, and par-ticipation; rights and responsibilities; option for the poor and vulnerable; the dignity of work and the rights of workers; solidarity; and care for God's creation.[33] CST then proposes "actions" that would help to ensure the protection of human dignity and the common good so that all may flourish. For example, in the marketplace, union issues, discriminatory actions, unjust wage earnings, and unsatisfactory work-ing conditions would be starting points for using this pedagogical method of CST.

Catholic social teaching capitalizes on the creation accounts in Genesis. Both stories describe a paradise in which God walks with humanity and all cre-ation thrives. CST strives to achieve that idyllic experience. The *Compendium* states that "*the permanent principles of the Church's social doctrine constitute the very heart of Catholic social teaching. . . . the dignity of the human person*, . . . which is the foundation of all the other principles and content of the Church's social doctrine; *the common good*; *subsidiarity*; and *solidarity*."[34] CST makes clear that its goals can be realized only with human cooperation. Genesis highlights this by identifying humans as stewards of all creation (Genesis 1:26–28). *Gaudium et spes* (Pastoral Constitution on the Church in the Modern World, 1965), a pastoral

---

32. Mary Irene Zotti, "The Young Christian Workers," *U.S. Catholic Historian* 9, no. 4 (Fall 1990): 387–400.

33. US Conference of Catholic Bishops, "Seven Themes of Catholic Social Teaching," *http://www.usccb.org/beliefs-and-teachings/what-we-believe/catholic-social-teaching/seven-themes-of-catho-lic-social-teaching.cfm*.

34. Pontifical Council for Justice and Peace, *Compendium of the Social Doctrine of the Church*, *http://www.vatican.va/roman_curia/pontifical_councils/justpeace/documents/rc_pc_justpeace_doc_20060526_compendio-dott-soc_en.html*, no. 160.

constitution promulgated at the Second Vatican Council, declared that faithful stewardship extends the range of responsibility for justice beyond oneself:

> It is imperative that no one, out of indifference to the course of events or because of inertia, would indulge in a merely individualistic morality. The best way to fulfill one's obligations of justice and love is to contribute to the common good according to one's means and the needs of others, and also to promote and help public and private organizations devoted to bettering the conditions of life. (No. 30)

In 1971, the World Synod of Catholic Bishops connected stewardship with the work of justice in "Justice in the World":[35]

> Action on behalf of justice and participation in the transformation of the world fully appear to us as a constitutive dimension of the preaching of the Gospel, or, in other words, of the Church's mission for the redemption of the human race and its liberation from every oppressive situation.[36]

Realistically, some people have been wise and faithful stewards, but other individuals and groups of people, including corporations, have not exercised biblical stewardship. In fact, they have turned their back on God and, in doing so, "sinned." As the Synod noted, some wander astray by co-opting or corrupting God's plan for creation.

The origins of CST can be traced back to the Bible and subsequent teachings of individuals called the Church Fathers. For instance, on the issue of whether it was morally right to hold private property, Saints Justin, Clement of Alexandria, and John Chrysostom condemned the Roman practice of absolute power and right and proposed different alternatives. However, the typical dating of *modern* CST begins in 1891 with *Rerum novarum*.[37]

---

35. Theologian Donal Dorr remarked that the 1971 synodol document is "one of the most important statements on social justice ever issued by Rome." See Donal Dorr, *Option for the Poor: A Hundred Years of Vatican Social Teaching* (Blackburn, Victoria: Collins Dove, 1992), 128.

36. Synod of Bishops, "Justice in the World," 1971 in *Catholic Social Thought: The Documentary Heritage*, eds. David J. O'Brien and Thomas A. Shannon (New York: Maryknoll, 1992), no. 6.

37. Michael Schuck allots considerable time to the "pre-Leonine" period (1740–1877) in his text *That They Be One: The Social Teachings of the Papal Encyclicals 1740–1989*. Schuck contends that ignorance of this period would be a mistake because it offers insight into some of the critiques of the claims of the Enlightenment that will prevail in subsequent encyclicals. The letters of this period challenge these claims by emphasizing community over the celebrated individualism and growing disuse for God, a characteristic of the Enlightenment. This pre-Leonine period is indeed critical to include as it demonstrates that justice accounts for not just one person's claims but also for justice always in relation to those in the wider human community. Michael J. Schuck, *That They Be One: The Social Teaching of the Papal Encyclicals 1740–1989* (Washington, DC: Georgetown University Press, 1991). See also Michael J. Schuck, "Early Modern Roman Catholic Social Thought, 1740–1890," in *Modern Catholic Social Teaching: Commentaries & Interpretations*, ed., Kenneth Himes, (Washington, DC: Georgetown University Press, 2004), 99–124.

In *Rerum novarum,* Leo XIII addressed the failures and abuses of the Industrial Revolution when massive migration to the cities transformed Europe, moving it from a society dominated by an agrarian lifestyle to one that was urban and industrial. The introduction of machinery, assembly lines, repetitive, unskilled tasks, and factories of mass production permanently altered the meaning of human labor, cheapening and eviscerating it at the same time. Leo XIII acknowledges the unjust byproduct of industrialization:

> Hence, by degrees it has come to pass that working men have been surrendered, isolated and helpless, to the hardheartedness of employers and the greed of unchecked competition. . . . To this must be added that the hiring of labor and the conduct of trade are concentrated in the hands of comparatively few; so that a small number of very rich men have been able to lay upon the teeming masses of the laboring poor a yoke little better than that of slavery itself. (*RN,* no. 3)

The pope turns to "principles which truth and justice dictate" in order to resolve the new urban reality of work. In *Rerum novarum,* Leo XIII provides a framework for economic justice. He challenges the human community to never sacrifice labor for capital; encourages the wealthy to be less greedy; supports the creation of unions; and reminds government of their purpose to ensure public and individual well-being.

Forty years later, Pius XI, in his encyclical, *Quadragesimo anno* (The Reconstruction of Social Order, 1931), tackled some painful economic realities following World War I and the Great Depression. The document tried to make sense of the social, political, and economic realities at a time of radical polarization, increasing violence, and the rising appeal of socialism.[38] In this encyclical, Pius XI attempted to reconcile the disparity between "individual and collectivism" that manifested itself in the tension between "capital or ownership and of work or labor." He notes,

> Relations of one to the other must be made to conform to the laws of strictest justice—commutative justice, as it is called—with the support, however, of Christian charity. Free competition, kept within definite and due limits, and still more economic dictatorship, must be effectively brought under public authority in these matters which pertain to the latter's function. The public institutions themselves, of peoples, moreover, ought to make all human society conform to the needs of the common good; that is, to the norm of social justice. If this is done, that most

---

38. What Pius XI and subsequent popes do is use Leo XIII's *Rerum novarum* as a baseline document. Pius and his successors first consider the successes since Leo's "magna carta" and then identify new pressing challenges.

important division of social life, namely, economic activity, cannot fail likewise to return to right and sound order. (No. 110)

Building upon his insight into commutative justice that exists between individuals or groups of people, Pius XI teaches that "charity will never be true charity unless it takes justice into account."[39] Mere occasional acts of charity do not shield Christians from the demands of justice.

John XXIII, in his 1961 encyclical, *Mater et magistra* (Christianity and Social Progress), and his 1963 encyclical, *Pacem in terris* (Peace on Earth), addressed the growing global nature of justice in relation to the glaring inequities in the world. John XXIII recognized this period in history as "opportune to point out how difficult it is to understand clearly the relation between the objective requirements of justice and concrete situations" (*PT*, no. 154). At the same time, justice in economic affairs can be realized "little by little" (*PT*, no. 161). Justice, for this pope, involved sacrifice in weeding out sin—structural sins in particular—and jettisoning self-serving habits whereby economic rights are understood more as entitlements.

The ecumenical gathering of bishops known as the Second Vatican Council proved a defining moment for the Roman Catholic Church. Bishops from around the world discussed how to engage the world in a profoundly new way. *Gaudium et spes* (*GS*), one of the sixteen documents of Vatican II, served as the blueprint for how the Church should move forward in protecting the poor while remaining faithful to its mission to others:

The joys and the hopes, the griefs and the anxieties of the men of this age, especially those who are poor or in any way afflicted, these are the joys and hopes, the griefs and anxieties of the followers of Christ. (No. 1)

It made clear that the pursuit of justice remained a central endeavor.

In 1967, Paul VI wrote the encyclical *Populorum progressio* (The Development of Peoples), in which he challenged the Church and the world to expand its socioeconomic political vision beyond traditional Western concerns. The pope condemned uncurbed capitalism that valued profits, competition, and an unrestricted right to private property over labor (no. 10). He recognized frustrated and oppressed citizens' temptation to engage in "a revolutionary uprising" to dismantle structures and cripple markets to correct unbridled capitalism that seemingly has no boundaries. However, the pope warned that such a "revolution" would only "produce new injustices," although yields to economic activism in areas "where there is manifest long standing tyranny which would do great damage to fundamental personal rights and dangerous

---

39. Pope Pius XI, *Divini redemptoris* (1937), *http://www.vatican.va/holy_father/pius_xi/encyclicals/documents/hf_p-xi_enc_19031937_divini-redemptoris_en.html*, no. 49.

harm to the common good of the country" (no. 31). As an alternative to violence, Paul VI suggested a global government "capable of acting effectively in the juridical and political sectors" (no. 78). Perhaps the most prolific and animated pope on economic concerns was John Paul II. Having experienced unjust economic conditions in his native Poland, John Paul II used the power of the papal office to transform fiscal realities that caused suffering and hardship. In *Centesimus annus* (One Hundred Years after *Rerum novarum*, 1981), *Sollicitudo rei socialis* (On Social Concern, 1987), and *Laborem exercens* (On Human Work, 1991), he offered insights about economic justice. Justice, he noted, demanded a living wage, access to trade unions, safe job conditions, and a respectful work environment:

> The justice of a socioeconomic system and, in each case, its just functioning, deserve in the final analysis to be evaluated by the way in which man's work is properly remunerated in the system. . . . Hence, in every case, a just wage is the concrete means of *verifying the justice* of the whole socioeconomic system and, in any case, of checking that it is functioning justly. It is not the only means of checking, but it is a particularly important one and, in a sense, the key means. (*LE*, no. 19)

Here, John Paul II established the just wage as the metric to measure justice.

This understanding of justice becomes clearer in its appropriation in the economic life. The *Catechism of the Catholic Church* makes several claims with respect to this. First, it teaches that all "economic activity, conducted according to its own proper methods, is to be exercised within the limits of the moral order, in keeping with social justice so as to correspond to God's plan for man" (no. 2426). Justice is a constitutive component of the marketplace that should influence the ends of work. Work should bring dignity and a deeper appreciation of one's gifts; generate a just wage to provide for one's and one's family's needs; and, to participate in the unfolding of God's creation (*CCC*, nos. 2428–2429 and 2433–2434).

Economic justice may be compromised by conflicting claims in the marketplace, for example, in the pursuit of profit. A business's quest for a greater profit cannot eclipse suitable working conditions, explicit contracts, and just wages (*CCC*, nos. 2431 and 2436). In extreme circumstances in which justice cannot be realized through any sort of negotiation, a strike is "morally legitimate." However, when a strike is marked by anything but peaceful demonstration, it "becomes morally unacceptable . . . or when objectives are included that are not directly linked to working conditions or are contrary to the common good" (no. 2435).

The Compendium of the Social Doctrine of the Church discourages any limitations on justice:

Justice is particularly important in the present-day context, where the individual value of the person, his dignity and his rights—despite proclaimed intentions—are seriously threatened by the widespread tendency to make exclusive use of criteria of utility and ownership. The full truth about man makes it possible to move beyond a contractualistic vision of justice, which is a reductionist vision, and to open up also for justice the new horizon of solidarity and love (nos. 201).

The Compendium jettisons any minimalist notions of justice, which it believes characterizes so much of contemporary marketplace relationships.

Faced with one of the more severe economic recessions in modern history, Pope Benedict XVI delayed publication of his encyclical *Caritas in veritate* (Charity in Truth) by two years. Originally, it was scheduled to be promulgated on the fortieth anniversary of *Populorum progressio*; but due to the economic crisis starting in 2007, it was delayed. After adjusting the text to respond to the financial meltdowns in the global markets, the pope promulgated it in 2009. *Caritas in veritate* (*CV*) discussed the interrelationship between charity and truth, especially as it related to the world financial crisis. Benedict XVI echoed Paul VI in his call for a world political authority to prevent further economic collapses and deal with its relative challenges (*CV*, no. 67). Although not universally embraced in the halls of economic power, Benedict XVI's overture put the G8 and World Monetary Fund, quasi "World Political Authorities," on notice. It also begged often-unspoken questions concerning justice with respect to the economy: "Who makes the decisions? How are they made? Are they inclusive and mindful of all?" These approximate the questions taken up by the US Conference of Catholic Bishops almost twenty-five years earlier in the pastoral letter *Economic Justice for All.*

Economic Justice for All

Supply-side economic policies popularly known as Reagonomics prevailed in the United States in the 1980s. In 1986, in response to the volatile economic reality the nation faced—and much to the chagrin of the corporate world who suggested that the Church had no place in boardroom decisions—US bishops issued the episcopal letter *Economic Justice for All* (*EJA*). The bishops wrote not as businesspersons, but as those charged with "the duty of scrutinizing the signs of the times and of interpreting them in the light of the Gospel" (*GS*, no. 4). They sought answers to three key questions: "What does the economy do *for* people? What does it do *to* people? And how do people *participate* in it?" (*EJA*, no. 1).

In the bishops' view, for far too long, "the economy" remained foreign to most people except those few insiders who knew how to operate, control, and manipulate it. The bishops wanted to persuade people to engage the economy instead of resigning themselves to being victims of it or mere cogs in its machinations. In this pivotal letter, the bishops encouraged people to reflect on their relationship with the economy and, in turn, pursue economic justice for everyone in society.

Building upon the Scriptures as a source of inspiration and direction in concert with the tradition of the Church, the bishops found that "the focal points of Israel's faith—creation, covenant, and community—provide a foundation for reflection on issues of economic and social justice" (*EJA*, no. 30). They used these three foci to develop their appreciation for economic justice. First, because God has created each person in God's own image, the concept of *imago dei*, every human deserves fair and just treatment. Ideally, Christians act justly not out of fear of God's retribution, but also because they believe the covenant they share with God demands it. This covenant calls them to respond to God's free promptings to work as a community of disciples toward the establishment of the reign of God and justice. The bishops called upon Christians to regularly evaluate their personal relationship with wealth as well as with the wealth of the entire nation. Christians have a rich, living tradition of reflecting on poverty and wealth that can serve as a beacon of hope for the wider global community (*EJA*, no. 19).

The US bishops followed up a decade later in 1996 with their document "A Decade After 'Economic Justice for All'"[40] As with papal and conciliar social teachings, the bishops considered "continuing principles, changing contexts, and new challenges." The bishops emphasized in this anniversary letter that "the pursuit of economic justice is not an option or add-on."[41]

---

40. U.S. Catholic Conference, "A Decade After 'Economic Justice for All'" (Washington, DC: United States Catholic Conference, 1996).

41. Mark Allman, *The Almighty and the Dollar: Reflections on Economic Justice for All* (Winona, MN: Anselm Academic Press, 2012). On the occasion of the twenty-fifth anniversary of *Economic Justice for All*, Mark Allman, a Catholic theologian at Merrimack College in Andover, MA, convened a group of scholars to reflect critically on the import and significance of the bishops' document in its history and for the future. *The Almighty and the Dollar: Reflections on Economic Justice for All* was the resultant text from their conversations. Allman's book contains engaging chapters and intriguing insights from professors and practitioners. David Hollenbach tackles the question of how economic justice might be achieved now that the market is global. Daniel Finn claims Roman Catholic social teaching can serve as an empirical claim for sustaining *prosperity* for all as opposed to riches for some in a global common good. Rebecca Todd Peters considers an economy branded with a framework of solidarity, a virtue discussed further elsewhere in this text. Mark Allman returns to the bishops' question and asks who is involved in the decision-making process using Amartya Sen's "development as participation" as his foundation.

Allman's text includes discussions of contemporary issues that are connected integrally to economic justice. Thomas Massaro, building upon his work on the 1996 US Welfare Act, demonstrates the influential nature of the Catholic Church vis-à-vis public policy and indicates contributions *Economic Justice for All* can make in the discussion of universal health care coverage. Alex Mikulich indicts the economy for its "white economic privilege and racial oppression" and suggests ways for moving beyond "whiteness in the struggle for economic justice." Maria Teresa Davila opens up the ever-present immigrant/day-laborer justice issue and proposes a "holistic vision for justice and solidarity." Margaret Pfeil links "food, liturgy, and the integrity of creation" in what she calls "synergoi" suggesting right relationship between these three is justice. Finally, Christopher Vogt writes on the "missed opportunity" he sees in connecting liturgy and justice.

Applications to Contemporary Business Settings

Distributive Justice and Corporate Governance

How a company organizes itself impacts its business culture, its products and services. Typically, a traditional publicly held corporation has a board of directors, an executive team, a cadre of middle managers, and finally, a slew of employees. History professor James Hoopes's book *False Prophets* identifies Frederick Taylor as the inventor of this top-down management style.[42] As a manager of industrial warehouses, he bullied his employees and dismissed his detractors.

This type of top-down management configuration works *for some* and is the organizational pattern most business schools teach. It offers a clear line of authority and, to a certain degree, protection knowing there is safety in obvious structures that make easy-to-define roles. However, this top-down decision-making process can hide infractions of justice and, in turn, make it easier for a corporation or business to let injustices fester. Some argue that, from the perspective of the option for the poor, the hierarchical structures represent a kind of injustice that relegates the majority to inferior status. They counter that the top-down management model tends to value the hierarchical management structure of the organization over and against the well-being of the workers.

Management experts Ron Ashkenas, Dave Ulrich, Todd Jick, and Steve Kerr have proposed "the boundaryless organization," which dismantles long-standing hierarchical structures, personal spaces, and allocated areas.[43] Their work has captured the attention of major corporations such as General Electric, which transformed the company by lowering boundaries levels of management while generating substantially higher profits.[44] This model has the potential to maximize justice by dismantling obstacles that can occlude suspicious behavior that may be antithetical to the promotion of justice or even criminal activity. The "wall-less" work environment has the capacity to ensure, through a new form of accountability, that all people are working for some common good.

When Michael Bloomberg became mayor of New York in 2002, he gave up the traditional corner office for what he called the bullpen. Everyone in his administration was expected to follow suit. Walls came down and open spaces replaced the traditional office arrangement. Bloomberg noted that one reason for his business success had to do with the rearrangement of the physical

---

42. James Hoopes, *False Prophets: The Gurus Who Created Modern Management and Why Their Ideas Are Bad for Business Today* (New York: Basic Books, 2013).

43. Ron Ashkenas, Dave Ulrich, Todd Jick, and Steve Kerr, *The Boundaryless Organization: Breaking the Chains of Organization Structure* (San Francisco: Jossey-Bass, 2002).

44. Dave Ulrich, Steve Kerr, and Ron Ashkenas, *The GE Work-Out: How to Implement GE's Revolutionary Method for Busting Bureaucracy & Attacking Organizational Problems—Fast* (New York: The McGraw-Hill Companies, 2002).

environment. He planned to bring that same success and openness to City Hall by literally knocking down the old barriers.

The bullpen is interesting nomenclature. Sports fans know it as the area where pitchers warm up by throwing to catchers. Often coaches and trainers observe and comment as the pitcher throws. Bloomberg credits this type of dynamic and engaging environment for the success of his financial data-services firm. Similarly, Google employees do not have private office space. Everything is done in common spaces. The "Googlopolis" has rooms for meetings, but even they remain open.[45]

In the end, in the interest of distributive and commutative justice, it seems as though the bullpen has the added potential to yield a revenue stream. At the same time, in its valuation of transparency and promotion of widespread participation in corporate policies and decisions, it can promote greater economic justice.

Participating in the Achievement of Social Justice: Microfinance

More than 1.4 billion people in the world live on less than $1.25 a day. This reality of extreme poverty strays far from the responsible stewardship presented in the book of Genesis. Poverty compromises human dignity and offsets the common good. Christians believe that their faith calls them to take responsibility for righting wrongs that trap people in poverty and to establish structures that facilitate sustainable development. In the Christian view, the relationship between God and humanity demands the work of justice.

Some have chosen to effect economic justice among the world's poor through the mechanism of microfinance, which builds upon the microcredit movement founded by Muhammad Yunus and Al Whittaker in the 1970s. As has been discussed in a previous chapter, microfinance can serve as an example of how the themes of CST are lived. A professor of economics, Yunus developed the concepts of microcredit and microfinance and implemented them in his Grameen Bank. Microcredit refers to the practice of providing small loans to candidates who do not qualify for a traditional bank loan to assist them in starting a business. Borrowers submit their requests, often via a website, and outline their business plans. Lenders pledge money and identify the payback period. Often, loans allow people, particularly women, to do so well that they develop a business relationship with their lender and secure larger loans that allow them to expand their business.

---

45. Although some companies and governments have incorporated the bullpen model into their business plans, most still have private offices, with special floors and spacious corner offices reserved for upper-level executives. Some businesses, such as American Express, have instituted a compromise model in which employees do not have permanent offices but "hotel," or sign up online for an available office space each week to encourage contact with a wide variety of colleagues.

Yunus's strategy offsets the plight of the poor by providing them a viable concrete means of development. Microfinancing connects a large array of stakeholders—borrowers, lenders, communities, governments and regulators, and speculators—to effect value creation through cooperation. Cyberspace has provided a rich platform for discovering need and investing and sustaining participation in a person or community's effort to eradicate poverty.[46] Every year, 5 percent of those who seek microcredit from the Grameen Bank emerge from poverty.[47] Microfinancing offers a venue for realizing justice.

Distributive Justice: Paying a Living Wage and Preventing Wage Theft

Just as well over a billion people live in extreme poverty, many workers live just above the poverty line. Two related reasons account for this reality: the failure of employers to pay a living wage and the theft of wages by employers.

In *Rerum novarum*, Leo XIII offers several insights that influence subsequent social teaching on a just wage. Leo XIII writes:

> Wages, as we are told, are regulated by free consent, and therefore the employer, when he pays what was agreed upon, has done his part and seemingly is not called upon to do anything beyond. The only way, it is said, in which injustice might occur would be if the master refused to pay the whole of the wages, or if the workman should not complete the work undertaken; in such cases the public authority should intervene, to see that each obtains his due, but not under any other circumstances. (No. 43)

Further on, Leo XIII observes that a higher "natural law" rather than market forces governs a wage:

> Let the working man and the employer make free agreements, and in particular let them agree freely as to the wages; nevertheless, there underlies a dictate of natural justice more imperious and ancient than any bargain between man and man, namely, that wages ought not to be insufficient to support a frugal and well-behaved wage-earner. (No. 45)

Further, he recommends the enactment of laws that "favor ownership, and its policy should be to induce as many as possible of the people to become

---

46. Jack J. Barry, "Microfinance, the Market and Political Development in the Internet Age," *Third World Quarterly* 33, no. 1 (2012): 125–141.

47. Anis Chowdhury, "How Effective is Microfinance as a Poverty Reduction Tool?" in *Poor Poverty: The Impoverishment of Analysis, Measurement and Policies*, eds. Anis Chowdhury and Jomo Kwame Sundaram (New York: Bloomsbury Academic, 2011),165–177.

owners" (no. 46). In its "Factsheet on Minimum Wage Legislation around the World," the Center for Public Policy Studies documented that 90 percent of the countries in the world have laws ensuring a daily minimum wage ranging from $2 to $40.[48]

Justice demands a just wage. However, the passage of just-wage legislation does not mean that businesses necessarily comply. Some employers do not pay the minimum hourly wage; others engage in wage theft. This may take the form of illegal payroll deductions, non-compensation for overtime or requested nonscheduled time, and failure to provide time for meals and breaks.[49] Workers' rights activist Kim Bobo calls it "the crime no one talks about" as employers pilfer billions of dollars from hard-working employees.[50] It is a violation of justice, and justice demands that anything that undermines the human as an *imago dei* and corrupts the common good be remedied.

Conclusion

For the most part, the Occupy Movement protests against unjust economic structures have simmered down. Some journalists have relegated the Occupy Movement to the morgue while others believe it is on life support.[51] Sociologist Marianne Manilov contends otherwise; she sees in the Occupy Movement hopeful signs that it can sustain the fight for economic justice.[52]

Economic justice is about the valuation of *people* living in a globalized economy, a marketplace in which human communities have an opportunity to access and participate in fiscal decisions that impact their lives. Ten years after the publication of its watershed document *Economic Justice for All*, the US Catholic Bishops amplified this as they identified ten principles for "A Catholic Framework for Economic Life":

---

48. Center for Public Policy Studies, "Factsheet on Minimum Wage Legislation around the World," *http://cpps.org.my/resource_centre/FACTSHEET%20ON%20MINIMUM%20WAGE%20 LEGISLATION%20AROUND%20THE%20WORLD.pdf*.

49. National Consumers League, "Workers Rights: Wage Theft: Six Common Methods," *http:// www.nclnet.org/worker-rights/148-wage-theft/525-wage-theft-six-common-methods*.

50. Kim Bobo, *Wage Theft in America: Why Millions of Working Americans Are Not Getting Paid— And What We Can Do about It* (New York: W.W. Norton & Company, Inc., 2009).

51. Meghan Barr, "1 Year on, Occupy Is in Disarray; Spirit Lives On," *Associated Press*, September 17, 2012.

52. See Marianne Manilov, "Occupy at One Year: Growing the Roots of a movement," *The Sociological Quarterly* 54, no. 2 (2013): 206–213. Although Manilov admits that the Movement has been growing more online than physically in the streets, given the reach of the World Wide Web and its historical impact in the Occupy Movement, online efforts toward a more just economy could prove to be more promising than the traditional protests.

1. The economy exists for the person, not the person for the economy.

2. All economic life should be shaped by moral principles. Economic choices and institutions must be judged by how they protect or undermine the life and dignity of the human, support the family, and serve the common good.

3. A fundamental moral measure of any economy is how the poor and vulnerable are faring.

4. All people have a right to life and to secure the basic necessities of life (e.g., food, clothing, shelter, education, health care, safe environment, economic security).

5. All people have the right to economic initiative, to productive work, to just wages and benefits, to decent working conditions as well as to organize and join unions or other associations.

6. All people, to the extent they are able, have a corresponding duty to work, a responsibility to provide the needs of their families and an obligation to contribute to the broader society.

7. In economic life, free markets have both clear advantages and limits; government has essential responsibilities and limitations; voluntary groups have irreplaceable roles but cannot substitute for the proper working of the market and the just policies of the state.

8. Society has a moral obligation, including governmental action when necessary, to assure opportunity, meet basic human needs, and pursue justice in economic life.

9. Workers, owners, managers, stockholders and consumers are moral agents in economic life. By our choices, initiative, creativity, and investment, we enhance or diminish economic opportunity, community life, and social justice.

10. The global economy has moral dimensions and human consequences. Decisions on investment, trade, aid, and development should protect human life and promote human rights, especially for those most in need wherever they might live on this globe.

Economic justice makes claims on the people and institutions for order, fairness, and giving to each his or her due. Catholic social teaching demands that corporate leaders fulfill the claims of justice. Without justice in the marketplace, scandals, abuses, Ponzi schemes, and the like will continue to favor some claims over others and, in turn, wreak havoc on the economy. Until justice pervades economic life, no enduring peace can prevail. In the words of Paul VI, "if you want peace, work for justice."[53]

---

53. "If You Want Peace, Work for Justice," *Message of His Holiness Pope Paul VI for the Celebration of the Day of Peace* (January 1, 1972), *http://www.vatican.va/holy_father/paul_vi/messages/peace/documents/hf_p-vi_mes_19711208_v-world-day-for-peace_en.html.*

Case Study

Day Laboring

The United States is a nation of immigrants. Some come legally, others illegally. Both groups, though, come for freedom and opportunity. Of the 38.5 million immigrants, 11.5 million have come from Mexico,[54] crossing dangerous borders in search of greater economic opportunity. Historically, Mexican immigrants have made their homes in metropolitan cities in Texas, California, and North Carolina. It was surprising to local residents when they settled in Farmingville, New York, a hamlet of approximately 15,500 people, mostly "Anglos."

About 1,500 Mexicans came to Farmingville in the late 1990s alone in search of job opportunities.[55] Farmingville offered easy access to the Long Island Expressway, a major thoroughfare for construction and landscaping trucks. The hamlet was also near many popular eateries, all of which were eager to hire immigrants, legal or otherwise.

The sheer number of undocumented residents provided a significant boost to the local economy. These women and men often worked long hours for low wages and took jobs few others would consider. Yet residents subjected the Mexican population to harassment that sometimes devolved into violence.

The people of Farmingville protested that Mexicans loitered at well-traveled corners and at "their" 7-11 convenience stores and Home Depots.[56] Local citizens were disturbed that Mexicans rented houses in their neighborhood and filled them beyond occupancy limits. The influx of undocumented residents divided the people of Farmingville. Some upheld the newcomers' right to stay. Critics countered, "We're being invaded and overrun."[57]

On one side of the protests was Margaret Bianculli-Dyber,[58] a concerned Farmingville resident who founded Sachem Quality of Life (SQL). In the movie

(continued)

54. Kate Brick, A. E. Challinor, and Marc R. Rosenblum, "Mexican and Central American Immigrants in the United States," A Report from Migration Policy Institute, 2011, *http://www.migrationpolicy.org/pubs/mexcentamimmigrants.pdf*. Ronald L. Mize and Grace Pena Delgado, *Latino Immigrants in the United States* (Malden, MA: Polity Press, 2012).

55. Jeffrey Passel, D'Vera Cohn, and Ana Gonzalez-Barrera, "Net Migration from Mexico Falls to Zero—and Perhaps Less," A Report from the Pew Research Hispanic Center, April 23, 2012, *http://www.pewhispanic.org/2012/04/23/net-migration-from-mexico-falls-to-zero-and-perhaps-less/*.

56. Denise Bonilla, Bart Jones, John Moreno Gonzales, and Theresa Vargas, "Farmingville: Where Controversy Lives," *Newsday*, January 29, 2006.

57. Candace Rondeaux, "Latino Laborers Targeted—Tolerance for Illegal Aliens Dropping," *National Catholic Reporter*, September 7, 2001, *http://natcath.org/NCR_Online/archives2/2001c/090701/090701d.htm*.

58. Bart Jones, "Farmingville: Why Here, Why Now? Probing the Tension, Fear, and Violence," *Newsday*, September 29, 2003.

Case Study   *(continued)*

Farmingville, which brought awareness of the day-laboring movement and established the hamlet as ground zero for immigration discussions, Bianculli-Dyber says that she never expected to become an activist.[59] The public nuisance, housing challenges, loitering, and increased crime rate in Farmingville prompted her to "protect her neighborhood." Despite Bianculli-Dyber's efforts, politicians greeted her protestations with suspicion and an unwillingness to act.

Ed Hernandez from Brookhaven Citizens for Peaceful Solutions and Joe Madsen, a Catholic religious brother and sympathetic accompanier of the Mexicans, led the other side, motivated by the belief that the Mexicans were good hard-working people, doing work that quite often others would not. In fact, as Hernandez and Madsen emphasize in *Farmingville*, if Mexicans did not provide the low-cost labor to the construction, landscaping, and restaurant businesses, the economy would experience a downturn. They accused the other side of racism and intolerance.[60]

The Farmingville situation came to some painful junctures for both sides during the course of the heated exchanges. First, Mexican laborers Israel Pérez and Magdaleno Escamilla were violently accosted and left seriously wounded in the basement of a home where they were told there was work.[61] They had been led there under false pretenses by perpetrators, two men with a known connection to a white supremacist group, who were later tried and convicted. This incident drew the attention of the press and increased sympathy for the Mexican laborers. A second incident increased the disdain *for* the Mexicans and further polarized the Farmingville community. In the early evening hours, a pregnant woman was struck down by an unlicensed immigrant worker.[62]

As a result, two significant efforts were made to resolve this situation. The first involved the establishment of hiring halls, central locations where Mexican day laborers could find secure work. This proposal generated hope as well as significant resistance. One group enlisted the help of the

(continued)

---

59. Carlos Sandoval and Catherine Tambini, *Farmingville*, 2004.

60. The efforts of Hernandez and Madsen complemented those of Matilde Parada. Working out the conference rooms of the local Catholic church, Parada helped the Mexican immigrants form Human Solidarity. The group aimed to build up the community of Mexicans in Farmingville; help them understand their rights as workers; and strategize how best to combat the verbal and physical harassment. To start the process, they organized a game of soccer, a sport central to their lives, playing on a local school field in exchange for taking care of it. The arrangement met with pushback from Bianculli-Dyber and her protest group, who took the Sachem School Board to task for permitting this.

61. Elissa Gootman, "Defendant Found Guilty in L. I. Beatings," *New York Times*, August 17, 2001, *http://www.nytimes.com/2001/08/17/nyregion/defendant-found-guilty-in-li-beatings.html*.

62. James Claffey, "Anti-immigrant Violence in Suburbia," *Social Text* 24, no. 3 (Fall 2006): 73–80.

Case Study *(continued)*

Federation for American Immigration Reform (FAIR), a national organization whose mission is to examine immigration trends and effects, to educate the American people on the impacts of sustained high-volume immigration, and to discern, put forward, and advocate immigration policies that will *best* serve American environmental, societal, and economic interests today and into the future. [emphasis mine][63]

The involvement of this national group only heightened the anti-Mexican sentiment and led to involvement of other national immigration watch groups. The pushback effectively stopped the proposal from moving forward.

Some twenty years have passed since the arrival of the first Mexicans in Farmingville. There are still no hiring halls, and day laborers continue to congregate at local stores in search of work. The situation, while still tense, has become somewhat less inflammatory than it was when the Mexicans first arrived. Aggravated residents have either moved out or become more tolerant.

Questions

1. Given that justice can be known from the experience of injustice, what does the experience of the Mexican immigrants in Farmingville say about justice?

2. Justice is something that continues to take root and flourish. In this case, though, polarization seems to have preempted solidarity, or has it? Why or why not?

3. Sacred Scripture reveals a God who has a special love for the "lost, last, and the least." How do the Mexicans compare with the *anawim* that the Judeo-Christian Scriptures referred to as highly favored by God?

4. What are the risks that undocumented immigrants take by staying in Farmingville and not applying for citizenship?

5. The United States is a land of immigrants. Why do some in the United States proudly acknowledge this and yet not accept immigrants in their neighborhoods?

6. Consider this case on immigration as the "see" in the see-judge-act methodology CST uses to assess unjust political, social, and economic situations. What principle(s) would you consider as helpful as an evaluative lens to "judge" this situation? What kind of "action" would you propose given what you "see" and "judge"?

---

63. "About FAIR," *http://www.fairus.org/about.*

Case Study

Sweet Justice or Sour Dough?

At the end of November 2012, Hostess Brands, Inc., announced it would permanently shut its manufacturing plants, leaving a sizable number of people jobless and bringing an end to delectable treats people have enjoyed since Hostess's inception in 1930.[64] Hostess ran 33 bakeries, 527 bakery outlet stores, 553 distribution centers, and about 5,500 delivery routes throughout the United States. A future without Hostess's iconic products, such as Twinkies, Ding Dongs, Sno Balls, and Dolly Madison Zingers, seemed unbearable to its loyal customers. The imminent ending of production caused people to run to grocery stores to purchase their favorite cake or bread product. When the shelves emptied, dedicated sympathizers turned to the web to buy Hostess snacks and its subsidiaries Wonder bread, Nature's Pride, Butternut Breads, and Drake's cakes.

The demise of Hostess signaled the end of an eighty-two-year-old company as well as the termination of 18,500 jobs. Despite eleventh-hour efforts to mediate an agreement between striking workers and Hostess Brands, Inc., the company could not be saved. New York Bankruptcy Judge Robert Drain attempted to work with both sides, serving as a mediator between the bakers' union and Hostess management. In the end, however, Hostess sought liquidation of its company in the face of low cash levels, increased overhead costs, deteriorating factories, and challenging union demands.

This round of financial woes following a history of fiscal challenges took its toll on Hostess. In October 2009, Interstate Bakeries Corp., Hostess Brands, Inc.'s original name, recovered from its 2004 bankruptcy with the assistance of Ripplewood Holdings LLC and lenders.[65] In January 2012, Hostess filed again for bankruptcy, acknowledging it owed $1 billion to creditors with a major financial claim coming from a union pension-benefit fund that represented 5,600 of its bakers.[66] In early November 2012, members of the Bakery, Confectionery, Tobacco Workers and Grain Millers Union initiated a strike against Hostess. The Teamsters, the union that represented many of Hostess's delivery workers, did not strike. In fact, the Teamsters

(continued)

---

64. Rachel Feintzeig, Mike Spector, and Julie Jargon, "Twinkie Maker Hostess to Close," *The Wall Street Journal* (November 16, 2012), *http://online.wsj.com/news/articles/SB10001424127887324 5563045781226325608426700.*

65. Interstate Bakeries Corp., 04- 45814, US Bankruptcy Court, Western District of Missouri (Kansas City).

66. Hostess Brands Inc., 12-22052, US Bankruptcy Court, Southern District of New York (White Plains).

Case Study

(continued)

conceded wage reductions of 8 percent as well as pension cuts.[67] Hostess communicated to its workers that it could not survive a work stoppage, and on November 20, after a round of mediations, Hostess's operations ceased. Judge Drain approved the liquidation plan, and Hostess workers were laid off immediately.

Following the judgment, a cache of more than one hundred prospective buyers emerged.[68] Hostess rivals Flowers Foods, owner of the "Nature's Own" brand; Mexico's Grupo Bimbo, the Mexican company that owns Sara Lee and Entenmann's; and private equity firms such as Sun Capital Partners, Inc., and Metropolous & Company expressed interest in manufacturing some Hostess products. Flowers Foods restructured its corporate loan agreements in an effort to consider "acquisition funding" and "expansion goals." Sun Capital Partners, Inc., made it a point that if they were to purchase the company, they would engage in more friendly relations with unions. In addition to these bidders, Wal-Mart Stores Inc. (WMT) and Kroger Company (KR) had made a move to purchase some of Hostess's assets. Hurst Capital LLP publicly expressed its interest in purchasing the company as well as its intellectual property and office supplies. In the end, in late April 2013, Apollo Global Management and Metropoulos & Company purchased Hostess Brands for $410 million.[69]

Hostess Brands, Inc., blamed its unprofitability, in part, on workers' unions, and the recent purchasers have announced their commitment to *nonunion* labor.[70] Because of union rules, Hostess bread products could not be carried in the same truck as its cakes. Additionally, drivers could not load or unload any trucks. In fact, Gregory Rayburn, the CEO of Hostess Brands, Inc., thought the company's labor contracts might actually deter prospective buyers. Financial analysts concurred that unionized labor proved a decisive factor in the demise of Hostess but also pointed to the company's failure to keep its facilities and equipment up to date with technological advances as contributing to its downfall.

(continued)

---

67. Many businesses have faced labor unrest in the recovery from the recession as they try to dial back benefits and wages and unions resist. In 2011, for example, there were nineteen major strikes and lockouts involving more than 1,000 workers, according to the Bureau of Labor Statistics, up from 11 in 2010. The 2011 strikes accounted for 1.02 million lost workdays.

68. "Hostess Liquidations Draws More than 100 Bidders," *http://www.nbcnews.com/business/hostess-liquidation-draws-more-100-bidders-1C7325957.*

69. "Twinkies (The Real Ones) Back on Shelves in July," *http://www.cnbc.com/id/100674792.*

70. "Twinkies Showdown Another Blow to Unions," *http://www.nbcnews.com/business/twinkies-showdown-another-blow-unions-6C9636035.*

Case Study *(continued)*

Union representatives indicated their membership conceded to as many demands as they reasonably could. Hostess, union leadership contended, was using unionized labor as a foil to deal with internal problems while asking its workers for wage and benefit cuts of about 30 percent. Union President Frank Hurt said, "The crisis facing Hostess Brands is the result of nearly a decade of financial and operational mismanagement that resulted in two bankruptcies, mountains of debt, declining sales and lost market share," and also that "the Wall Street investors who took over the company after the last bankruptcy attempted to resolve the mess by attacking the company's most valuable asset—its workers."[71]

The union leadership has a case. While Hostess asked union members to take wage cuts, its top executives enjoyed considerable pay increases. In addition to bonuses totaling $1.8 million dollars for nine top executives, Hostess also tripled its CEO's pay.[72] Hostess also misused funds intended for retiree benefits to offset the company's operations' shortfall. On behalf of its membership and with an eye to the common good, union leaders are pointing out the economic injustices of executive compensation, misuse of funds, and garnishing of retirement funds. These economic moves by Hostess, in addition to placing blame where it does not belong, violate giving all their fair share and just due.

Questions

1. Some financial analysts have suggested that the privately held Hostess Brands, Inc. is a brilliant example of vulture capitalism perpetuated by Wall Street hedge fund managers. Lots of money was made, particularly in the end. Does an understanding of justice informed by CST support amassing of such wealth. Why or why not?

2. Who is to blame for the demise of Hostess? Explain whether you believe management or unions are more responsible for the shuttering of Hostess.

(continued)

---

71. The Bakery, Confectionery, Tobacco Workers and Grain Millers' International Union, "Hostess in Current Condition Because of Failed Management," *http://www.bctgm.org/2012/11/hostess-in-current-condition-because-of-failed-management/*.

72. Travis Waldron, "Hostess CEO Cuts Worker Pay, But Leaves Own Salary Untouched," *http://thinkprogress.org/economy/2012/12/04/1278131/hostess-ceo-cuts-worker-pay-but-leaves-own-salary-untouched/?mobile=nc*.

Case Study   *(continued)*

3. Does union leadership have any sort of fiduciary responsibility toward fired Hostess workers? Why or why not?

4. Could union leadership have used other means to avoid losing this worksite?

5. Do you believe that Apollo Global Management and Metropoulos & Company made the decision to hire only nonunion workers too quickly? Why or why not?

6. Consider this case on unions as the "see" in the see-judge-act methodology CST uses to assesspolitical, social, and economic situations. What principle(s) would you consider as helpful as an evaluative lens to "judge" this situation? What kind of "action" would you propose given what you "see" and "judge"?

For Further Reading

Barrera, Albino. *Market Complicity and Christian Ethics (New Studies in Christian Ethics)*. Cambridge, UK: Cambridge University Press, 2011.

Cahill, Lisa Sowle. *Global Justice, Christology and Christian Ethics (New Studies in Christian Ethics)*. Cambridge, UK: Cambridge University Press, 2013.

Groody, Daniel G., and Peter C. Phan. *Globalization, Spirituality, and Justice (Theology in Global Perspectives)*. Maryknoll, NY: Orbis Books, 2011.

Heagle, John. *Justice Rising: The Emerging Biblical Vision*. Maryknoll, NY: Orbis Books, 2010.

Horsley, Richard A. *Covenant Economics: A Biblical Vision of Justice for All*. Louisville, KY: Westminster John Knox Press, 2009.

Hughson, Thomas. *Connecting Jesus to Social Justice: Classical Christology and Public Theology*. Lanham, MD: Rowman & Littlefield Publishers, 2013.

Massaro, Thomas. *Living Justice: Catholic Social Teaching in Action*. Lanham, MD: Rowman & Littlefield Publishers, 2011.

McCracken, Vic. *Christian Faith and Social Justice: Five Views*. New York: Bloomsbury Academic, 2014.

Power, David, and Michael Downey. *Living the Justice of the Triune God*. Collegeville, MN: Michael Glazier, 2012.

Sullivan, Susan Crawford, and Ron Pagnucco. *A Vision of Justice: Engaging Catholic Social Teaching on the College Campus*. Collegeville, MN: Michael Glazier, 2014.

Wolterstorff, Nicholas P. *Journey toward Justice* (*Turning South: Christian Scholars in an Age of World Christianity*): *Personal Encounters*. Grand Rapids, MI: Baker Academic, 2013.

Chapter 6

Subsidiarity in the Midst of Globalization

Elizabeth W. Collier

Introduction

The discussion of the Occupy Movement in the last chapter is a good starting point for the topic of this chapter, subsidiarity. The Occupy Movement illustrates the central feature of subsidiarity, which gives preference to local, grassroots organization. When North Americans think about organization, they often imagine hierarchical structures that are built from the top down and depend on an established authority for legitimacy. Subsidiarity is a principle that turns that logic on its head and is manifested when organizations develop from the ground up and are accountable primarily to immediate constituents rather than to established authorities. In this way, subsidiarity is subversive; it reconfigures common understandings of authority and the distribution of power in the global economy.

Subsidiarity is a term rarely cited in the United States outside of Catholic social thought. Pope Pius XI used the term to explain the preference for making decisions at local levels rather than at state levels whenever possible and practical to do so. This preferential option for local decision making correlates well with the other preferential option in Catholic social theory—the preferential option for the poor. Both affirm the need for the participation of those likely to be otherwise excluded from decision-making processes. Subsidiarity, in particular, has significant practical applications for business settings.

The Local Gets Lost in the Global

Feats of human ingenuity can be seen in executive boardrooms, on college campuses, and in local public-library branches across the country every day. Wireless networks allow students to submit assignments to online-course-management systems and enable social network users to update their Facebook status from almost anywhere. People can Skype with friends on other continents anytime of day for free. A person in the United States can participate in a webinar with someone in Africa or watch someone jump out of a capsule twenty miles above Earth's surface. Technology has globalized information and put it instantly within reach. Every year the technology not only gets faster, lighter, and more compact, but it also offers increasingly more options. Advances in technology, communications, and travel have given small and large businesses global-supply chains and manufacturing, marketing, and distribution options unavailable at any other time in history.

Globalization has brought many positive changes to people's lives. People in impoverished regions and countries have access to jobs due to outsourcing and global expansion of many industries. People in well-off regions and countries have access to mass-produced, inexpensive goods and to meat and produce throughout the year, no matter the season or growing conditions in the local region. They also have almost immediate access to information about happenings around the world.

Along with benefits, globalization carries significant hidden costs. Many US companies have outsourced manufacturing jobs to countries with few environmental regulations. As a result, entire waterways in regions outside the United States have become unfit sources of potable water. Consumers in the United States are often unaware of the pollution caused by some production facilities and the suffering it causes people living in the vicinity of these places. The wages associated with many manufacturing jobs outsourced to other countries do not allow workers to pull themselves out of poverty. In addition, many companies provide inadequate oversight of safety conditions and bar workers from forming unions, which would give them a voice in negotiating with the employers. Workers are rarely allowed to speak to investigators about the reality of their employment either. Furthermore, when inexpensive goods are mass produced outside the United States, these products—often poor in quality—quickly end up in landfills. While out of the sight of most consumers, these landfills often negatively impact local communities. These communities typically do not have the leverage to force change and neither is their plight reported in the press or widely known. The people who buy the products may have no way of knowing the effect on the local communities where the goods were produced.

When examining ethical issues that arise in business today, what happens at the local level often lies at the center of the issue. The practices of many businesses make it difficult to identify the primary decision makers affecting the communities in which goods are produced. Those affected at the local level often don't have the political or economic power to bring attention to injustices harming their communities. Some businesses neglect the concerns of local producers and consumers and instead make decisions from afar and at levels so high in the organization that decision makers are insulated from the repercussions of their choices. Some companies are very secretive about where they manufacture their products for reasons related to cutting-edge technology, patent applications, and overall market share. The supply chains of many companies contain subcontractors, who are intertwined with others in their industry, making it difficult for multinational entities to know the realities of labor practices and environmental realities at the local level. These examples are the antithesis of subsidiarity.

Complex markets and their myriad local manifestations give rise to concerns that may seem unique to modernity. However, since the time of the Roman Empire, empires and subsequent nation-states have grappled with how best to govern. What can or should be done at the local level and how can it be done? What can or should be done at a higher level of organization? What are the costs and benefits of organizing things globally and centralizing decision-making? What issues or situations require local influence? These are timeless questions for markets and their managers. Catholic social teaching advocates subsidiarity as the organizing principle that will often lead to answers in accord with human dignity, common good, preferential option for the poor, and the requirements of justice.

Roots of Subsidiarity in Catholic Social Teaching

Catholic social teaching (CST) takes a complex and dynamic approach to ethical reflection and decision making. Rather than providing specific directions for proceeding with social, political, and economic matters, CST offers foundational concepts and principles to use as a guide in working through complex issues.

The following four concepts are foundational:

- The human person, created in the image and likeness of God, should be treated with dignity and respect and able to live a life of flourishing;
- Humans are social beings, created to live in relationship with others. There is to be a constant dialectic between the individual and the community;
- All of the goods of the earth are to be understood as gifts from God. They have a "social destination," meaning that they are not solely for the use or enjoyment of the person in possession of them, but for the overall community as well;
- Poverty is a scandal—poverty would cease to exist if human dignity, common good, and stewardship governed the reality of individual and communal life.

These four concepts form part of the Catholic framework for thinking about what it means to be human and how to live together as a community. Because they are interrelated, striving to realize one of them requires striving toward all. As communities reflect on these concepts in the context of their daily lives and economic and political decisions, additional concepts flow from them. These succeeding layers make more specific demands and offer more detailed guidance about specific issues. One of these concepts is subsidiarity—a negotiating principle that when implemented can help particular communities organize their social, economic, and political lives with the aim of meeting the needs and respecting the rights of all community members.

Fundamentals of the Principle of Subsidiarity

The principle of subsidiarity relates to the individual; to the communities in which an individual lives, works, or participates; and to the civil and political structures within which communities exist. (The Latin word *subsidium*, from which *subsidiarity* is derived, means to offer help.) In order for one's human dignity to be fully realized and exercised, one must participate in the various communities to which one belongs. Each person's passions, talents, and resources offer that person different choices about how to participate in the community. Though the nature of one's participation in community life will vary throughout one's life journey, it is by contributing to the lives of others that one is able to fully realize one's human dignity. In this sense, human dignity, stewardship, and subsidiarity intimately relate to one another. Becoming a steward of one's passions, talents, and resources enhances one's dignity. Choosing not to participate or being unable to participate due to barriers created by one's community/society negatively impacts human dignity.

In addition to its connection with dignity, the principle of subsidiarity integrally relates to how stewardship facilitates the common good. Realization of the common good depends on everyone contributing his or her passions, talents, and resources, all of which are required for the smooth functioning of society. CST holds that if someone chooses not to participate or is not able to participate, then the individual, the community, and the overarching common good suffer. This nonparticipation results in a deficiency in the community and the common good. The greater the number of nonparticipants, the greater is the harm to the community. The onus, is not simply on the individual though, but also on the community to organize itself in such a way as to encourage individuals to participate and to facilitate that participation.

Intermediary groups or associations provide one major avenue for facilitating the participation of individuals in society. Intermediary groups, which range from small to large, national or even international, basically consist of groups of people working together for a common cause. They frequently pool their resources and their voices to increase their influence. An example of an intermediary group is a union, which allows workers to negotiate better wages, benefits, and working conditions. Unions are also often politically active in supporting candidates with positions on economic issues and collective bargaining that are favorable to laborers and to particular industries. Religiously affiliated intermediary groups lobby for causes such as universal health care, fair housing laws, and fair, just, and legal treatment for workers.[1] These intermediary groups function at every possible level of society and can vary greatly in size, function, and impact.

Catholic social teaching sees the functioning of society in terms of a dynamic interdependent system. In order for this system to protect and promote human dignity, stewardship, and the common good, all levels must function well and in accordance with the principle of subsidiarity: Anything that can realistically and reasonably be done on a local level should be done at that level. The people at the level at which issues arise have a certain understanding of them, know what resources they have for tackling them, and are likely more invested in resolving them.

Although a large, complex organization or entity can help a small local group with expertise, resources, or other needs, CST cautions against having a larger, higher-level entity take over: "It is an injustice and at the same time a grave evil and a disturbance of right order to transfer to the larger and higher collectivity functions which can be performed and provided for by lesser and subordinate bodies."[2] According to CST, when a larger entity takes over something better handled at a local level, the larger organization usurps or inhibits the dignity of those at the local level.

Implementing subsidiarity requires identifying the societal or organizational level that can most appropriately accomplish a task. The level will vary widely, based on the type of problem in need of resolution, the resources available at various levels, and the general state of affairs of government, private entities, and intermediary organizations. CST offers no single formula for determining how things should be done. The principle of subsidiarity helps guide one's decision-making process by offering questions and considerations to help establish the appropriate level of participation for individuals or a community.

Historical Development of Subsidiarity

While many of the foundational concepts in CST are grounded in biblical teaching, others such as subsidiarity come from theological and philosophical methods, concepts, and principles that inform the Catholic Church's moral teaching.

---

1. See Interfaith Worker Justice for an example of such a group, *http://www.iwj.org/*.

2. Pius XI, *Quadragesimo anno* (1931), no. 79, *http://www.vatican.va/holy_father/pius_xi/encyclicals /documents/hf_p-xi_enc_19310515_quadragesimo-anno_en.html*.

The principle of subsidiarity has roots in ancient social, legal, and political questions. The Church identifies subsidiarity as a principle of social philosophy.[3]

The principle of subsidiarity emerged implicitly in the late nineteenth century before the promulgation of *Rerum novaum* (On the Condition of Labor, 1891) by Pope Leo XIII but developed further between then and the period when *Quadragesimo anno* (The Reconstruction of Social Order, 1931) was drafted. During this time, complex changes took place in Western Europe, as it adjusted to the breakdown of the feudal system in the preceding decades. The dismantling of this system ushered in a variety of changes, including:

- the onset of mechanization and the Industrial Revolution
- the migration of labor to urban areas resulting in an oversupply of workers
- the rise of capitalism, which views labor as a commodity to be paid for according to the laws of supply and demand

The modern concept of subsidiarity began to take shape in the early twentieth century when Pope Pius XI commissioned the drafting of *Quadragesimo anno*. Although published under the name of the pope who promulgates it, an encyclical often includes contributions from various people working behind the scenes. One of the primary drafters of *Quadragesimo anno* was a German Jesuit, Oswald von Nell-Breuning. His task consisted, in part, of commemorating and explaining the significance of the first official social encyclical, *Rerum novarum*. Nell-Breuning was also charged with reflecting on social questions that had persisted or emerged in the forty years since *Rerum novarum*.

These new social and economic realities raised important questions about wages, working conditions, the length of the work week, child labor, women in the workplace, the relationship between owners, managers, and laborers, and the purpose of work and income, among many others.

Origins of Subsidiarity in Legal Theory

In the mid-nineteenth century, Germany faced challenging questions about how to reorganize its civil society. One consideration related to the "rule of law." At that time, two main schools of thought held sway. The *ius commune*, or "choice of law," system, aimed to balance the customs, contexts, and laws of local communities with universal and unifying political and legal influences. This understanding drew on ancient Roman law and rose to prominence among German theorists because of its use by Martin Luther and

---

3. See *Compendium of the Social Doctrine of the Catholic Church*, no. 187, *http://www.vatican.va/ roman_curia/pontifical_councils/justpeace/documents/rc_pc_justpeace_doc_20060526_compendio-dott-soc_en.html#Origin%20and%20meanin*.

Philipp Melanchthon to maintain peace and order during the upheaval of the Reformation.[4]

The ancient Roman Empire covered an immense territory and governed peoples of many different languages, religions, histories, and even levels of political organization. In an attempt to maintain order, the Roman system recognized that legal cases at the local level occurred in varying contexts. Before a case could be tried, authorities needed to determine where the case should be tried and identify the relevant laws. This process reflected the idea that the laws applied in any given case should come from the most local level held in common by those involved in the case, while also considering the requirements of universal justice, equity, and impartiality.[5] The Romans intended this system to balance lawlessness and potential rebelliousness leading to revolution on the one hand and imperialist tendencies of a centralizing authority on the other.[6]

The second main school of thought in Germany, "concept jurisprudence," argued for a uniform code of law for everyone. Deeming the *ius commune* an overlapping mess of traditions, procedures, and jurisdictions, this group sought to "erect a wholly rational system using universal principles and rigorous rules of reason."[7] This legal system defined the role of the judge as one who looked at the "perfectly logical and closed system" of "universal principles and axioms" and applied them to the case before the court.[8]

Friedrich Karl von Savigny (1779–1861), one of the most important jurists in nineteenth-century Germany, was a proponent of the first main school of thought, the *ius commune*.[9] Much of his support stemmed from his belief that the ways people organize themselves into social and political groups are part of their nature. Savigny drew on Catholic beliefs about human dignity and human nature as ordered to community as he advanced the theoretical underpinnings of the *ius commune*. In particular, he emphasized that what happens in local communities and how local communities organize themselves, relates to the nature of humanity and community: "Human community benefits from the law, but it is neither created by it, nor determined by it. Similarly, the great achievements of language like literature or song cannot be reduced to grammar, although grammar is, nonetheless, an essential aspect of human language."[10]

---

4. Martin O'Malley, "Currents in Nineteenth Century German Law, and Subsidiarity's Emergence as a Social Principle in the Writings of Wilhelm Kettler," *Journal of Law, Philosophy and Culture* 2, no. 1, (2008): 109. This article provides more information about the two schools of thought and how they influenced Kettler.

5. Ibid., 108.

6. Ibid., 106.

7. Ibid., 110.

8. Ibid., 110–111.

9. Ibid., 105.

10. Ibid., 115–16, includes footnote of O'Malley for Savigny, *supra* note 45, at 15.

The work of Savigny is important for understanding the development of the principle of subsidiarity because of its influence on Wilhelm Emmanuel von Kettler, one of the most significant figures in the German Roman Catholic Church hierarchy of the nineteenth century. Introduced to Savigny and his work as a young man, Kettler would have been familiar with Savigny's thoughts on the relationship between the local and the universal before entering law school.[11] Kettler attended a law school sympathetic to Savigny's school of thought.[12] In addition to his legal education, Kettler pursued a theological education and decided to become a Catholic priest. During this time he was influenced by several theologians whose work "emphasized the intertwining organic development of communities and their constitutive rules and doctrines."[13] His theological and legal studies both would have emphasized the importance of understanding local communities and their ways of life.

Kettler had concerns about the effects of the Industrial Revolution, such as poverty, low wages, and poor working conditions, on ordinary Germans. These circumstances left people feeling powerless, and he believed similar conditions had fostered revolutions in other times and places. Because of his legal and theological training, with its emphasis on the centrality of the local level and its role in the natural order of things, he thought it necessary to speak on behalf of the ignored and marginalized suffering from injustice. He believed that the church could have an important and productive role in this work of advocacy. These factors influenced the reform proposals that he put forth in speeches and writings.

Kettler believed in the freedom of the individual, the role of various communities in one's life, and the value of subsidiarity for resolving tensions between individuals and the communities within which they live and work. He believed that humans are free to make decisions and contribute resources, gifts, and talents to the wider community.[14] This freedom exists within the context of many different groups, such as the family and local municipalities. Intermediary associations also give people a voice and help them make a difference at the local and nongovernmental levels. Drawing on the principle of stewardship, people determine where their participation is required:

---

11. Savigny was Protestant, and there was significant conflict between Protestants and Catholics in Germany at this time. There was also philosophical pressure from others, including Kant, to minimize the influence of the churches in the political and civil realms, which Savigny did not support. He saw the churches as being important participants in civil society. Ibid., 118.

12. Ibid., 118.

13. O'Malley, footnote 56, p. 118.

14. As will be explained in chapter 8, "Rights against Responsibilities," in Catholic thought, every right brings with it a corresponding duty. Kettler understands *freedom* as freedom to do things—positive freedoms and rights. When someone has a right to make decisions and contribute to the community, that person has a duty to do so. The principle of subsidiarity only works if people in the local communities participate in the life of the community to the extent that they can and is appropriate.

People live freely when they are able to enjoy the rights and functions proper to each subsidiary level of human society: in their families, their local religious and neighborhood communities, and successively more universal governing structures. The ultimate telos (goal/aim) is the free self-government of the population, with Kettler's principle of subsidiarity indicating that each successively larger community, from the family to the nation should be granted as much freedom as it can properly exercise for its own flourishing. True to the organic model, the practice of freedoms on the lower levels fosters the competence for freedoms in more universal forms of governance.[15]

In order for the principle of subsidiarity to be implemented, individuals must be free to participate in the life of their local communities. Individuals and communities must also determine the proper scope of their decision-making capabilities. If the most local or lowest level of organization cannot serve the common good, then succeeding higher-level organizations can take on the task. According to the principle of subsidiarity higher-level organizations function as "helpers." If an organization or the state addresses an issue, it aims to help, not take unilateral control; otherwise, it may negatively impact the dignity of those at the local level by impeding their participation and stewardship. Kettler and others influenced those writing *Quadragesimo anno* with this understanding of human dignity, the proper role of government, intermediary organizations, and participation.

Subsidiarity in Catholic Social Teaching

The milieu within which subsidiarity developed sheds light on the inclusion of the principle in *Quadragesimo anno*. Pope Pius XI asked several German Jesuits[16] to help draft an encyclical that would commemorate the fortieth anniversary of *Rerum novarum* and further develop the social teaching in ways that could speak to the situation of workers and business in the late 1920s and early 1930s.

Well-steeped in the ongoing discussion about the legal system in Germany, these Jesuits reflected on the two dominant economic systems in existence at that time, namely capitalism and communism. They considered what type of economic system could most closely adhere to the concepts and principles of CST, which had expressed reservations about certain characteristics of both of these systems.

---

15. O'Malley, 128.

16. Jesuits are members of the Society of Jesus, which is a worldwide, Roman Catholic religious order of priests and brothers founded in 1540 by Saint Ignatius of Loyola.

They criticized capitalism because of its over emphasis on individual rights and the idea that individuals must make their own way in the world.[17] They also criticized capitalism's emphasis on private property and its corresponding downplaying of the social destination of goods (stewardship). In the capitalist view, a person buying a property or good is free to use or dispose of it as he or she wishes. This view does not consider that the community may have a claim on that good or property as well.

The German Jesuits were also concerned about how capitalism views the worker. In line with the teaching on human dignity, CST views people as "ends" in and of themselves, not as a means to an end. Capitalism, on the other hand, tends to see workers in terms of how they can contribute to production in an efficient and cost-effective way. In *Rerum novarum* and *Quadragesimo anno,* the Catholic Church raised concerns about workers not having a voice in free-market capitalism. This concern for workers underlies the Church's ongoing support of unions. Through collective bargaining, the threat of strikes and litigation, and political influence, unions give workers some power in a system that generally excludes them from decision making.

Just as capitalism receives its share of criticism by those drafting *Quadragesimo anno,* so too does communism. The command economy in communism is wholly dictated and managed by the government. It is contrary to the concept of human dignity because individual rights are subsumed to the government and society. The drafters also criticized communism's understanding of private property. Although the concept of stewardship includes the belief that property and goods have a social destination, it does not assert that society takes ownership of them. The Catholic Church considers owning property a natural right that comes from God. The state can regulate property in order to serve the common good, but the property remains in the possession of the owner and, to some extent, at the owner's disposal (*RN*, no. 35).

The period preceding the drafting of *Quadragesimo anno,* particularly in Germany, found economists, theologians, business owners, and others grappling with what type of economic system would best approximate the values of Christian social theory in light of the economic struggles and increasing centralization occurring in the early twentieth century. The main alternative proposed by Catholics was the "corporatist" model, which reflects a desire to find ways for people in similar professions or industries to work together in a more community-oriented way. Some proposed bringing back a version of the medieval guilds, with professional standards and an apprenticeship system. Once a person became a master of a trade, he or she could work with others on supply-chain

---

17. In the United States, this tends toward a libertarian understanding of negative rights—individuals have a right not to be interfered with or coerced into anything, but they do not really have rights *to* many things.

resources and the marketing and sale of products.[18] Some Catholic theorists believed that this was a more cooperative system, one that did not view workers simply a means to enhancing the wealth of the capitalists with little hope of improving their own economic station in life.

For all of the complex legal, political, and economic reasons stated, and in conjunction with the intellectual formation of the German Jesuits writing in consultation with Pius XI, the principle of subsidiarity found its way into *Quadragesimo anno* as can be seen in this oft-quoted passage:

> As history abundantly proves, it is true that on account of changed conditions many things which were done by small associations in former times cannot be done now save by large associations. Still, that most weighty principle, which cannot be set aside or changed, remains fixed and unshaken in social philosophy: Just as it is gravely wrong to take from individuals what they can accomplish by their own initiative and industry and give it to the community, so also it is an injustice and at the same time a grave evil and disturbance of right order to assign to a greater and higher association what lesser and subordinate organizations can do. For every social activity ought of its very nature to furnish help to the members of the body social, and never destroy and absorb them.
>
> The supreme authority of the State ought, therefore, to let subordinate groups handle matters and concerns of lesser importance, which would otherwise dissipate its efforts greatly. Thereby the State will more freely, powerfully, and effectively do all those things that belong to it alone because it alone can do them: directing, watching, urging, restraining, as occasion requires and necessity demands. Therefore, those in power should be sure that the more perfectly a graduated order is kept among the various associations, in observance of the principle of "subsidiary function," the stronger social authority and effectiveness will be the happier and more prosperous the condition of the State. (Nos. 79–80)

Some applauded the Catholic Church's reflection and suggestions for reconstructing the social order to relieve the suffering of many and advance the human flourishing of all, especially workers. Many others complained about the Church making suggestions for the organization of business and professions.[19] While *Quadragesimo anno* and the principle of subsidiarity did not result in any concrete, measurable changes, the explicit inclusion of the principle of subsidiarity and the ways it enhances the interrelated concepts of human dignity, social

---

18. Mich, Marvin L. Krier, *Catholic Social Teaching and Movements* (Mystic, CT: Twenty-third Publications, 1998), 12–13.

19. See overview of reactions to the document in Hinze, "Commentary on *Quadragesimo Anno (After Forty Years)*," in *Modern Catholic Social Teaching*, 171.

justice, stewardship, and the common good would prove important to the development of Catholic social thought going forward.[20]

Since *Quadragesimo anno*, this principle has continued to appear in the Church's official teaching. Pope John XXIII promulgated his first social encyclical *Mater et magistra* (Christianity and Social Progress) in 1961.[21] He was interested in helping the Catholic Church adjust institutionally to the changes taking place in society. John XXIII was concerned about the centralization of authority in the political and business realms and in their intersection as well. In *Mater et magistra*, he states in relationship to *Rerum novarum*: "It should be stated at the outset that in the economic order first place must be given to the personal initiative of private citizens working either as individuals or in association with each other in various ways for the furtherance of common interests" (no. 51). He also talks about the proper role for government in the economy (no. 52) and refers to *Quadragesimo anno* for how this should occur: "And in this work of directing, stimulating, co-ordinating, supplying and integrating, its guiding principle must be the 'principle of subsidiary function' formulated by Pius XI in *Quadragesimo anno*" (no. 53). The succeeding paragraphs of the document explain that while the government has a greater role in managing various aspects of the economy, there exists a dialectic tension between the government's appropriate economic role and the common good. Individuals and lower-level intermediary groups need to be integrally involved.

Pope John XXIII discussed the tension between proper higher-level intervention and the need for individual and local participation as a characteristic of the way society was developing in general. His writings mention the many ways society was changing and the growing level of interdependence. He did not see this as a bad thing but was optimistic about what such developments could offer the human community. At the same time, he cautioned against what might happen if higher-level organizations subsumed the role of the individual and the local. Here, in addition to the realities of modern development and technology, the pope had in mind the reality of communism and central government planning. He explains,

> As these mutual ties binding the men of our age one to the other grow and develop, governments will the more easily achieve a right order the more they succeed in striking a balance between the autonomous and active collaboration of individuals and groups, and the timely coordination and encouragement by the State of these private undertakings. (*MM*, no. 66)

---

20. The Vatican's social teachings give the broad strokes of definition and application. In the spirit of subsidiarity, it is up to regional and national bishops' conferences to apply the themes and principles of CST to local situations.

21. John XXIII, *Mater et magistra* (1961), no. 66, *http://www.vatican.va/holy_father/john_xxiii/encyclicals/documents/hf_j-xxiii_enc_15051961_mater_en.html.*

The pope is striving to balance the dignity of the individual, the social nature of the human person, and the need for participation. These principles encourage the realization of stewardship, social justice, and the common good.

This understanding of subsidiarity that developed in theological circles up through the 1960s and of the dialectic between the global and the local, the higher-level organization and the individual or local community, continues to appear, albeit implicitly, in the later papal documents. For instance, Pope Paul VI's *Populorum progressio* (The Development of Peoples, 1967) discusses development and economic initiative and their impact on the rich and poor. Paul VI argues that programs of development and economic initiatives should serve human nature. The pope goes on to say:

> Economics and technology are meaningless if they do not benefit man, for it is he they are to serve. Man is truly human only if he is the master of his own actions and the judge of their worth, only if he is the architect of his own progress. He must act according to his God-given nature, freely accepting its potentials and its claims upon him. (*PP*, no. 34)

This emphasis on the individual and personal freedom should be understood within the context of the social nature of the human person and the duty toward the common good. The pope puts emphasis on the individual out of concern that the state and certain types of economic activity do not maintain the importance and freedom of the individual in their proposals. The pope does not use the phrase "principle of subsidiarity," but his message and his discussion of "intermediary groups" serve as sure signs that he has this principle in mind.[22]

John Paul II, pope from October 1978 through April 2005, wrote prolifically and had an incredible influence on both the Roman Catholic Church and the world. He grew up in Poland during a time when the communist government of the USSR ruled Eastern Europe. Having experienced the Soviet political and economic control of Poland and their suppression of the Catholic Church, John Paul II entered the pontificate with an intimate understanding of how communism impacts Catholic notions of freedom, flourishing, individual initiative, and vocation as well as local communities (and states in this case) and their proper functions.

This first-hand knowledge most notably impacts his social encyclical *Centesimus annus* (One Hundred Years after *Rerum novarum*, 1991), which the pope wrote to commemorate the one-hundredth anniversary of *Rerum novarum*. In *Centesimus annus*, John Paul II explicitly mentions subsidiarity, coupling it with a

---

22. For more on this and Pope Paul VI's discussion of poverty in *Populorum progressio*, nos. 33–42, see Allen Figueroa Deck, S.J., "Commentary on *Populorum progressio* (On the Development of Peoples)," ed. Kenneth Hines, *Modern Catholic Social Teaching: Commentaries & Interpretation* (Washington, DC: Georgetown University Press, 2004)

relatively new concept in CST, solidarity. After discussing the suffering of workers and the state's role in protecting workers, he says,

> The State must contribute to the achievement of these goals both directly and indirectly. Indirectly and according to the *principle of subsidiarity*, by creating favourable conditions for the free exercise of economic activity, which will lead to abundant opportunities for employment and sources of wealth. Directly and according to the *principle of solidarity*, by defending the weakest, by placing certain limits on the autonomy of the parties who determine working conditions, and by ensuring in every case the necessary minimum support for the unemployed worker. (*CA*, no. 15)

In no. 48, he explains the proper role of government in the economic sphere. It entails "guarantees of individual freedom and private property, as well as a stable currency and efficient public services." The government also has "a duty to sustain business activities by creating conditions which will ensure job opportunities, by stimulating those activities where they are lacking or by supporting them in moments of crisis." The state or government has the right "to intervene when particular monopolies create delays or obstacles to development" and in extreme circumstances, to perform a "substitute function" when social or business sectors cannot perform their functions properly. He then explicitly cites the principle of subsidiarity:

> Here again *the principle of subsidiarity* must be respected: a community of a higher order should not interfere in the internal life of a community of a lower order, depriving the latter of its functions, but rather should support it in case of need and help to coordinate its activity with the activities of the rest of society, always with a view to the common good. (*CA*, no. 48)

In his discussion of subsidiarity, the pope clearly emphasizes the freedom and initiative of the individual. He uses solidarity as the complementary concept to maintain the tension between individualism and the place of the community in human nature. He refers to solidarity fifteen times in the document. The pope appeals to the possibility of a deep social bond existing within and across communities that drives people to action on behalf of others in order to ensure the dignity of fellow humans and the common good of all.

European vs. US Context

A Google search of the term *subsidiarity* will most likely bring up articles related the European Union (EU). In the EU, many different countries have come together to create a political and economic entity that they hope benefits the entire region. The various countries have had broad discussions about subsidiarity while deciding individually and collectively what policies the EU can and should deal with and what can and should be left to individual nations or entities within nations. This has not been an easy process, especially with the global economic crisis and the involvement of countries with vastly different cultures; attitudes toward work, taxes, and banks; initial monetary systems; and historically strained relationships. Some countries had to bail out other countries and impose strict and unpopular austerity measures in order to keep the overall system intact. Many of these countries have more communitarian systems internally, so individual sacrifice for the common good is not foreign to them. For instance, in several countries people willingly pay much higher income taxes in order to have universal health care and free education through college. Taking on this more communitarian disposition toward other nations, though, has proven difficult, especially when the benefits to the home country are not obvious to much of the population. Therefore, the concept of subsidiarity has figured into many of these conversations and on both sides of the issue.

In the United States, the term *subsidiarity* remains relatively unknown. Most people have never heard of the principle. Every once in a while a fiscally conservative politician will try to use the principle of subsidiarity to bolster arguments about the free market and opposition to any government interaction with the markets. They tend to espouse libertarianism. The political and economic theory undergirding that position, argues for individual liberty, autonomy, and free markets. Libertarians do not believe in "positive rights." They think of rights in negative terms—people have a right *not* to be interfered with and *not* to be coerced. As long as a person does not infringe on another person's rights and associations are voluntary, then a person should proceed as he or she wishes. The government should not be involved. In this view, the government's role consists of keeping internal order, defending the country, and upholding contracts. Libertarians do not want government regulations or processes, preferring to leave individuals and communities to regulate their own spheres. If a need arises in the community, then the community can decide whether to deal with that need.[23]

A few Catholics involved in government, academia, and industry have proposed that the principle of subsidiarity supports such libertarian values. As understood in CST though, subsidiarity strikes a balance between the freedom and initiative of the individual and local communities on the one hand and the striving of the common good, to which individuals, community groups, intermediary organizations, and the state all contribute on the other. Faith communities

---

23. The following link includes a quiz that illustrates libertarian positions on economic and social issues. It gives a score at the end of the quiz to show how the score compares to libertarian responses. Note the language used in the questions and the place of noninterference, noncoercion, and voluntary association in the thought, *http://www.theadvocates.org/quiz.*

and other intermediary groups in civil society help people reach their potential and meet their needs within a system that allows for commutative, distributive, and social justice.[24] CST clearly asserts that the proper role of government includes helping to set up systems that serve these ends and to intervene when crises tax the systems in such a way that local levels cannot effectively respond. Despite the caution against unnecessary or prolonged government intervention, CST nevertheless delineates a role for government.

In 1983, the US bishops took on the task of writing a document on the US economy. Between 1983 and 1986, two drafts of this document, *Economic Justice for All* (*EJA*), were written and widely disseminated for comment. Theologians, ethicists, Nobel Prize-winning economists, businesspeople in different industries and many others submitted more than 90,000 responses over the course of the three years. In 1986, the bishops published the final document. Although the public, for the most part, is not aware of the document or its contents, scholars and teachers use it in research and in the classroom. It has also had a significant impact on some in the business world. Although some Catholic business leaders do not use the explicit religious language as they make decisions, CST undergirds their decision making on matters such as wages, benefits, and what companies to do business with.[25]

In the introduction to *Economic Justice for All*, the bishops explicitly reaffirm many aspects of CST and mention *subsidiarity*. They explain that "Catholic social teaching calls for respect for the full richness of social life. The need for vital contributions from different human associations—ranging in size from the family to government—has been classically expressed in Catholic social teaching in the 'principle of subsidiarity'"(no. 99). They cite the classic definition of *subsidiarity* from *Quadragesimo anno* and then discuss the "institutional pluralism" inherent in this principle. That means every individual, organization, and institution must determine its place within the social constructs of the human community, such that dignity, stewardship and the common good can be realized. As it relates specifically to the economy, the bishops note that every person and institution has a role to play in a just and robust economy. Participation in the building up of such an economy is a right and duty of each person.[26]

In *Economic Justice for All*, the bishops address the government's relationship to the principle of subsidiarity. They reiterate Church teaching on the role of government in the economy and specifically refute the claim of libertarians that government should be as minimal as possible.

---

24. Commutative justice is fairness in contracts and agreements. Distributive justice is fair allocation of money, power, and resources. Social justice is about participation in one's community.

25. If you Google "Business Leaders for Excellence, Ethics and Justice" you will find information about one group that met for decades in Chicago.

26. See chapter 8, "Weighing Rights against Responsibilities."

This does not mean, however, that the government that governs least governs best. Rather [CST] defines good government intervention as that which truly "helps" other social groups contribute to the common good by directing, urging, restraining, and regulating economic activity "as occasion requires and necessity demands" [(*QA*, no. 80)]. This calls for cooperation and consensus building among the diverse agents in our economic life, including government. (*EJA*, no. 124)

All actors in the economy must determine how to contribute to it and work with others to achieve the ends of the economy. The government has a role, but it must strike a balance between helping and directing when necessary and allowing for the participation of all.

Application of Subsidiarity in a Contemporary Business Setting

How does this principle relate to business? While the practical application of subsidiarity and intermediary associations does not comprise part of the official CST tradition, there are many theoretical intersections. One aspect is the development or expansion of business. The relatively new arena of social entrepreneurship, for example, uses established business practices to alleviate some aspect of poverty, marginalization, or environmental degradation. Social entrepreneurs believe that business can bring a unique perspective and problem-solving skills as well as a drive for efficiency and return on investment that differs significantly from what charitable organizations can or have done.

For instance, in *Alleviating Poverty through Profitable Partnerships: Globalization, Markets and Economic Well-Being*, Patricia Werhane and her coauthors argue that traditional philanthropic initiatives and national and international aid programs have inherent limitations. In contrast, they believe that global corporations have developed initiatives that show great promise for profit-making *and* poverty alleviation: "By developing new markets for their products and creating new jobs and opportunities for economic development, profitable partnerships hold the potential to create value-added for shareholders as well as for these new stakeholders."[27] These authors contend that multinational corporations have global systems in place and the resources for expanding the markets for their products into areas where—if it views the poor as producers and consumers who can participate in the business expansion of the companies—the company can

---

27. Patricia H. Werhane, Scott P. Kelley, Laura P. Hartman, and Dennis J. Moburg, *Alleviating Poverty through Profitable Partnerships: Globalization, Markets and Economic Well-Being* (New York: Routledge, 2010), 1.

expand its markets and increase revenue while also providing jobs and products to people without the infrastructure, political stability, or resources to create such enterprises from scratch.

Many scholars and nongovernmental organizations (NGOs) have highlighted the economic situation of those at the base of the pyramid as those living in extreme poverty. Famine, war, drought, lack of access to resources, political corruption, and social instability comprise just some of the reasons the economic systems in which these people live do not facilitate their involvement in entrepreneurship. Werhane and her coauthors, in particular Scott P. Kelley,[28] claim that an information economy exists in places of extreme poverty. Businesses investigating new markets, however, tend to view the extremely poor as a sector of society entirely without economic resources. If these people live on one to two dollars a day, how could profit-seeking shareholders get a return on their investment in such communities?

Werhane challenges this developed-nation assumption about profits. It may seem counterintuitive to think of people in extreme poverty as consumers or as entrepreneurs who market and sell products to their neighbors. In reality, though, numerous projects in just such markets end up as successful profit-making ventures. Many assume that a top-down model works best at alleviating situations of extreme poverty, and the specific communities that have shaped most developed-nation thinkers differ significantly from the villages, cities, and cultures found in developing countries.

The Children's Development Bank in India provides an example:[29] Fully staffed by and exclusively serving street children, the volunteer-run bank is only open for one hour a day. No other banks would serve the children, so the National Foundation of India gave them seed money. The bank takes deposits for the street children and gives them 3.5 percent interest. It also provides loans to students who could advance their vocational skills with some additional financial resources. In 2008, the bank had a membership of 8,000.

Werhane and her coauthors explain:

> our minds actively interact with the data of our experiences, selectively filtering and framing that data. . . . Thus mental models function as selective filters for dealing with experience. All the mental models we employ are socially acquired and altered through socialization, educational upbringing, our religious commitments and other experiences.[30]

---

28. Scott Kelley, "Subsidiarity: Challenging the Top Down Bias," *Journal of Religion and Business Ethics* 1, no. 2, Article 2 (2010), *http://via.library.depaul.edu/jrbe/vol1/iss2/2*.

29. Ibid., 44–45.

30. Ibid., 46.

The mental models that are challenged then are those that would keep people from coming up with the idea of having a bank for homeless children that the children run themselves. Part of the problem is that people typically have preconceived notions of what others need or don't need or how to solve their problems. Having some experience of the local communities proves essential to seeing how business might serve the interests of the community and also of the business itself. The principle of subsidiarity challenges top-down models of aid and suggests that by understanding the circumstances in local communities, helping them set up intermediary associations, and giving them opportunities for commerce and other social goods, grassroots efforts can help communities elevate the economic and social situation of its members in ways that NGOs and international government aid have not.

Other elements of Werhane's work expand on the requirements of the principle of subsidiarity. The book discusses the "bird's eye view" versus the "worm's-eye view," noting:

> One of the greatest challenges to addressing poverty is getting beyond mental models that view the poor from a . . . self-referential point of view. Imagining what life must be like on less than US $2 per day or trying to identify what the commonalities might be among those at the BoP is far less informative than listening to those who do it every day.[31]

Highlighting another characteristic of subsidiarity, Werhane and her colleagues also caution against a one-size-fits-all mentality. Different communities even within the same urban area may have vastly different resources, needs, challenges, and local leaders. Developing intermediary associations and capitalizing on the different assets in the community can empower residents to utilize the resources available to them and make a difference in their own communities. Cookie-cutter resolutions diminish the community involvement and do not enhance the dignity and participation of the local community members.

These concepts can be applied to the communities within which we all live. Recently a group of MBA students wanted to help former felons find work in their local community. They found a local nonprofit organization that worked with people recently released from prison. The MBA students first got to know the people looking for work to get a sense of their job skills and where they might fit in the local job market. They then went into the community to investigate the employment options. Not one business would agree to even interview someone who had spent time in prison. After moving their search into the surrounding communities, the students found that only through their personal relationships could they secure interviews for the job seekers.

---

31. Ibid., 51.

The MBA students learned through their research and canvassing of the area that, despite their many unmet economic and employment needs, no opportunities existed for people seeking employment after time in prison. The students' belief that they could help individuals find employment in their surrounding community was not based on realities in the community itself.[32]

Werhane and her colleagues advocate for "deep dialogue" in order to tackle the complex needs of local communities:

> Deep dialogue with stakeholders emanates from an attitude of identification and sense of solidarity that only comes from prolonged contact with local stakeholders . . . companies choose strategies for engaging with these stakeholders that are not just respectful of stakeholder customs, but also that represent the perhaps unspoken wishes, habits and practices of these groups.[33]

They argue that deep dialogue moves beyond what the business community traditionally thinks of as "market research" and relates more to moral imagination. They have proposed moral imagination as a constitutive element in business, describing it as "the ability to escape from defective mental models that dominate a particular situation, to envision new possibilities that are not so contextually dependent, and to evaluate and act on those possibilities."[34]

Underlying beliefs about business and profit making, the culture of companies, and the price of "risk" when bucking conventional wisdom make it difficult to activate the moral imagination, engage in deep dialogue, and take a worm's-eye view in many business settings. These "risky" values though are all in line with the principle of subsidiarity and the elements of CST related to it. If entrepreneurs and corporations are willing to invest the time and resources needed to learn about the needs of BoP populations from their perspective and can discover what the higher-order organizations can do in partnership, it's a win-win-win situation. The entrepreneurs and corporations have a new market. The local populations can have employment opportunities that enhance their stewardship and human dignity and the common good. The worldwide community has more local communities able to contribute and participate. In addition to what it provides to all of these people, it also decreases the need for aid, the exploitation of marginalized workers and peoples, and the exploitation of local resources. The

---

32. When another group of MBA students several semesters later proposed a restaurant in the area, they found that one of the two prior independent restaurants had closed, decreasing the already small number of employers, gathering places, and everything else that small businesses provide in a community.

33. Ibid., 81.

34. Ibid., 75.

principle of subsidiarity and its related concepts call people to humanizing, creative, innovative relationships that serve humanity.

Conclusion

In the midst of an ever-increasing globalized business world, CST asserts that the principle of subsidiarity is an important concept for businesspeople to consider. In order for human dignity, stewardship, the common good, and the preferential option for the poor to all be addressed, the participation of those at the most local level must occur. Other higher-level organizations (government, NGOs, and private entitites) can be involved in addressing problems or expanding business and services, but they must work in a way that respects the dignity, community, and participation of the locals.

These concepts are particularly important when dealing with the issues experienced by those at the BoP. Using a "worm's-eye" view, challenging mental models that ignore the experience and input of those at the local level, and engaging in systems thinking are consistent with the principle of subsidiarity.

Case Study

Toyota Motor Corporation and Employee "Suggestion" System

The principle of subsidiarity can be applied to business settings for reasons that go beyond poverty alleviation. The practices of a division of Toyota Motor Corporation are a case in point.

In 2012, Toyota sold more cars than any other company in the world, with an estimated 9.71 million vehicle sales.[35] It has spent many years at the top of the sales list and although it has had some issues with recalls in the past several years and leadership stumbles, overall it is highly respected and regarded as an innovative company. One reason for this is the Toyota Production System (TPS), which differs significantly from the systems that have historically been used in US car production.

A joint collaboration in Fremont, California, between General Motors (GM) and Toyota that began in the early 1980s illustrates the differences in

(continued)

---

35. Hiroko Tabuchi, "Toyota Is Back on Top in Sales," *New York Times*, January 28, 2013, *http://www.nytimes.com/2013/01/29/business/global/toyota-returns-to-no-1-in-global-auto-sales.html?ref=toyotamotorcorporation.*

Case Study *(continued)*

the US and Toyota systems and how the principle of subsidiarity relates.[36] There had previously been a GM plant in Fremont, but it was the worst production facility in the US system due to the systems in place there, the relationship between management and workers, and the poor work ethic and drug and alcohol culture of workers. After it was shut down, it sat idle and no new industry moved into the facility. Toyota suggested this site as a place where GM and Toyota could collaborate. Toyota offered to teach GM all of its production facility secrets if GM taught Toyota how to work within the US market. Although Toyota had been exporting cars to the United States, it wanted to open production facilities here.

The first step of the working relationship involved former Fremont United Auto Workers workers going to Japan to for two-week training sessions. Then when enough employees were trained, the California location could open and begin production. When the US workers first arrived at the Toyota plant in Japan, they could not believe how different the production line was. In the TPS, managers and employees work together. Everything has a team-based approach. Each individual has a job to complete, but each is part of a group and a team with a leader. If someone makes a mistake or cannot keep up with production or there is some issue on the line, the worker will pull a cord that alerts others with a light and a happy little song that there is an issue. If the worker and others who come to help cannot resolve the issue, they pull the cord again and stop the entire production line. As soon as the issue is resolved, the line begins again.

After the issue is resolved, someone at the company would later find out how the issue could be dealt with in the future so there is no need to stop the line. If an employee offers a suggestion for a different type of tool or a different arrangement for storage and availability of tools or anything else that ultimately saves the company money due to a smoother production process, that employee will receive several hundred dollars in a bonus. This is part of what the Japanese call *kaizen*, or continuous improvement. Everyone is expected to make suggestions to improve the production process and maintain a focus on the quality, not the quantity, of the products.[37] This explains why the US workers saw mats for the workers to stand on, cushions for them to kneel on, and shelves that travel along with them while they're working to make reaching for tools easier and more efficient.

(continued)

---

36. Unless otherwise noted, the information related to the NUMMI collaboration comes from the March 26, 2010, *This American Life* episode that details the termination of a collaboration between GM and Toyota in California. It further explains the Toyota Production System. *http://www.thisamericanlife.org/radio-archives/episode/403/nummi.*

37. *http://www.thisamericanlife.org/radio-archives/episode/403/nummi.*

Case Study   *(continued)*

Although recent information is not available, the phenomenon of the Creative Idea Solution System was documented in the the 1980s and early 1990s. The system was begun in 1951 and between that time and 1988, about 20 million suggestions were turned in.[38] It got to the point at which two million suggestions were turned in each year at a rate of forty suggestions per year per worker. About 95 percent of employees participated in the program and their suggestions were adopted at an astonishing 96 percent rate.[39] This system made it very clear to employees that they were an integral part of the team, they were an expert in what they did on the line, their feedback was critical to the company's success, and quality of process and product were highly valued.

In contrast, the US workers explained that they were trained not to ever stop the production line for any reason whatsoever. Henry Ford's focus on the production line from the very beginning was quantity. If there was an error, the car should continue through the production process and could be fixed later. Everyone had to keep up with the timing of the system in order to maintain the quantity targets. The Fremont workers explained that if the bumper for a different type of car was on the line to be placed on the wrong car, they were to put on the wrong bumper and everything else around it and then it would be brought out to a lot to be fixed later. Workers could earn overtime fixing the cars, even though they might not have the expertise for the particular type of work they were doing. Not only did the workers have to continue the movement of the line if a car part was wrong or installed incorrectly but also if someone fell into a pit or had a heart attack, everything was to continue. No one ever asked the workers how consistent issues could be fixed. The workers and management did not get along at all and even though the system made costly errors and had sacrificed quality for quantity, the system remained in place.

The US workers interviewed discussed how embarrassed and ashamed they were at seeing the systems in Japan and knowing how flawed the US system was. A YouTube video created on the twentieth anniversary of the collaboration explains that the workers learned the five cornerstones of the Toyota system: mutual trust and respect, involvement, teamwork, safety, and equity.[40] UAW workers discussed how easy it was to say something like mutual trust and respect need to be part of the workplace, but that it

(continued)

---

38. Yuzo Yasuda, *40 Years, 20 Million Ideas: The Toyota Suggestion System* (Cambridge, MA: Productivity Press, 1991), 70–75.

39. Ibid.

40. *NUMMI 20th Anniversary* Video, *http://www.youtube.com/watch?v=ZkiwJSAXgLw.*

Case Study *(continued)*

is something that must be part of the culture and must be worked toward. Although the plant itself won many awards after it opened, the UAW leadership explained that the real winners were the workers on the line who were making good wages, making a top-quality car, and keeping a previously closed plant alive for the workers' jobs. Workers described their happiness, enjoyment of their jobs, pride at the products they produced, and the way they were able to support their families.[41] [42]

Questions

1. What elements of the principle of subsidiarity do you see or not see in the differences between the GM and Toyota systems?

2. In the context of this case, how is human dignity related to the principle of subsidiarity?

3. In the context of this case, how does the implementation of systems consistent with the principle of subsidiarity relate to productivity and profitability?

4. Are there other principles from CST that can be applied to this case?

Case Study

Homeboy Industries

Los Angeles, California, has long been known as the Gang Capital of the World. According to the Los Angeles Police Department, there are approximately 45,000 people in Los Angeles who are members of more than 450 gangs.[43] Gang activity has devastating consequences for the neighborhoods, businesses, schools, members, and nonmembers in the areas where they

(continued)

---

41. Ibid.

42. This case study only discusses the employee-suggestion system. There are other elements of TPS, including its team-based approach and multitiered leadership development that also relate to the principle of subsidiarity.

43. Cindy Y. Rodriguez and Jacqueline Hurtado, "Homeboy Industries' Business Model: A Way Out of Gang Life," CNN.com, Cable News Network, September 5, 2013, *http://www.cnn.com/2013/08/23/us/gang-rehabilitation-program/*.

Case Study
(continued)

flourish: the rates of robberies, rapes, homicides, unemployment, high school dropouts, and poverty are all very high. Children see little opportunity or options in the midst of a violent neighborhood and opt for gang life to offer themselves protection, income, and some semblance of community.

An area of Los Angeles called Boyle Heights had more gang members as a percentage of the population in the 1980s than anywhere else in the United States.[44] In the mid-1980s, Fr. Greg Boyle, S.J., asked to work in an impoverished area and was assigned by his Jesuit superior to work in that neighborhood at the Dolores Mission Church. The church was the poorest parish in the archdiocese of Los Angeles and was located in the midst of the largest public housing grouping in the western half of the United States.[45]

While pastor of the Dolores Mission, Fr. Greg and the leaders of the parish decided to open up the doors of the parish grounds to keep young people off the streets and learn what their needs were. Fr. Greg presided over many funerals of young people he knew, befriended many in prison where he regularly said Mass, and sat with the women of the parish who cried when their own or others' children were murdered or incarcerated. As he got to know the gang members and their families and neighbors, he realized that many obstacles faced those who wanted to leave gang life and start anew. Finding work was impossible in a neighborhood where few businesses existed and leaving the neighborhood did not seem to be an option. Banks would not lend to someone wanting to start a business in the area and people from outside the neighborhood were afraid to come anywhere near.

Antigang initiatives throughout Los Angeles focused on a heavy police presence, increased incarceration rates, "3 strikes and you're out," and other heavy-handed penalties. Fr. Greg came to understand that there were no alternatives for many of the children, other than gangs. Fr. Greg tried to figure out how to help with employment. One of the most basic issues faced by many of the gang members was that they were heavily tattooed, including on their face, neck, and entire forearms, and often had many gang symbols visible. Teens could not be in school with these tattoos, and employers would not offer a job to someone with them. To alleviate this issue, the Dolores Mission created a tattoo-removal clinic. Today they have thirty volunteer doctors who remove an average of 745 tattoos *every month* for free.[46]

(continued)

44. Homeboy Industries, *http://www.homeboyindustries.org/why-we-do-it/*.

45. Gregory Boyle, S.J., *Tattoos on the Heart: The Power of Boundless Compassion* (New York, NY: Free Press, 2010), Kindle Edition, p. 1 of introduction.

46. Homeboy Industries, *http://www.homeboyindustries.org/what-we-do/tattoo-removal*.

Case Study

The only businesses with job possibilities in the area were factories. The Dolores Mission decided to start a Jobs for a Future initiative. Hundreds of women passed out fliers to the foremen of factories located near the parish, trying to get interviews for people in the neighborhood.[47] When nothing materialized from those attempts, Dolores Mission developed jobs in the area and worked hard to fund the salaries itself. Although the parish was not in a financial situation to fully fund the businesses within its regular budget, surprise donations or other contributions would always materialize at the last second so the enterprise could stay afloat.[48] Fr. Greg found that a job opportunity was 80 percent of what the people in the neighborhood needed in order to make better decisions about their future.[49]

A wealthy Hollywood director called Fr. Greg to brainstorm many different ways that he could invest in initiatives to help the gang members get off the streets. Fr. Greg says that he had to "respectfully dismiss" all of the ideas that the director came up with. When the exasperated director finally asked Fr. Greg if there was anything that could be done, Fr. Greg asked him to buy an old, closed bakery, so they could start a business called The Homeboy Bakery.[50]

In spite of a fire that had originally burned the place down, bomb threats, death threats, and hate mail,[51] the bakery survives to this day and the overall Homeboy Industries now includes Homegirl Café and Catering, Homeboy Diner, Homeboy Farmers Markets, Homeboy Grocery, and Homeboy Silk Screening and Embroidery. These enterprises allow people to learn the basic skills of showing up on time (every time they're scheduled) putting up with a boss, and working alongside their former enemies. The Homeboy Industries budget for 2012 was approximately $14,700,000, with the social enterprises bringing in around $3,500,000. The goal is not to ultimately make money in these social enterprises. Fr. Greg says, "We don't hire homies to bake bread, we bake bread to hire homies."[52]

If the 80 percent need for employment skills is taken care of, Fr. Greg says that there is a 20 percent need for other types of services for those formerly in gangs. In addition to the tattoo removal, an employment services division acts as an intermediary between the clients looking for work and

(continued)

---

47. Boyle, *Tattoos on the Heart*, Location 152, Kindle Edition.

48. Ibid. Location 164, Kindle Edition.

49. Homeboy Industries, *http://www.homeboyindustries.org/why-we-do-it*.

50. Boyle, *Tattoos on the Heart*, Location 198, Kindle Edition.

51. Ibid, Location 259, Kindle Edition.

52. Homeboy Industries, *http://www.homeboyindustries.org/what-we-do/faq/*.

Case Study

(continued)

the potential employers.[53] The division has a mental health, substance abuse, and domestic violence prevention program[54], as well as a full-time lawyer who can help with the many of the issues that former gang members face.[55] The employment services division also offers extensive education classes, with more than 400 trainees and community clients, engaged in forty-five different classes each month, ranging from high school equivalency classes, to financial literacy courses and even "Baby and Me" classes.[56] People from the neighborhood utilize these services as do people released from the prison, the detention center, and the juvenile probation camps.

Homeboy Industries has been a resounding success. Fr. Greg Boyle is invited to speak all over the country about Homeboy Industries and often brings some of the homies with him. Other communities in the United States and around the world have asked how to build the Homeboy model of their own. Fr. Greg says that the goals of Homeboy Industries is not to "franchise" their model but for other communities to understand their own situation and the types of ownership required in their location: "We have a hyper-reverence for the dynamics of other communities rather than a need to import our model. We are not proposing a one-size-fits all model, but a way of proceeding. We help others understand elements of our own culturally-competent model so that they can develop and refine their own."[57]

Questions

1. What elements of the principle of subsidiarity do you see present in Fr. Greg's approach to gang issues in his parish neighborhood?
2. How is the principle of subsidiarity evident in the exchange with the Hollywood director who wants to help?
3. How is the principle of subsidiarity evident in Fr. Greg's approach to spreading the Homeboy Industries' model to other communities?
4. Fr. Greg claims that the primary, but not only, need of gang members was employment. How does this align with the principles of CST?

---

53. Homeboy Industries, *http://www.homeboyindustries.org/what-we-do/employment-services/*.

54. Homeboy Industries, *http://www.homeboyindustries.org/what-we-do/mental-health/*.

55. Homeboy Industries, *http://www.homeboyindustries.org/what-we-do/legal-services/*.

56. Homeboy Industries, *http://www.homeboyindustries.org/what-we-do/mental-health/*.

57. Homeboy Industries, *http://www.homeboyindustries.org/why-we-do-it/*.

For Further Reading

Clark, Meghan, "Subsidiarity Is a Two-Sided Coin," Catholic Moral Theology Blog, *http://catholicmoraltheology.com/subsidiarity-is-a-two-sided-coin/.*

Kelley, Scott (2010) "Subsidiarity: Challenging the Top Down Bias," *Journal of Religion and Business Ethics*: 1: 2, Article 2, *http://via.library.depaul.edu/jrbe/vol1/iss2/2.*

Kelly, John E., "Solidarity and Subsidiarity: 'Organizing Principles' for Corporate Moral Leadership in the New Global Economy," *Journal of Business Ethics*, 52: 283–295, 2004.

Chapter 7

The Challenge of Solidarity in a Competitive Business Environment

Thomas O'Brien

Introduction

Outside of select social justice circles, the word *solidarity* is used sparingly, to the extent that many might struggle to come up with an adequate definition on the spot. Those familiar with recent European history might associate the term with the *Solidarność* trade union formed by Gdansk, Poland, shipyard workers in 1980. In fact, this example provides a good place to begin the discussion, in light of a Polish pope's push for the widespread adoption of solidarity as a central theme of Catholic social teaching. Pope John Paul II had been a staunch supporter of Lech Walesa and the Polish Solidarity movement that eventually led to the downfall of the Polish communist state.[1] John Paul II promulgated the encyclical, *Sollicitudo rei socialis* (On Social Concern, 1987), and most scholars assume the pope had the situation in his own country in mind when he defined and expounded at length on the theme of solidarity.[2]

In common usage, the word *solidarity* implies a sense of unity among a select group of people and often describes a kind of social harmony existing between individuals and groups that have formed an unusual or unexpected bond. Discussions about solidarity often use the kind of language usually reserved to

---

1. For more information about this moment in Polish history, see Timothy Garton Ash, *The Polish Revolution: Solidarity* (New Haven, CT: Yale University Press, 2002).

2. Kenneth Himes, Charles Curran, David Hollenbach, and Thomas Shannon, eds., *Modern Catholic Social Teaching: Commentaries and Interpretations* (Washington, DC: Georgetown University Press, 2005), 416–17.

describe the concord and mutual support found among small, close-knit groups, such as extended families. However, the term itself normally applies to cases in which blood relationships do not necessarily or obviously exist. In this way, the term *solidarity* connotes a form of social adoption between individuals and groups, who do not, as a matter of course, share any kinship association. For instance, family members sacrificing themselves for or passionately defending one another is certainly a sign of solidarity, but it is not normally singled out as such because this kind of behavior is generally expected from people sharing an intimate familial bond. However, when 10 million people, representing virtually all classes and ethnicities in a society, come together to form a peaceful, united opposition movement, as the Poles did in the 1980s, then this massive, cohesive, and cooperative social phenomenon warrants being labeled a special kind of *solidarity*.[3]

This relatively new idea closely relates to other themes in Catholic social thought and has been integrated into the constellation of principles that constitute what is broadly referred to as Catholic social teaching. It tightly connects to the concepts of the common good[4] and the option for the poor.[5] Like the common good, solidarity prioritizes the good of others over self-centered goods. In its call for universal solidarity among all peoples, the Church shows its concern for achieving a greater good on a global scale in ways that closely mirror the goals of the common good. The phrase "we are all really responsible to all" from *Sollicitudo rei socialis* could equally be ascribed to both principles (no. 38).

In a similar way, the concept of solidarity overlaps with and reproduces aspects of the preferential option for the poor. This rings particularly true when solidarity is encouraged among poor and marginalized groups. For these reasons, the preferential option for the poor and solidarity are often accused of being biased and exclusionary,[6] when in reality the intention behind them is precisely the inclusion of those people who have hitherto been excluded from full social participation. Both the preferential option for the poor and solidarity figure prominently in various campaigns for social justice as well as in the conversations many Catholics are having about the need to listen to voices that have not been heard.

Recent work in Catholic theology, for instance, has explored American immigration policy and immigrant rights, in part due to the significant increase in migration across the southern border of the United States over the last few decades. Catholic theologians have generally criticized the deterrence policies of

---

3. Peter Ackerman and Jack Duvall, *A Force More Powerful: A Century of Non-Violent Conflict* (New York, NY: Palgrave, 2000), 152.

4. Himes, et al., 429–30.

5. Ibid., 432.

6. Catherine Cowley, "Philia and Social Ethics," *Forum Philsophicum* 14 (2009): 30.

the American government and its use of police and military power to intimidate potential Latin American immigrants and to deport those who have been arrested and lack documentation. Theologian Patricia A. Lamoureux calls on Catholics to form bonds of solidarity with immigrants by avoiding discrimination and welcoming them into full participation in the American economy.[7] Other theologians, such as Kristin Heyer, echo this sentiment, blaming free-trade agreements for destroying the livelihoods of small farmers in Latin America as well as the consumerist lifestyles of North Americans that creates the demand for the cheap labor that underemployed people from Latin America often provide.[8] Heyer concludes that, "in the light of the biblical call to live 'like foreigners, uprooted in this world, as a sign of the new creation that makes itself present,' our solidarity with contemporary sojourners must become a genuine reality."[9]

While the issue of immigration clearly calls for the development of new social bonds between strangers, other social justice causes have also drawn on the principle of solidarity as both a norm and a method. For instance, social justice advocates have spent a great deal of time and effort getting to know sex workers around the world to better understand how they live and work and how they characterize their role in society.[10] In addition to being exploited and denigrated, this group has also traditionally been ignored or silenced by Western culture.

The reconciliation processes in war-torn areas of the world, which foster healing and peace in the wake of civil conflicts, offer another example of how solidarity functions as both a norm and a practice. In places such as South Africa, Rwanda, Bosnia, and Chile, truth-and-reconciliation commissions invited both perpetrators and victims to give public statements at public hearings about their experiences of the conflict. The point of these hearings was not to prosecute or punish criminals but to reestablish bonds of solidarity sundered by the violence.[11]

History and Development of the Idea of Solidarity

Like most other concepts of social philosophy in Western culture, solidarity has its roots in ancient Greek philosophy. Aristotle first used this notion to describe

---

7. Patricia A. Lamoureux, "Immigration Reconsidered in the Context of an Ethic of Solidarity," in *Made in God's Image: The Catholic Vision of Human Dignity*, eds. Regis Duffy and Angelus Gambatese (New York, NY: Paulist Press, 1999), 127.

8. Kristin E. Heyer, "Strangers in Our Midst: Day Laborers and Just Immigration Reform," *Political Theology* 9.4 (2008): 426, 442, 443, 445, 447.

9. Ibid., 451.

10. Laura Maria Augustin, *Sex at the Margins: Migration, Labor Markets and the Rescue Industry* (New York, NY: Zed Books, 2007), 175.

11. Lisa Cahill, "Goods for Whom? Defining Goods and Expanding Solidarity in Catholic Approaches to Violence," *Journal of Religious Ethics* 25, no. 3 (1998): 209, 212.

the virtues underlying relations of reciprocity and good will necessary to the smooth functioning of society. According to Aristotle, citizens had to view one another as political equals so that democratic institutions did not deteriorate into chaos and mutually exclusive camps.[12] Solidarity served as the glue that held individuals and groups together in a unified whole. The Romans assimilated this concept of solidarity and codified it into Roman law as the *obligation in solidum*, which defined a joint liability for a debt.[13] In the hands of the Romans, solidarity began to connote advocacy and taking up the burden of others.

In more modern times, revolutionaries designated solidarity as one of the three key virtues of the liberated French republic, as can be seen in the tripartite slogan of the French Revolution, *"liberté, egalité, fraternité"* (liberty, equality, fraternity). Immanuel Kant's categorical imperative, especially his concept of the Kingdom of Ends,[14] reflected this eighteenth-century ideal of solidarity as "fraternity." From the perspective of the Kingdom of Ends, a person was obligated to treat other persons as ends unto themselves and never merely as a means to one's own ends. Later, in the nineteenth century, Karl Marx and other more radical thinkers took up the idea of *fraternité*, or solidarity, in order to describe the principle that a revolutionary vanguard should share in the experience of oppression with the working class and other marginal groups in society.[15] Only in this intimate sharing of fates would the revolutionaries fully appreciate the suffering they were working to overcome.

Today solidarity is a rich concept that can refer to both a normative orientation as well as a practice of engagement. Therefore, in common usage, solidarity is held as a principle or a virtue to be honored, while at the same time, it describes the types of actions a person or a group should pursue. "It refers to the citizenly capacity to act in ways characterized by public spiritedness or reciprocity," writes Juliet Hooker, in her book *Race and the Politics of Solidarity.* "The concept of political solidarity as it is generally understood thus denotes the ability of individuals to engage in relations of trust and obligation with fellow members of a political community whom they may see as inherently 'other' in some fundamental way."[16] Solidarity refers to relations of trust and obligation developed between individuals and groups who are not normally understood as having close personal connections.[17]

---

12. Juliet Hooker, *Race and the Politics of Solidarity* (New York, NY: Oxford University Press, 2009), 23.

13. Max Pensky, *The Ends of Solidarity: Discourse Theory in Ethics and Politics* (Albany, NY: State University of New York Press, 2009), 6.

14. Ibid., 2.

15. Ibid., 7.

16. Hooker, *Race and the Politics of Solidarity*, 1.

17. Ibid., 22–23.

Many contemporary philosophers, such as Thomas E. Reynolds, claim, "solidarity is a dialectical achievement."[18] By this he means that solidarity, as both a concept and a practice, is shot through with diverse interpretations and practical inconsistencies, which can make it both a fascinating and an ambiguous subject. Paul DeBeer and Ferry Koster, in their book *Sticking Together or Falling Apart?* have identified many of these dialectical elements. They define *solidarity* as "a situation in which the well-being of one person or groups is positively related to that of others."[19] They explain how solidarity can refer to a relationship of dependence, in which some rely on others for things they cannot provide for themselves or to a cooperative relationship in which people achieve something together that they could not have achieved alone.[20] Solidarity can be one-sided or two. It can refer to acts of assisting others without expecting anything in return or to assistance that is mutual and that includes expectations of reciprocity.[21] Additionally, solidarity can be voluntary or compulsory. It can refer to an attitude or an act, be it formal and organized or informal and spontaneous. The scope of solidarity can be local, national, or global; and it can take the form of time, money, or in-kind donation.[22] *Solidarity* can refer to a feeling of affection, responsibility, and duty, or it can be more calculating in the sense of an enlightened egoism that understands the achievement of its own good as dependent on achieving the good of others.[23] Finally, it can refer to a normative ethical principle as well as describe the actions of individuals or groups.[24]

Social theorists see two main challenges to closer social bonding in modern culture: individualization and globalization. For some, individualization is an attitude or concept claiming the superiority or primacy of the individual over the group and demonstrating a preference for freedom of choice in public policy. However, sociologists have an entirely different definition, which treats individualization as a fact imposed by modern institutions. They define it as a context in which traditional structures such as the family and the church, which treat people as part of a group, are progressively replaced by state and corporate institutions, which treat them as individuals.[25]

---

18. Thomas E. Reynolds, *The Broken Whole: Philosophical Steps toward a Theology of Global Solidarity* (Albany, NY: State University of New York Press, 2006), 103.

19. Paul DeBeer and Ferry Koster, *Sticking Together or Falling Apart? Solidarity in an Era of Individualization and Globalization* (Amsterdam, Netherlands: University of Amsterdam Press, 2009), 12.

20. Ibid.

21. Ibid., 19–20.

22. Ibid., 21–22. See also Hooker, *Race and the Politics of Solidarity*, 30.

23. Ibid., 23–24. See also Hooker, *Race and the Politics of Solidarity*, 39.

24. Pensky, *The Ends of Solidarity*, 3–4.

25. DeBeer and Koster, *Sticking Together or Falling Apart?* 55.

Individualization also entails what DeBeer and Koster refer to as "detraditionalization," or the emancipation from social groups and institutions that once provided structure and content for one's attitudes and behaviors.[26] It also involves "heterogenization," a situation in which "people no longer appeal to traditional institutions for guidelines for their conduct and increasingly make their own choices"[27] in relation to one another. Hence, greater variety and plurality develop in the culture, further accentuating individualization—or so the theory goes. The only problem with the theories of increasing individualization eroding solidarity in modern societies is that, according to DeBeer and Koster, such a trend toward greater individualization could not be empirically established when they reviewed the data taken since the 1970s.

Sociologists are not the only ones focusing on the problems resulting from a culture that seems to isolate individuals from their social moorings. Catholic authors also raise concerns about individualization eroding a sense of community and shared destiny. However, rather than devaluing the individual or preaching collectivist solutions, Catholic thinkers have responded by taking a balanced approach that affirms both human dignity and solidarity.[28] One should balance the other, for "when the personal concentrates on itself, it slides toward individualism, and when the structural (social) concentrates on itself, it tends toward oppressive collectivism."[29] Spiritual literature expresses this balanced approach in terms of the creative tension between solitude and solidarity, which give birth to each other and remain incomplete without the other.[30] Catholic theology resists the temptation to conceptualize the human person in exclusively atomistic, individual terms or as merely a cog in the greater collective, and it condemns either extreme as "sinful."

The fear that globalization erodes a sense of solidarity in community suffers the same fate as fears about individualization. Using a simple definition of globalization as "increasing cross-border interactions,"[31] DeBeer and Koster reviewed the empirical sociological literature to find correlations between

---

26. Ibid.

27. Ibid., 56.

28. Pope Pius XI expresses this Catholic bias toward balancing the individual and social natures of humanity in his encyclical *Quadragesimo anno* (The Reconstruction of Social Order, 1931): "Accordingly, twin rocks of shipwreck must be carefully avoided. For, as one is wrecked upon, or comes close to, what is known as 'individualism' by denying or minimizing the social and public character of the right of property, so by rejecting or minimizing the private and individual character of this same right, one inevitably runs into 'collectivism' or at least closely approaches its tenets" (no. 46).

29. Uzochukwu Jude Njoku, "Re-Thinking Solidarity as a Principle of Catholic Social Teaching: Going Beyond Gaudium et Spes and the Social Encyclicals of John Paul II," Political Theology 9, no. 4 (2008), 540.

30. Gus Gordon, *Solitude and Compassion: The Path to the Heart of the Gospel* (Maryknoll, NY: Orbis Books, 2009), 61.

31. DeBeer and Koster, *Sticking Together or Falling Apart?* 105.

globalization and the erosion of the collective willingness to enact government policies for the welfare of fellow citizens. Contrary to the common presumption that globalization leads to a progressive breakdown of socialization and solidarity, the authors conclude that "most of the empirical studies report a positive relationship between economic openness and the welfare state, and quite a few other studies indicate no relationship."[32] They also conclude that social cohesion has not disappeared because of increasing globalization. In fact, based on the evidence they gathered, one could argue that globalization "increases the need for community relations."[33]

Many Catholic authors have something to add to the debate about the potential effects of globalization on solidarity. Lisa Cahill affirms that "it is the issue of solidarity, not the issue of knowing the goods for humans, that is the most important and most difficult problem in social ethics, in global ethics, and, likewise, in Christian ethics."[34] In spite of the empirical studies cited that might contradict this fear, many Catholic authors continue to express the concern that globalization dilutes the collective sense of responsibility.[35] They are concerned that globalization blurs the lines of demarcation and frees people from the connection to local spaces that ground the idea of community.[36] A number of Catholic authors fear that globalization replaces religious traditions "with doctrines of consumerism and the canons of technological positivism."[37] This supposed disintegration of overall solidarity has led some to identify a multiplicity of different solidarities "that jostle for primacy within [a] cultural-political landscape, of shifting, contingent, and multiply-determined solidarities engendered by the dynamics of complex societies."[38] These solidarities can compete with one another and undermine efforts to achieve justice and equality.[39]

In spite of these threats, many Catholic authors also see new opportunities arising in the increasingly global moral landscape.[40] Some point to a revival of religion as the basis of identity formation in the wake of blurred national and territorial boundaries. In this scenario, religion becomes an alternative to

---

32. Ibid., 153.

33. Ibid., 189.

34. Cahill, "Goods for Whom?" 198.

35. Cowley, "Philia and Social Ethics," 32.

36. James Fredericks, "Dialogue and Solidarity in a Time of Globalization," *Buddhist-Christian Studies* 27 (2007): 54–55.

37. Daniel Groody, "Globalizing Solidarity: Christian Anthropology and the Challenge of Human Liberation," *Theological Studies* 69 (2008): 252.

38. Pensky, *The Ends of Solidarity*, 2.

39. Paul Routledge and Andrew Cumbers, *Global Justice Networks: Geographies of Transnational Solidarity* (New York, NY: Manchester University Press, 2009), 207. See also Nathalie Karagiannis, *European Solidarity* (Liverpool, UK: Liverpool University Press, 2007), 2.

40. Groody, "Globalizing Solidarity," 254.

other national, political, and economic identities.[41] While this reintegration of identity based on religion carries many dangers—not the least being the potential for radicalization and its occasionally violent manifestations—some see in it the promise of a transcultural ethic capable of addressing the needs of an interdependent world.[42] Theologians such as Daniel Groody claim that such a transcultural ethic has the potential to challenge the erroneous anthropological assumptions of the reigning capitalist culture, which misunderstands humans as primarily defined by their economic endowments and their integration into the system of production and consumption.[43] The new ethic would reconfigure human priorities by placing relationship to God and other humans ahead of economic characteristics and by defining inner endowments as having primacy over material and financial ones.

Theological Conceptions of Solidarity

One of the first steps toward rearranging the ethical landscape, according to Catholic theologian Christopher Vogt, consists of rediscovering the paradigm of covenant as an organizing principle for human community. The current organizing paradigm is the contract, which views humans as isolatable individuals who have no prior relationship or obligations toward one another. Contract theory considers people as solitary vessels, whose interests have no necessary connection and occasionally compete with each other. This explains the need for contracts that regulate and adjudicate these various competing interests. The idea of covenant, as it exists in a number of different religious traditions, counters the individualistic claims of contract theory and contends that people are formed in community, and human nature is, therefore, essentially social.[44] The social does not obliterate the individual. It does, however, by necessity, place individuals within a context and never allows those individuals to divorce themselves entirely from the constellation of relationships that have formed them.

Because humans are essentially social, according to traditional Catholic theology, personal and moral character traits are formed in community and developed in a broader social context. Therefore, the virtues are formed in solidarity with others, and solidarity—the capacity to feel compassion for others and act upon that compassion in community—becomes a virtue in and of itself.[45] In a global context in which solidarity is understood as a virtue but in which

---

41. Fredericks, "Dialogue and Solidarity in a Time of Globalization," 57.

42. Cahill, "Goods for Whom?" 193.

43. Groody, "Globalizing Solidarity," 266.

44. Christopher P. Vogt, "Fostering a Catholic Commitment to the Common Good: An Approach Rooted in Virtue Ethics," *Theological Studies* 68 (2007): 396–98.

45. Ibid., 398–400.

progressively larger numbers of people from distinct cultures find it increasingly difficult to talk meaningfully to one another, dialogue is also recognized as a type of ethic unto itself. As James Fredericks puts it, "interreligious dialogue, now and in the foreseeable future, needs to be recognized as a civic virtue."[46] In the face of greater religious and cultural diversity, an increasingly interdependent world must begin to recognize the work of dialogue as an essential part of the moral landscape.[47] Fredericks notes, "Interreligious dialogue should be seen as a concrete way to put into practice the virtue of solidarity."[48]

According to many Catholic theologians, the close bonds formed in a community of dialogue are akin to the bonds of love.[49] In solidarity, people come to intimately *know* one other and their communities in the same way family members can claim to know one another. Like any real family, the types of families created in solidarity experience both love and tension, both joy and frustration, but rarely apathy or indifference.[50] Indifference, not hate, is the opposite of genuine solidarity.[51] Learning about the actual, specific, and concrete injustices suffered by people around the world fosters love and develops a shared experience of oppression[52] along with a concern for those least well-off. Those who enter into relationships of solidarity "share 'a common fight' and 'a common sense of suffering,' in the face of which religious distinctions tend to 'melt away.'"[53] In this way, solidarity serves as a necessary precondition for justice,[54] which, in turn, requires greater and greater degrees of inclusion from all sectors of a society. "Solidarity demands the universal and symmetrical inclusion of persons into an ever-expanding community of reciprocal recognition."[55]

The unity, or *solidus*,[56] that individuals should feel toward one another and the whole of society rests on a foundation of compassion, which, according to

---

46. Fredericks, "Dialogue and Solidarity in a Time of Globalization," 59.

47. Ibid., 60–62. See also Heyer, "Strangers in Our Midst," 447.

48. Ibid., 63.

49. Vogt, "Fostering a Catholic Commitment to the Common Good," 404.

50. Njoku, "Re-Thinking Solidarity as a Principle of Catholic Social Teaching," 535–36.

51. Cowley, "Philia and Social Ethics," 32.

52. Ann E. Patrick, "Conscience and Solidarity with Victims," in *Conscience: Readings in Moral Theology*, ed. Charles E. Curran, no. 14 (New York, NY: Paulist Press, 2004), 190. See also Pensky, *The Ends of Solidarity*, 10; Hooker, *Race and the Politics of Solidarity*, 30.

53. Paul D. Numrich, *The Faith Next Door* (New York, NY: Oxford University Press, 2009), 118.

54. Clare Weber, *Visions of Solidarity: U.S. Peace Activists in Nicaragua from War to Women's Activism and Globalization* (New York, NY: Lexington Books, 2006), 138–139.

55. Pensky, *The Ends of Solidarity*, 182.

56. Uzochukwu Jude Njoku, "Re-Thinking Solidarity as a Principle of Catholic Social Teaching," 526.

Vogt, "is a prerequisite for the ability to develop solidarity."[57] The empathetic feelings associated with compassion provide "the motivation for a person to act to dismantle injustice and relieve the suffering of other people."[58] Then the privileged and the oppressed can initiate a dialogue in which they can develop feelings of mutuality and establish genuine solidarity.[59] Once solidarity takes hold, it has the power to shatter the old ethic based in more selfish and individualistic ideas of the human person,[60] with new notions of the common good and a proactive universal respect for human dignity[61] taking their place.[62]

Catholic theologians stress that authentic solidarity is not a kind of noblesse oblige—an attitude of charitable condescension by those with greater privilege toward those who are less well off. According to Catholic pedagogue Joseph Gerics, noblesse oblige has the potential to demean those it intends to serve, tends to inculcate an overly personalistic and individualistic understanding of justice, and legitimates the status quo rather than challenging a social order that fosters injustice.[63] Instead, solidarity should instruct Catholics about the social nature of the human person, "the equality of all in dignity and rights, and the common path of individuals and peoples toward an ever more committed unity."[64] It underscores intersubjectivity by emphasizing the ways people are bound together in definite relationships that fulfill real and perceived needs.[65] From this perspective, human communities are not merely a collection of individuals thrown together haphazardly but rather people who belong together and whose togetherness has a purpose.

Solidarity in Catholic Social Teaching

Like other Christians, Catholics trace their most basic principles back to scriptural witness, and more particularly, to the example of Christ himself: "As the New Testament portrays it, discipleship entails the concrete and practical reconfiguration of social relations under images such as love of neighbor, love

---

57. Vogt, "Fostering a Catholic Commitment to the Common Good," 405.

58. Ibid., 408.

59. Ibid., 409.

60. Ibid., 410.

61. For a more in-depth reflection on the relationship between solidarity and the sense of human dignity, see Lamoureux, "Immigration Reconsidered in the Context of an Ethic of Solidarity," 110.

62. David Hollenbach, *The Common Good and Christian Ethics* (New York, NY: Cambridge University Press, 2002), 189.

63. Joseph Gerics, "From Orthodoxy to Orthopraxis: Community Service as *Noblesse Oblige* and as Solidarity with the Poor," *Religious Education* 86.2 (1991): 58–60.

64. *Compendium of the Social Doctrine of the Church* (Vatican City: Pontifical Council for Justice and Peace, 2004), 84.

65. Pensky, *The Ends of Solidarity*, 9.

of enemy, forgiveness, mercy, cross, Resurrection, body of Christ, and brothers and sisters in Christ."[66] In short, discipleship implies solidarity. William O'Neill, among others, looks to the parable of the Good Samaritan (Luke 10:25–37) as a paradigm of good discipleship and solidarity.[67] In this story, a person is robbed, beaten, and left to die at the side of the road. A number of travelers pass by without assisting the man because they are either too busy or too afraid. After a while, a Samaritan—a member of a sect that was hated and considered blasphemous by the Israelites—comes along and takes pity on the man, mends his wounds, places him on his donkey, and takes him to the nearest inn where he puts him up for the night. This parable highlights what O'Neill refers to as "anamnestic solidarity," a kind of Christ-like solidarity that overlooks differences and injuries of the past in order to seek new relationships of compassion, hospitality, and reciprocity.[68]

The Catholic tradition also looks to its long theological history, and especially to the philosophy of Thomas Aquinas, in order to make sense of the virtue of solidarity. Aquinas reaffirms that humans are, by nature, social creatures:[69] "Solidarism in its Thomistic sense is a term which connotes the golden mean between individualism and collectivism; it is the middle position between two extremes of absolute centralization and absolute decentralization."[70] From this starting point, Aquinas anchors his ideas about the goodness and necessity of solidarity. Although Aquinas uses the term *solidarity* sparingly, his philosophy develops the related term *philia,* or friendship, to a much greater extent.[71] "St. Thomas tells us that friendship is a form of love, which involves a certain capacity for being reciprocated."[72] In this conception of friendship, reciprocity becomes the key to overcoming self-centeredness and opens the human person to a world of relationships that build positively upon one another, ultimately creating a web of mutually reinforcing, supportive social connections known collectively in Catholic social theory as the common good.[73] For this reason the Catholic Church "seeks persistently for more than justice. She warns men [*sic*] that it is by keeping a more perfect rule that class becomes joined to class in

---

66. Cahill, "Goods for Whom?" 184.

67. William O'Neill, "Christian Hospitality and Solidarity with the Stranger," in *And You Welcomed Me: Migration and Catholic Social Teaching,* eds. Donald Kerwin and Jill Marie Gerschultz (New York, NY: Lexington Books, 2009), 150.

68. Ibid., 151.

69. Lamoureux, "Immigration Reconsidered in the Context of an Ethic of Solidarity," 111.

70. Sister Mary Joan of Arc Wolfe, *The Problem of Solidarism in St. Thomas* (Washington, DC: The Catholic University of America, 1938), 15.

71. Cowley, "Philia and Social Ethics," 18.

72. Kevin Doran, *Solidarity: A Synthesis of Personalism and Communalism in the Thought of Karol Wojtyla* (New York, NY: P. Lang, 1996), 94.

73. Cowley, "Philia and Social Ethics," 33.

the closest neighborliness and friendship."[74] Solidarity is a kind of friendship broadly cast and applied to individuals one does not necessarily know personally but to whom one is connected in this web of relationality. True solidarity, like true friendship, is not a fair-weather phenomenon but is tested in the fires of suffering and oppression.[75] That explains why so many authors turn to illustrations of suffering in order to demonstrate authentic solidarity.

In addition to *friendship*, the Catholic Church uses the term *social charity* to express the essence of solidarity. Pius XI coined the phrase in his encyclical *Quadragesimo anno* (The Reconstruction of Social Order, 1931), in which he fuses it to the idea of social justice (no. 88). In this context, social charity is the sole and affective inspiration for social justice. It becomes the motivating force that propels individuals to choose the difficult path of social justice, rather than avoiding suffering and tolerating injustice. In this way, these two ideas are interdependent and cannot be properly understood in isolation from one another.[76] In his encyclical, *Populorum progressio* (The Development of Peoples, 1967), Pope Paul VI reframes this idea of social charity as "universal charity" (no. 44).

It is only with the papacy of John XXIII that the term *solidarity* appears in Catholic social theory in more than just passing references.[77] During the 1960s, the Catholic Church began to embrace modern and liberal philosophies that it had, until that time, either condemned outright or kept at arm's length. The ancient conception of an organic society organized around the metaphor of the human body[78] gave way to more modern contractual and voluntaristic notions of social arrangement. John XXIII uses the word *solidarity* on seven separate occasions in his encyclical *Mater et magistra* (Christianity and Social Progress, 1961); and in his encyclical *Pacem in terris* (Peace on Earth, 1963), he expands the notion of the common good to the global community. There, he affirms that,

> justice cannot be accomplished by elites working in abstraction from the complex factors leading to social conflict. Rather moral discernment in "our age" must start from the facts that the "working classes" are insisting on their own rights, that women "will not tolerate" affronts to "their human dignity," and that the colonial era is over.[79]

---

74. Leo XIII, *Rerum novarum* (1891), 18, *http://www.vatican.va/holy_father/leo_xiii/encyclicals/documents/hf_l-xiii_enc_15051891_rerum-novarum_en.html*.

75. Ibid., no. 34.

76. Doran, *Solidarity*, 99.

77. Pius XII uses the term more frequently than his predecessors, but he never produces an encyclical in the social tradition.

78. Lamoureux, "Immigration Reconsidered in the Context of an Ethic of Solidarity," 112. "In sum, the preconciliar writings reveal an understanding of solidarity that is organic and conflict-free. It presumes a mutually interdependent order of cooperation and harmony of interests between all groups and classes in society, motivated by charity and justice" 115.

79. Cahill, "Goods for Whom?" 198.

The Vatican II document *Gaudium et spes* (Pastoral Constitution on the Church in the Modern World, 1965) mentions *solidarity* nine times and develops the concept to a limited degree.[80] This document contributes to the understanding of solidarity as the principle of unity that should constantly increase until it ultimately leads humans to that perfect union with God in the act of salvation (*GS*, no. 32). One year after the close of Vatican II, Pope Paul VI issued the encyclical, *Populorum progressio* (The Development of Peoples), which further develops solidarity as an international and global ethic. It considers solidarity more than just a privilege that bestows benefits on everyone engaged but an obligation of mutual aid that falls disproportionately on the shoulders of wealthier nations (nos. 17, 44). The encyclical calls for dismantling trade relations tainted by the sins of colonialism and racism and establishing new agreements based on trust and collaboration (nos. 52, 62).

These scattered references to solidarity offer brief glimpses of its potential as a theme of Catholic social thought, but the concept does not receive a full theological treatment in official Catholic documents until the papacy of John Paul II. In 1987, John Paul II promulgated the document *Sollicitudo rei socialis* (On Social Concern) on the anniversary of Paul VI's *Populorum progressio,* and while the development of solidarity certainly was in harmony with the spirit of his predecessor, clearly this Polish pope had other, more concrete, inspirations for stressing this particular term in his encyclical. The decade of the 1980s had seen the unprecedented success of the Solidarity labor union opposing the policies of the communist government in Poland. Eventually, this opposition would lead to the downfall of the government, which would, in turn, precipitate events that led to similar changes in the rest of the eastern bloc and the Soviet Union. However, in 1987, Solidarity was still fighting the good fight, and the Communists still had their hands on the rudder of the Polish ship of state. Much of what the pope says in this encyclical can be understood as an address in support of his fellow Polish citizens who are united in solidarity (both figuratively and literally) against the injustice of communist rule.

In *Sollicitudo rei socialis,* John Paul II begins his exegesis of solidarity in no. 38, in which he engages in a theological interpretation of current world events. Evidence for solidarity can be seen around the world in the growing recognition of interdependence among all peoples.[81] The quality of this interdependence is a moral concern because, while it could serve human flourishing, it might just as easily lead to exploitation and misery.[82] *Sollicitudo rei socialis* treats solidarity

---

80. For a more detailed analysis of solidarity in *Gaudium et spes*, see Njoku, "Re-Thinking Solidarity as a Principle of Catholic Social Teaching," 529–531.

81. See also the US Catholic Bishops, *Economic Justice for All,* no. 28, *http://www.osjspm.org/economic_justice_for_all.aspx*; and Vatican II, *Gaudium et spes,* no. 4.

82. See also Paul VI, *Populorum progressio,* no 17; John XXIII, *Mater et Magistra,* no. 146.

as a virtue, which is "not a feeling of vague concern or shallow distress at the misfortunes of so many people both near and far" (no. 38). Rather, it is a "firm and persevering determination to commit oneself to the common good; that is to say to the good of all and each individual because we are really responsible for all" (no. 38). Therefore, the virtue of solidarity strives to achieve full authentic development of both the person and society. The "desire for profit" and a "thirst for power," however, can undermine solidarity by shifting the focus away from the value of humans and their flourishing.[83]

Sollicitudo rei socialis notes that the commitment to the good of others, the hallmark of authentic solidarity, is the antidote against the infection of the structural sins caused by unbridled desires for wealth and power (no. 38).[84] Solidarity empowers one to sacrifice for the sake of others, rather than exploit them for personal advantage (*SRS*, no 38). It is put into practice when a person recognizes the human dignity of another. The pope explains that each class of society has a responsibility to contribute to the good of everyone else: the wealthy and powerful have a special responsibility to the poor; the poor themselves should remain actively engaged in order to contribute to the common good and avoid passivity; and the intermediate classes need to avoid focusing social resources on their own particular interests and mistaking their own concerns for the concerns of the common good (*SRS*, no. 39).[85]

Signs of solidarity in contemporary society can be witnessed in especially powerful ways among the poor and "their efforts to support one another and their public demonstrations on the social scene which, without recourse to violence, present their own needs and rights in the face of the inefficiency or corruption of the public authorities" (*SRS*, no. 39). According to the pope, the church has a special responsibility to stand beside the poor and support their efforts to discern the right path forward and work for justice.[86] Solidarity operates at the personal, group, social, and even international levels, in which it fosters cooperation and a global common good.[87] The virtue of solidarity is marked by a capacity to recognize other people, groups, and nations as "neighbors" who deserve a share in "the banquet of life" on a par with one's own (*SRS*, no. 39). Solidarity offers the path to true peace and genuine development; it undermines

---

83. These sentiments echo those expressed by the US bishops, who claimed that extreme inequalities were a threat to solidarity because they fostered "deep social divisions and conflict" (*Economic Justice for All*, no. 74; see also no. 185).

84. The US Bishops believe that sin shatters the solidarity of human community (*EJA*, no. 33).

85. See also Paul VI, *Populorum progressio*, no. 84; John XXIII, *Mater et magistra*, no. 155; US Catholic Bishops, *Economic Justice for All*, no. 102.

86. See also US Catholic Bishops, *Economic Justice for All*, no. 88.

87. See also Paul VI, *Populorum progressio*, nos. 44, 48; John XXIII, *Pacem in terris*, no. 98, Vatican II, *Gaudium et spes*, nos. 57, 85, 90.

the logic of economic, military, and political imperialism and transforms "mutual distrust into collaboration" (*SRS*, no. 39).

As a virtue, solidarity is closely related to love, "the distinguishing mark of Christ's disciples" (*SRS*, no. 40).[88] A commitment to the virtue means going beyond oneself and offering oneself as a gift to others—especially those who are suffering and marginalized.[89] The pope believes that Christians have the advantage of a tradition that regularly reminds them of their creaturely kinship with every other person and all of creation (*SRS*, no. 39). The Christian sees other people as living representations of the triune God (*SRS*, no. 40). As an icon of God, "one's neighbor must therefore be loved, even if an enemy, with the same love with which the Lord loves him or her; and for that person's sake one must be ready for sacrifice, even the ultimate one to lay down one's life for the brethren" (*SRS*, no. 40).

In the end, the pope observes, a Christian commitment to solidarity should lead the believer to "a new model of the unity of the human race" (*SRS*, no. 40). The universal bond holding together all people around the world mirrors the intimate bonds that exist between the three divine persons: the Father, the Son, and the Holy Spirit. Solidarity, in this way, functions as a sacrament to the extent that it is a concrete, temporal sign pointing to an eternal divine truth (*SRS*, no. 40). Solidarity closely relates to, and often overlaps with, other themes of Catholic social thought, especially love and the preferential option for the poor (*SRS*, no. 47).[90] For individual Christians, it serves as both a virtue and a duty that recognizes and acts on the value of the interdependence of all humanity (*SRS*, nos. 10, 23, 31). The state pursues solidarity "by defending the weakest, by placing certain limits on the autonomy of the parties who determine working conditions, and by ensuring in every case the necessary minimum support for the unemployed worker" (*CA*, no. 15).

Paradoxes and Terminological Problems

Like all general principles, one can interpret solidarity from a number of different angles and define and apply it in many ways. However, it is the kind of philosophical concept associated with certain paradoxes and contradictions simply by virtue of the way people have understood and practiced it. The first problem for solidarity theorists consists of addressing the postmodern dilemma of what ought to draw people together.[91] Perhaps humans should seek closer bonds with

---

88. See also Paul VI, *Populorum progressio*, no. 67; and US Catholic Bishops, *Economic Justice for All*, nos. 64–67.

89. See also John XXIII, *Pacem in terris*, no. 107.

90. See also John Paul II, *Centesimus annus*, no. 49.

91. Karagiannis, *European Solidarity*, 5.

one another and seek situations of mutuality and reciprocity, but most people come together around a point of reference. Mutuality assumes that something is shared; reciprocity presumes some sort of common pretext. This, in turn, raises the more-prickly questions: "Around what center or cause can individuals, groups, and societies come together in solidarity with one another? Should they gather around God? Church? Nation? Culture? Class? Race? Ethnicity? Gender?" Each of these rallying points presents problems if one is trying to achieve the universal solidarity that Catholic social theorists have written about for so many decades. The literature rarely even mentions this issue, let alone addresses it at length or in detail.

In addition to the postmodern problem, solidarity is dogged by a set of three paradoxes. The first—the inclusion/exclusion paradox—simply acknowledges that forming social bonds with one group assumes the exclusion of others who do not share such a bond. If by some stroke of luck or divine grace, people everywhere found themselves included in this close-knit society, then some would argue that solidarity would immediately be rendered moot.[92] The second paradox, referred to as equality/inequality, observes that while solidarity may aim to make all people equal, solidarity itself can only arise in an existing situation of inequality. Only in the presence of wealthy and poor, oppressors and oppressed, mainstream as well as marginal, can an act of solidarity be inclusive and, therefore, have any meaning.[93] Once again, some claim that in a world in which *solidarity* is a universal achievement, it becomes a meaningless term.

A final problematic aspect of the use and application of solidarity has to do with its "already, but not yet" quality. In case studies, social justice authors identify the ways solidarity already exists within certain groups, while, at the same time, has not yet been fully realized.[94] Thomas Reynolds, for one, refers to solidarity as a type of "dialectical pluralism" that is "both an 'always already' and a 'not yet.' It is, on the one hand, a fact and on the other, a task stretching infinitely forward, intimating the ever-deferred possibility of a maximally inclusive horizon of conversational solidarity among differences."[95] This logical paradox is one of many encountered by Catholic theologians, who also have the task of making sense of a God who is both immanent and transcendent, a church that is both sinful and graced, and a savior who is both human and divine. At the Second Vatican Council the bishops equated the Church to the Kingdom of God, which, like solidarity, also has an "already, but not yet" quality. It is already present through the incarnation of Christ and the ongoing existence of the Church,

---

92. Ibid. See also Hooker, *Race and the Politics of Solidarity*, 32–33.

93. Ibid., 6.

94. Ibid., 6–7.

95. Reynolds, *The Broken Whole*, 102.

but also, at the same time, not yet present in its fullest sense. That can only come at the end of time.[96]

Solidarity in a Business Context

Evaluating the overall capitalist business climate in North America based solely on the public image presented in advertising might lead to the conclusion that consumerism is one of the primary vehicles of solidarity. Advertising is filled with powerful and compelling images that, among other things, suggest North Americans are blissfully united by the products they consume and, moreover, that these products are symbols of camaraderie and fellowship. For instance, a recent series of Miller High Life commercials depicts a beer-distribution truck driver with an attitude against elitism that crashes a variety of mixed-class events, taking Miller High Life from the wealthy in their aristocratic settings and giving it to the folksy middle class in the main arena. The advertising industry often uses this kind of faux solidarity to procure an artificial variant of something that consumer culture in reality cannot deliver.[97] Most people realize that advertisers' commercials are replete with unfulfilled promises, but in the case of solidarity, the promise was never theirs to make. That is to say, consumerism in a capitalist marketplace is not a likely pathway to the development of tight-knit bonds between individuals within a community. In fact, consumerism often leads to feelings of envy, resentment, and competition. So, how can a capitalist business culture truly embrace solidarity as a virtue, and what needs to change in order to make that happen?

Competition vs. Cooperation

Free competition is a primary principle of all theories of modern capitalism. It is based on the idea that rational consumers and their demands will drive a variety of producers to develop superior products at progressively lower prices. Clever, nimble, and hard-working producers will eventually win the day, developing the best products at the lowest prices. Producers less well-adapted to the competitive environment will fall by the wayside and go out of business. According to the theory, the free and open context of "the market" sets the stage for the cumulative improvement in products coupled with diminishing prices. The question for those convinced of the free-market logic is, "What

---

96. Vatican Council II, *Lumen gentium* (The Dogmatic Constitution on the Church, 1964), no. 48, *http://www.vatican.va/archive/hist_councils/ii_vatican_council/documents/vat-ii_const_19641 121_lumen-gentium_en.html.*

97. Lloyd E. Sandelands and Andrew J. Hoffman, "Sustainability, Faith, and the Market," *Worldview* 12 (2008): 142.

could be wrong with this arrangement, and who could possibly be against this elegant, simple, and natural solution?"

The answer to that question is less obvious than one might imagine. Many economists acknowledge that in order for markets to work as described, the people who engage in those markets must share common values of truth, freedom, justice, and love and must be willing to consistently behave in a virtuous manner.[98] Copious evidence from history and the social sciences shows that individuals do not always behave themselves, and some regularly misbehave in ways that put the good of others at risk. Psychologist Detlef Fletchenhauer, who has studied personal interactions in a social context, reinforces this observation and claims that the solidarity and pro-social behavior necessary for smooth economic transactions rely on subjective interpretations and situational perceptions.[99] In the end, one's capacity to behave in solidarity with others is determined, largely, by one's definition of a situation.[100] For instance, the degree of prosocial behavior exhibited by a company when a competing business changes its marketing strategy depends on whether that marketing strategy is perceived to be relatively fair and honest. Such interpretations and perceptions can just as easily lead to antisocial and, therefore, antimarket behavior under certain circumstances. Psychology, sociology, and personal experience all point to humans as "highly altruistic in some situations, but are brutally selfish in others."[101]

For this reason, markets require some fundamental degree of solidarity and cooperation in order to function properly. Competition informed by the mutual and reciprocal vision of solidarity likely results in markets that work like the theories predict. However, competition that is self-centered, arrogant, and focused on the destruction of the competitors, rather than on the production of excellent products at fair prices, undermines markets, as can be witnessed in the recent global financial meltdown.[102] Moreover, an obsessive focus on individual freedom and the pursuit of dog-eat-dog competition has contributed greatly to the underdevelopment of starving and suffering peoples around the world.[103] In

---

98. Kenneth J. Arrow, "Methodological Individualism and Social Knowledge," *American Economic Review* 84.2 (May 1994): 2.

99. Detlef Fletchenhauer, Siegwart Lindenberg, Andreas Flache, and Abraham P. Buunk, "Solidarity and Prosocial Behavior: A Framing Approach," in *Solidarity and Prosocial Behavior: An Integration of Sociological and Psychological Perspectives*, ed. Detlef Fletchenhauer (Groningen, The Netherlands: University of Groningen, 2010), 11.

100. Ibid., 10.

101. Ibid., 3.

102. Kathleen M. Gounaris and Maurice F. Prout, "Repairing Relationships and Restoring Trust: Behavioral Finance and the Economic Crisis," *Journal of Financial Service Professionals* 63, no. 4 (July 2009): 75–84.

103. Mark Duffield, *Development, Security and Unending War: Governing the World of Peoples* (Malden, MA: Polity Press, 2007), 233.

solidarity with the least well-off, theologian Ann Patrick asks if their voices can be heard and if the business world can respond with values more efficacious than freedom, competition, or acquisitiveness.[104] "Solidarity challenges first-world levels of consumption, expressions of preference, and understanding of freedom as immunities from our responsibilities to others," says Maureen O'Connell in her book *Compassion: Loving Our Neighbor in an Age of Globalization.* "It highlights that all persons struggle to flourish under the yoke of privilege."[105]

People vs. Profit

In *Sollicitudo rei socialis,* Pope John Paul II refers to a "cult of having," which prioritizes the accumulation of wealth and material things over the basic human needs of the poor and marginal groups around the world (no. 28). This notion emphasizes the interconnected nature of global capitalism and how indulging the desire for unrestrained freedom for some connects to "the totalitarian poverty for others."[106] It recognizes that many of the low-cost consumer products purchased at a discount in North America can be traced back to the low wages and Dickensian working conditions in the developing world, or how the seemingly unlimited energy resources enjoyed by some can be linked to the environmental disasters suffered by others, or how the voluntary segregation of the gated community can be tied to the involuntary segregation of the slum. In response, the pope calls on modern business to incorporate practices of solidarity and act on behalf of all humankind.[107] "A financial economy that is an end unto itself is destined to contradict its goals, since it is no longer in touch with its roots and has lost sight of its constitutive purpose . . . of serving the real economy, and, ultimately, of contributing to the development of people and the human community."[108]

These kinds of admonitions have led some Catholic businesspeople to reflect on the ways good public health is threatened by the disintegration of solidarity[109] and how they can promote genuine mutuality and reciprocity among their constituents. Many businesses question the assumption that what is best for capital is also best for everyone[110] and have begun to experiment with new

---

104. Patrick, "Conscience and Solidarity with Victims," 192.

105. Maureen H. O'Connell, *Compassion: Loving Our Neighbor in an Age of Globalization* (Maryknoll, NY: Orbis Books, 2009), 86.

106. O'Connell, *Compassion,* 87.

107. Hoffman, "Sustainability, Faith, and the Market," 141.

108. Pontifical Council on Justice and Peace, *Compendium of the Social Doctrine of the Church* (Washington, DC: US Conference of Catholic Bishops, 2004), 369.

109. Chuck Collins and Mary Wright, *The Moral Measure of the Economy* (Maryknoll, NY: Orbis Books, 2007), 70.

110. Christine Firer-Hinze, "Social and Economic Ethics," *Theological Studies* 70 (2009): 170.

models of organization, development, and production. Experiments in workplace democracy, in which workers have a say in corporate governance and policy, provide a good example of this trend.[111] Many businesses have committed to sustainability programs that focus on environmental impact to both human and nonhuman life.[112] Other business trends that point in the direction of solidarity include the widespread adoptions of corporate social responsibility charters, which take a broad look at the social impact of all operations in a company and seek to minimize negative impacts while maximizing value.[113] These and other efforts made by contemporary businesses help to build faith in a capitalist system that has endured a decade of dramatic moral failures. They also help to combat the impression that businesses focus myopically on making a few owners wealthy while damning the rest of the world to live in an apartheid society made up of "haves" and "have-nots."[114]

Stockholder vs. Stakeholder

Another way business leaders have demonstrated an interest in solidarity is through the relatively recent focus on stakeholder value, as opposed to the traditional focus on stockholder value. Stockholders represent the relatively limited group of people who have purchased shares in a company. Traditional management theory stresses the need to maximize return on investment to convince current stockholders to hold onto their shares and to attract new investors to their company's stock, which also increases the share price. However, many within both the business community and the ethical community have raised questions about focusing on the interests of such a narrow audience and have proposed a broader perspective that takes into account all of the parties impacted by corporate decisions, such as employees, consumers, suppliers, government agencies, the community, and the environment.[115] Managing from a stakeholder model, though, has its own problems and complexities, different from the more straightforward task of managing to achieve maximum return on funds invested. Stakeholders represent a multitude of seemingly ever-expanding interests, many of which conflict with one

---

111. Janice R. Foley, and Michael Polanyi, "Workplace Democracy: Why Bother?" *Economic and Industrial Democracy* 27.1 (February 2006): 173–191.

112. Heather Elms, Stephen Brammer, Jared D. Harris, and Robert A. Phillips, "New Directions in Strategic Management and Business Ethics," *Business Ethics Quarterly* 20.3 (July 2010): 401–425.

113. Paul C. Godfrey, Craig B. Merrill, and Jared M. Hansen, "The Relationship between Corporate Social Responsibility and Shareholder Value: An Empirical Test of the Risk Management Hypothesis," *Strategic Management Journal* 30.4 (April 2009): 425–445.

114. Collins, *The Moral Measure of the Economy*, 70.

115. Rickard Garvare and Peter Johansson, "Management for Sustainability—A Stakeholder Theory," *Total Quality Management & Business Excellence* 21.7 (July 2010): 737–744.

another.[116] For instance, the demand for higher pay and better benefits on the part of employee stakeholders normally will come at the expense of some profits, which, in turn, will harm shareholder value in the short term.

Catholic social theorists claim that focusing too narrowly on profit and shareholders runs the risk of eroding a sense of moral obligation.[117] Using the language of the common good, it can lead to a "tragedy of the commons," which refers to the neglect of those aspects of economic and social life that are shared and in danger of falling into collapse or ruin if people within a society cannot come together to support, develop, and protect these common resources.[118] While stakeholder theory moves management practices in the right direction, many social theorists still sense the need to broaden these stakeholder notions to include more of the constituents, both human and non-human, who are positively and adversely affected by corporate activity.[119] The extreme individualism that informs much management theory and practice denies the social dimension of human nature, as conceived by Catholic theology.[120] In turn, these individualized notions of human happiness and fulfillment can lead to the injustices associated with the privatization of market successes and the socialization of failures, as can be seen in the recent financial and automotive bailouts.[121] These catastrophes, in ironic ways, highlight the inescapable interdependence of a globalized economy and demonstrate the urgent need for an ethic of solidarity.[122]

Participative vs. Command Model of Leadership

Economic crises drive home the point that virtually all humans are integrated into the fate of the world economy whether they like it or not. Because of this, people have begun to acknowledge this de facto solidarity and form more participative leadership structures that consider the needs, desires, hopes, and dreams of a much larger and more representative sampling of the people affected by this economic activity: "The issue of participation, and of solidarity as the attitude facilitating it, arises out of the fact that the person is not an isolated subject in

---

116. For a more detailed discussion of the issues of conflicts between stakeholder interests, see Paul T. M. Ingenbleek and Victor M. Immink, "Managing Conflicting Stakeholder Interests: An Exploratory Case Analysis of the Formulation of Corporate Social Responsibility Standards in the Netherlands," *Journal of Public Policy & Marketing* 29.1 (Spring 2010): 52–65.

117. Collins, *The Moral Measure of the Economy*, 84.

118. Hoffman, "Sustainability, Faith, and the Market," 131.

119. Heyer, "Strangers in Our Midst," 448–49.

120. Collins, 84.

121. Firer-Hinze, "Social and Economic Ethics," 170.

122. Ibid.

a world of objects, but rather a subject among subjects."[123] Many Catholic social theorists characterize the current state of affairs in global capitalism as exclusive, dictatorial, and elitist, rather than inclusive, democratic, and participative.[124] Therefore, many of these same authors call for greater democracy in the global economy so that the voices of those who have been excluded from the conversations and decisions can exert some control over the ways their markets function.[125] As mentioned, greater workplace democracy, increased awareness of corporate social responsibility, and the broadening of stakeholder definitions indicate that many corporations already understand the need for more participative business models in this expanding, interdependent global economy.

Conclusion

Solidarity seeks to subvert the privatization of the ethical life in the world of corporate capitalism, which raises the privatization of ownership to a first principle.[126] In business environments that strive to maximize profit and shareholder return on investment, international solidarity seeks to maximize hope and inspire trust.[127] Catholic social theorists maintain that solidarity has the capacity to inspire business leaders to construct a new story that "incorporates rather than obliterates difference."[128] In this way, these businesses can become agents of "tolerance, accommodation, compromise, and cooperation, rather than hatred, division, competition, and dominance."[129] Achieving these lofty goals in a global context will require business leaders to expand their inclusive visions beyond even the broadest conceptions of stakeholder value and recognize the essentially interconnected and interdependent nature of all reality. Businesses will have to employ more cooperative strategies and embody more participative structures to build a livable, sustainable world and not just one that can be temporarily exploited for profit and then discarded. More than ever before in human history, businesses have the power to transform the world for the better. A laser focus on the virtue of solidarity offers a good place to begin this journey.

---

123. Doran, *Solidarity*, 171.

124. O'Connell, *Compassion*, 87.

125. Christopher J. Voparil and Richard J. Bernstein, eds., *The Rorty Reader* (Malden, MA: Wiley-Blackwell, 2010), 209.

126. Cowley, "Philia and Social Ethics," 35.

127. Routledge, *Global Justice Networks*, 212.

128. Cahill, "Goods for Whom?" 208.

129. Ibid.

One Acre Fund

Andrew Youn's career path seemed to be headed in a predictable direction. After graduating with honors from Yale and finishing his MBA at the prestigious Kellogg School of Management, this son of Korean immigrants who grew up in St. Paul, Minnesota, dreamed of becoming a strategic consultant for a large *Fortune* 500 company.[130] However, after an extended internship in rural Kenya, where Andrew had the opportunity to interview subsistence farmers, he began to refocus his entrepreneurial drive. He realized that the lives of African farmers could be radically transformed by a relatively minuscule investment. According to Youn, "The sheer magnitude of what we can accomplish from a humanitarian perspective with very little resources is just staggering."[131]

Youn and cofounder John Gachunga's epiphany gave birth to the One Acre Fund (OAF), which provides microfinance, supplies, and insurance to rural African farmers. While OAF is a nonprofit organization driven by compassion, it does not treat farmers as charity cases and does not function as a charitable organization that simply hands out cash and resources without any obligation to repay. In fact, OAF was designed to function on a sustainable business model that lends money and resources to farmers and expects repayment based on a schedule determined by seasonal harvests and market conditions rather than by the more rigid schedules of traditional microfinance.

One of the problems Youn recognized during his internship in rural Africa was the way traditional microfinance had been designed around the needs of people who sold products and services in urban markets. This supported an unsustainable growth of urban micro-entrepreneurs to the neglect of farming and rural development. Because the income of farmers is not constant, but rises and falls according to the seasonal harvest, they had a difficult time attracting microfinance dollars because most of these monies were offered only under regimented repayment conditions that the farmers could not meet. Because of this lack of credit, supplies, and training, rural farming communities were languishing, and farmers were consigned to live in persistent conditions of poverty.

In response to these circumstances, the One Acre Fund sought to work with rural farmers in Burundi, Rwanda, and Kenya to provide a

(continued)

---

130. *http://www.skollfoundation.org/entrepreneur/andrew-youn/.*

131. *http://www.pbs.org/newshour/rundown/2012/04/one-acre-fund-a-nonprofits-business-approach-to-helping-small-farmers.html.*

Case Study

package of agricultural goods and services that would change the market equation that had left the farmers no better off than when they began. The fund set up its training, credit, supplies, and insurance programs so that the farmers would pay for these on a schedule tied to the harvest cycle. The farmers repay their loans at harvest time, and those repayments are recycled back into the fund so that other farmers can then use those monies to support and expand their operations. D. Stephanie Hanson, the director of policy and research at OAF, claims, "Because we're charging for the good or service it means we can [ensure financial] sustainability as an organization."[132]

The flexible loan terms set OAF programs apart from other nonprofit microfinance organizations. In many ways, OAF gives farmers the capacity to set their own repayment schedule with the caveat that the loan must be paid in full after the harvest. In addition, the program makes provisions for drought, crop failure, or other natural disasters that would prevent repayment and offers farmers the opportunity to purchase insurance to protect them from these adverse circumstances. Loans can also be forgiven in extreme situations in which farmers face unforeseen calamities.

Over its first half-decade of existence, the OAF received numerous grants and awards for its innovative approach to development financing from such prestigious foundations as the Echoing Green Fellowship, the Draper Richards Foundation, the Pershing Square Foundation, and the Skoll Foundation. In many cases, the awards were made not only on the basis of OAF's unique and innovative approach to rural farming microfinance but also in response to the values espoused and put into practice. The One Acre Fund lists six key values that inform its operations:

1. Humble Service—We meet farmers in their fields and we get our shoes muddy. Farmers are our customers and we serve them with humility.

2. Hard Work—We work hard everyday. We execute with world-class professionalism and business excellence. Farmers deserve nothing less.

3. Continual Growth—We improve every season. We work with determination to meet our goals and then stretch ourselves by raising the bar even higher.

4. Family and Leaders—We bring together the best leaders and build long-term careers. We care for team members like family.

(continued)

---

132. *http://www.csmonitorcom/World/Making-a-difference/Change-Agent/2012/0321/One-Acre-Fund-helps-Africa-s-small-farmers-keep-in-their-fields.html.*

Case Study   *(continued)*

5. Dreaming Big—We envision serving millions of farm families. We build for scale with every idea and solution.

6. Integrity—We do what we say, and our words match our values.[133]

After six years of operation, the results speak for themselves. OAF has experienced rapid growth in the number of families served, from 5,000 in 2006 to 125,000 in 2012. Like many other microfinance organizations, OAF enjoys a very high repayment rate on its loans and services—99 percent. On average, farmers who use the fund triple their yields in the seasons following their enrollment in the program.

Questions

1. What do you think about Andrew Youn and John Gachunga's decision to launch the OAF after graduate school? Is this a good way to apply the skills acquired by these talented young businessmen? Should business schools promote this kind of social entrepreneurship in their MBA programs?

2. In what ways do you think the OAF was inspired by a genuine sense of solidarity? How does solidarity inform the ongoing operation of the fund?

3. Do you think the six values of the OAF are adequate and helpful for employees of the OAF? Would you add other values to this list? Do any seem unnecessary? Have you ever worked at a company that had an explicit set of values or a code of conduct? How did it compare to the list of values at OAF?

4. Can you think of a need that could be met using the same kind of moral imagination Youn and Gachunga used when they conceived of a better way to finance rural farming in Africa?

---

133. *http://www.oneacrefund.org.*

Case Study

The Solar Suitcase

Dr. Laura Stachel went to northern Nigeria in 2008 to investigate the high mortality rates among women who were having their babies in state hospitals. She never imagined that it would ultimately lead her to establish her own nonprofit solar business, but that is exactly what happened when she took on the challenges posed by unreliable energy sources in the developing world.

Dr. Stachel is an obstetrician/gynecologist who had returned to graduate school at the University of California, Berkeley, for graduate study in public policy. During her course of study, she researched the unusually high rate of maternal mortality in Nigeria, which accounts for 10 percent of all maternal deaths during birth worldwide. Her research brought her to Nigeria where she could witness firsthand the standard practices used during delivery in state hospitals. She discovered that the fundamental problem was not in the policies and procedures of the hospitals, but in something far more basic— the lack of light. Dr. Stachel says, "I witnessed deliveries by kerosene lantern, nursing care by candlelight, and was present at a C-section when the lights went out. I saw women who died when blood transfusions were delayed (due to lack of blood banking) and stillbirths that occurred when doctors could not be located for emergency C-sections."[134]

Fortunately for Nigeria and the rest of the developing world, Stachel knew where to turn to find a workable solution to this lack of reliable electricity. Her husband, Hal Aronson, was a solar educator, and he began experimenting with ways that portable solar energy could be employed to address these critical medical issues. Eventually, they came up with a solar electrical system that could function independently of the Nigerian electrical grid.[135]

They designed their first system to replace the vital electrical systems of an entire hospital,[136] but then Hal and Laura received requests for smaller, portable systems that could be used at clinics in more rural settings. This gave birth to the Solar Suitcase—literally a baggage-sized case filled with a battery, LED lights, and solar cells. The solar cells convert sunlight into electricity, which is stored in the batteries and then used to run the LEDs at dark

(continued)

---

134. Ariel Schwartz, "A Solar Suitcase to Treat Medical Emergencies in the Dark," *http://www.fastcoexist.com/1679942/a-solar-suitcase-to-treat-medical-emergencies-in-the-dark*.

135. We Care Solar website: *http://wecaresolar.org/*.

136. Schwartz, "A Solar Suitcase to Treat Medical Emergencies in the Dark."

Case Study   *(continued)*

or if the electrical grid fails. Now Nigerian delivery rooms could continue to safely function at night, even when the power failed.[137]

Originally, the systems were built by hand, using parts and supplies available over the counter and a volunteer labor force. However, with the assistance of grants and foundations, We Care Solar developed a design that could be factory manufactured, taking advantage of economies of scale to ramp up production, while at the same time keeping costs reasonable for cash-strapped health clinics in developing countries.

As with the One Acre Fund, the results speak for themselves. In one hospital, maternal deaths decreased by 70 percent after the Solar Suitcase was installed. Clinics no longer turn away patients at night, so the number of patients served by these caregivers has increased by 16 percent overall.

Dr. Jacques Sebisaho, founder of Amani Global Works, a health-care organization told one of the most inspiring stories. He used the Solar Suitcase on a recent trip to Idjwi Island on Lake Kivu in the Congo where he was treating cholera at an outdoor infirmary. For the first time in the history of the region, no one died during the cholera outbreak. The normal mortality rate for a cholera outbreak in the area is 50 percent—80 percent of which happen at night.[138]

At this point in the history of their fledgling enterprise, the main concern of We Care Solar is their ability to meet demand. So far, the company has produced and installed hundreds of suitcases, but Stachel estimates that 300,000 or more are needed in clinics around the world. They also are trying to bring the cost of each unit down from its current $1,500 price tag to somewhere under $1,000.[139] This will make the units more affordable and will reduce their replacement cost.

Questions

1. Like the One Acre Fund, We Care Solar decided to organize its business around a nonprofit model. Are there advantages to this business model? Why do you think these companies decided to use this model?

2. In what ways does the principle of solidarity apply in this case? When and how did the founders demonstrate solidarity?

(continued)

---

137. Spencer Michaels, "Saving Lives with Solar Power," *http://www.pbs.org/newshour/rundown/2012/04/delivering-in-the-dark-we-care-solar.html.*

138. Schwartz, "A Solar Suitcase to Treat Medical Emergencies in the Dark."

139. Michaels, "Saving Lives with Solar Power."

Case Study

(continued)

3. What considerations—other than price and quantity—might We Care Solar consider as they continue to refine their product to better meet the needs of their customers?

4. Using We Care Solar as a model, can you think of other circumstances in which the application of a relatively simple technology or service made an important difference in the lives of a large number of people?

For Further Reading

Bouchard, Marie J. *Innovation and the Social Economy: The Québec Experience.* Buffalo, NY: University of Toronto Press, 2013.

Gordon Nembhard, Jessica. *Collective Courage: A History of African American Cooperative Economic Thought and Practice.* University Park, PA: Pennsylvania State University Press, 2014.

Heller, Chaia. *Food, Farms & Solidarity: French Farmers Challenge Industrial Agriculture and Genetically Modified Crops.* Durham, NC: Duke University Press, 2013.

Hillenkamp, Isabelle, Frédéric Lapeyre, and Andreia Lemaître. *Securing Livelihoods: Informal Economy Practices and Institutions.* New York: Oxford University Press, 2013.

Holmes, Seth M. *Fresh Fruit, Broken Bodies: Migrant Farmworkers in the United States.* Berkeley: University of California Press, 2013.

Räthzel, Nora, and David L. Uzzell. *Trade Unions in the Green Economy: Working for the Environment.* New York, NY: Routledge, 2013.

Roman, Richard, and Edur Velasco Arregui. *Continental Crucible: Big Business, Workers and Unions in the Transformation of North America.* Winnipeg: Fernwood, 2013.

Spillman, Lyn. *Solidarity in Strategy: Making Business Meaningful in American Trade Associations.* Chicago, IL: The University of Chicago Press, 2012.

Chapter 8

Weighing Rights against Responsibilities

Thomas O'Brien

Introduction

It has become commonplace in North American culture to employ the language of *rights* to publicly advocate for a particular position on a controversial topic. Those who use this language often leave the term undefined as they consider it self-explanatory. However, when proponents of different sides of a polarized issue, such as abortion, both claim to protect the fundamental rights of Americans, it raises questions about what having an inherent *right* to certain goods and behaviors actually means. Some claim to fight on behalf of unborn citizens for the right to life itself, which they consider the most fundamental right of all. They argue that if this right is violated or even mitigated, it will devalue human life everywhere and foreshadow a dark future in which "inconvenient" people can be eliminated for little or no reason whatsoever. Others claim to champion a woman's right to make her own decisions about what happens to her body, which they affirm as a fundamental right long denied women due to their second-class status in patriarchal societies of the past. If this right is violated or even mitigated, they claim, women will remain hostage to their biology in a social milieu dominated by male priorities.

The abortion debate is not the only current issue that employs competing conceptions of human rights. Mass shootings in schools and other public venues have generated vigorous debate about the right to bear arms. This right to arm oneself is balanced against the rights of citizens to be safe and secure in their own communities. Many argue that securing the right to safe schools, streets, and other public venues requires placing limitations on the right to bear arms.

Others claim that any restrictions on a person's right to own and use firearms compromises American citizenship.

The contemporary debate about same-sex marriage, or marriage equality, also relies on *rights* language. Advocates of marriage equality claim that denying same-sex couples the right to marry violates their right to fair and equal treatment especially regarding those laws that confer privileges to legally married couples. They argue that denying them the right to marry the person they choose treats their relationships as frivolous and denies them their full human dignity in society. Opponents of marriage equality point to their right to uphold the institution of "traditional marriage" between a man and a woman. They assert that marriage equality compromises the ideal of marriage and jeopardizes the sacred bond of the traditional family.

These contentious issues—abortion, firearm ownership, marriage equality—serve as a good starting point for discussing rights because all sides of the debates regularly and powerfully invoke this language, and all sides seem to deny, or at least minimize, the rights claims of the other camps. In turn, this raises questions about the self-evident nature of the very rights being advocated as well as the essentials of human rights and how they are acknowledged and instituted in a society. Are people born with rights, that is, are rights built into human nature, or does society confer rights on its members when they follow the rules and contribute to its survival and advancement? Who has the authority to define, confer, and enforce these rights? Are these rights divinely sanctioned or merely products of social, economic, and political development? Are rights just a list of things people want and would like to see realized in their lives or essential elements of a genuinely and thoroughly human existence that bring the full dignity of the person to fruition?

As evident from the three issues described, infusing a debate with the language of human rights has profound implications for how those issues are discussed and whether they can be resolved. A popular definition defines a right as an entitlement to certain goods or benefits that cannot, or should not, be infringed upon by other individuals or by society as a whole. This entitlement, if genuinely a right, should be recognized, protected, and even promoted by the state. From the perspective of Catholic social teaching (CST), the dignity of the human person stands at the heart of every authentic right. Therefore, violating or compromising another's rights devalues his or her human dignity in the process.

These features of human rights make them both morally compelling and uniquely divisive, both essentially empowering and deeply uncompromising. For these reasons, human rights can serve as an outstanding foundation for a moral vision of society; at the same time, they can be politically impractical due to the uncompromising spirit they inspire. Rights language tends to raise the stakes of any practical issue, turning an otherwise simple weighing of possible consequences into a pitched battle over one's essential identity. The issue of gun ownership in the United States provides a good example of an issue that, under normal circumstances, would appear rather easy to resolve. Gun ownership tends to raise little debate in other societies around the world. Like the ownership of any consumer item with the potential to do great harm, gun use and ownership is legally limited and carefully regulated. In the United States, however, gun ownership has been steeped in the language of rights because of the Second Amendment of the Constitution, making the use and possession of firearms a symbol of national identity. This, in turn, means that laws governing the use and ownership of this consumer item do not function as simply practical means to the end of protecting public safety. In this case, and others like it, the use of rights language has made legal resolution of the issue much more contentious.

Such circumstances explain why Catholic social thought has consistently paired its interpretation of human rights with corresponding responsibilities. This perspective does not view rights as absolute entitlements but primarily as contingent privileges based, in part, on responsible participation in society. Understood in this way, one's right to health care, for example, depends on a willingness to maintain a healthy lifestyle. Pairing a right with a responsibility makes sense in a society in which everyone, as a community, has agreed to pick up the bill for each individual's medical expenses. Irresponsible, unhealthy behavior increases the cost of living in that society for everyone; therefore, society has an interest and a *right* to impose legal limits and sanctions against those who engage in that sort of behavior.

Human Rights: Philosophical, Biblical, and Theological Foundations

As discussed in prior chapters, human dignity underpins the notion of human rights, and the concept of the common good grounds discussions of personal responsibility toward others in society. What, then, makes human rights a topic distinct from human dignity? Furthermore, how does the idea of human rights expand the understanding of one's duties in society beyond that encompassed by the notion of the common good?

Human rights and responsibilities in the context of this discussion function as a practical and concrete application of the principles of human dignity and the common good. As controversies arise and are resolved in social, economic, and political settings, understandings of human dignity and the common good are codified as rights and duties. Eventually, they become institutionalized in constitutions, laws, regulations, public policies, and social practices. These particular rights and duties, based on a broader understanding of human identity and worth, express the essence of human rights and constitute a distinct and practical application of the common good and human dignity theory in specific social settings. Catholic social thought has consistently sought to balance the rights of individuals, which protect the dignity of the human person, with the duties each individual owes to society, which protects and maintains the common good.

The Philosophical Development of Human Rights Theory[1]

In addition to human dignity and the common good, the historical development of the concepts of justice and equality also informs the philosophy of human rights and responsibilities. Experts in the field of human rights frequently cite passages from Plato's *Republic*, Aristotle's *Politics*, Cicero's *On the Laws*, Aquinas's *Summa Theologica*, and Grotius's *The Rights of War and Peace*, along with many other great works of the ancient and medieval world.[2]

A number of conceptual building blocks form the foundation of the contemporary edifice of human rights theory. Working from the insights of the ancient notion of the natural law, John Locke, in his *Second Treatise on Civil Government*, affirmed that humans had natural rights to life, liberty, and property and that these had a foundation independent of the laws and customs of any particular society.[3] These universal rights were not privileges conferred by an authority or by consensus but an essential characteristic of the human person.[4] In the state of nature, with no agreed upon judge or authority to intervene, humans were free and equal, a situation that could lead to conflict when one person's exercise of freedom impinged upon another's rights and freedoms.[5] This picture of a potentially unruly state of nature, leading to a state of war, to a state of slavery, and so forth, grounds Locke's justification for a legitimate government based on a social contract in which people freely transfer some of their rights to the government in order to establish and maintain a secure and stable context for the enjoyment of their life, liberty, and property.

---

1. In many ways, the struggle to say something new in the last chapter of a book about the philosophical roots of this theme highlights one of the main characteristics of the themes of CST; that is, their interconnection. Each of the major themes is principally linked to the others in such a tight web that a thorough explication of one theme implicitly introduces the reader to the others. By the time one has studied seven of eight themes, there can be a sense of redundancy in the presentation. For this reason, the discussion of the philosophical foundations of human rights and responsibilities will focus on modern themes, rather than on the more typical ancient and medieval sources, which have already been mentioned in some detail.

2. For a good example of this sort of historical treatment of human rights, see Patrick Hayden, *The Philosophy of Human Rights* (St. Paul, MN: Paragon House, 2001).

3. Jack Mahoney, *The Challenge of Human Rights: Origin, Development and Significance* (Malden, MA: Blackwell Publishing, 2007), 129.

4. C. Fred Alford, *Narrative, Nature, and the Natural Law: From Aquinas to International Human Rights* (New York, NY: Palgrave MacMillan, 2010), 123–27.

5. John Locke, *Two Treatises of Government* (New York, NY: Cambridge University Press, 2003), 268–278.

Locke's understanding of rights emphasizes another essential element of contemporary human rights theory—rights are an outgrowth of the interrelatedness of humans.[6] In the absence of relationships, human rights are mere abstractions derived from a theoretical state of nature. Only when people encounter one another and start figuratively rubbing up against each other do they recognize the need to compromise their primal equality and freedom so that all might live together and enjoy a common good. Living in society with other humans necessarily obliges individuals to acknowledge the equality and freedom of others. This relational notion of rights reflects "two broad ways that we understand and use rights (1) as empowerments or signs of what I get to do, and (2) as protective securities against what you (meaning any agent) might want to do to me."[7] This mutual acknowledgment and respect becomes the basis for a broader social contract that requires each individual to respect the rights of everyone else and society itself to remain cognizant of the rights of individuals to exercise their basic freedoms as long as these do not seriously infringe upon the rights of others.

Most renditions of contemporary human rights theory discuss the difference between positive and negative rights. The latter refer to the government *refraining* from action; thus, *negative* rights assure individual citizens that the state will not encroach upon their freedom to fundamentals such as life, liberty, and the pursuit of happiness. A *positive* right, on the contrary, refers to the prerogative of an activist government to pursue what it deems a public good, such as education or health care.[8] A number of modern theorists claim that the state can only legitimately protect negative rights.[9] However, a majority of authors disagree with this narrow reading of the obligation of government to its citizens; they allow for at least a limited set of positive rights, such as the right to safety and security, which in practical terms enables the government to establish and maintain a police force and a military.

Catholic social teaching sides with those human rights theorists who have a rather liberal interpretation of both the negative and positive rights. The litany of rights appearing in the official documents of the Catholic Church corresponds closely to the list found in the UN Declaration on Human Rights, which includes both negative rights, such as the freedom from discrimination, slavery, and torture, as well as positive rights, such as the right to marriage and a family, social security, rest and leisure, and an education.[10]

---

6. David Boersema, *Philosophy of Human Rights: Theory and Practice* (Boulder, CO: Westview Press, 2011), 13–16.

7. Ibid., 15.

8. For a concise discussion of negative and positive rights, see Jack Donnelly, *Universal Human Rights in Theory and Practice* (Ithaca, NY: Cornell University Press, 2003), 30–31.

9. For a more thorough treatment of this controversy, see Thomas Cushman, ed., *Handbook of Human Rights* (New York, NY: Routledge International, 2012), 110–17.

10. The declaration can be found online, *http://www.un.org/en/documents/udhr/*.

The language of the UN Declaration raises another issue related to negative and positive rights: the apparent conflict between freedom and entitlement. Some theorists object to positive rights because the provision of entitlements such as education and health care requires the government to levy higher taxes, which they interpret as an encroachment on an individual's ability to freely own and control property. Negative rights, for the most part, do not require extensive government outlays of programs and tax dollars, although the protection of negative rights (life, liberty, and property) necessitates a police force and a military. Positive-rights advocates respond by claiming any society that does not guarantee basic positive rights will likely devolve into a dysfunctional society with higher crime rates, increased poverty, public-health crises, and other disasters, all of which would cost society far more to police and clean up than the funds needed to implement government programs that address these basic human needs.

In philosophical language, positive-rights advocates claim that proportionality should guide deliberations in instances in which rights and freedoms collide. They argue that freedoms can be limited or even sacrificed in circumstances in which the consequences of neglecting the entitlement and allowing freedom to reign raises more of a threat to the public good than restricting the freedom and allowing the entitlement.[11]

The positive right to an education illustrates how some use proportionality to justify positive rights. Both the decision to educate and the decision not to educate its youth will incur costs for a society in one way or the other. Public education will cost a predictable amount based on various well-established formulae, and this cost will be levied relatively fairly through tax increases. On the other hand, the costs of neglecting public education are more unpredictable and will be felt as massive losses of opportunity for those in society who already occupy the lowest income brackets. The poor will likely become poorer, requiring greater direct assistance in the forms of housing, food, clothing, and other necessities. Crimes of desperation will likely increase, which will raise the cost of social services and police protection. An undereducated population that is less creative and productive will, in economic terms, impact the overall competitiveness of that particular society in the global marketplace. In the end, its proponents argue, the costs to society of providing the right to education appear much lower than the cost of neglecting this entitlement. They claim that the argument that the provision of a public education infringes on the freedom to own property does not stand up to closer examination. In fact, they find the opposite to be true—to neglect the entitlement

---

11. Andrew Chapman, *Human Rights: A Very Short Introduction* (New York, NY: Oxford University Press, 2007), 97–101.

to a public education has a greater overall negative impact on an individual citizen's right to own property.[12]

Another issue that comes up regularly in philosophical debates about human rights is whether groups and associations have rights or whether human rights belong only to individuals.[13] Philosophers do not contest the idea that individuals have rights based on their common human dignity; however, many question the validity and even the existence of the collective rights of groups: "The right to *collective self-determination* entitles a group to limit the full exercise of its members' human right to act as they wish whenever the group determines that this exercise endangers the identity of the group."[14] The Catholic Church's request for an exemption (2011) from certain aspects of the Affordable Care Act that the Church claimed would compromise its teachings on contraception provides one contemporary example of a group right in a North American context. From the earliest official social teaching documents, the Church has vigorously supported the notion that groups have rights. *Rerum novarum*'s (On the Condition of Labor, 1891) support of unionization and worker's associations offers yet another example of the Church's support for collective rights as something that positively augments individual human rights.[15]

In concert with a number of other human rights advocates, the Catholic Church also insists on connecting any discussion of rights to the corresponding duties owed to each other and to society as a whole. Often referred to by philosophers as the *correlativity thesis*, it claims that rights and duties relate to one another and imply each other: "One agent's right implies another agent's duty and vice versa."[16] Often the implied duty consists merely of not interfering with the fulfillment of the right, as is the case with the constitutional right to life in which the duty is simply not to murder. Other duties involve a more proactive stance on the part of the agents. The right to public education, for example, requires citizens to attend school through a certain grade level, pay taxes, and support government structures that facilitate the accomplishment of this right for everyone in society.

Biblical and Theological Roots of Rights and Responsibilities

As the previous section demonstrated, the concept of human rights—as commonly understood today—is relatively modern with mainly indirect links to

---

12. This argument assumes society equitably shares the burden for all the social costs mentioned in this case.

13. Paul Gordon Lauren, *The Evolution of International Human Rights* (Philadelphia, PA: University of Pennsylvania Press, 2011), 96.

14. Cushman, *Handbook of Human Rights*, 277.

15. Leo XIII, *Rerum novarum* (1891), no. 48, *http://www.vatican.va/holy_father/leo_xiii/encyclicals/documents/hf_l-xiii_enc_15051891_rerum-novarum_en.html*.

16. Boersema, *Philosophy of Human Rights*, 16.

ideas and practices from the ancient and medieval world of Christianity. For instance, most of the societies responsible for Christian Scriptures, early Christian theology, and later medieval developments were built on the notion of the divine mandate to rule. In fact, these cultures had no conception of civil self-rule, in which a people might come together in order to constitute a government and elect representatives to make and enforce the laws of the land. In these societies, emperors and kings ruled, and citizens of the realm had rights only to the extent that the monarchical authorities allowed such rights to exist. These same citizens were compelled to perform the duties assigned to them, and these responsibilities could change at a moment's notice depending on the whims of the ruling class. In other words, today's sense of human rights and responsibilities is of recent vintage. Therefore, ancient and medieval Christian ideas that relate, in some way, to contemporary, secular concepts of human rights and responsibilities do so for reasons unrelated to any direct experience of such privileges by those ancient authors.

The Covenantal Roots of Rights and Responsibilities

While secular, philosophical conceptions have profoundly influenced Catholic social thought on human rights, the Church's teachings rest more fundamentally on the ancient Judaic notion of the *covenant*. Simply stated, a covenant is a kind of contractual arrangement, usually between two parties of unequal power, in which both parties enjoy certain privileges but also carry a burden of duties toward each other. In the Hebrew Scriptures, a covenant is a reciprocal relationship initiated by God that establishes the rights and responsibilities of Israel in its dealings with God. Numerous covenants are set up throughout the Hebrew Scriptures. God established the very first with Adam in the Garden of Eden, giving Adam and Eve the privilege of living life in paradise as long as they did not eat fruit from the tree of knowledge of good and evil (Genesis 2:4b–3:22). Inevitably, humans broke the covenant by neglecting their duty and eating from that tree. God held these human representatives accountable for their transgression of the covenant promise and drove them from paradise into a world filled with suffering and death.

This first covenant between God and humanity sets the precedent for future covenants in which a faithful and loving God takes a chance on imperfect humans and strikes a generous covenantal agreement, only to be spurned and disappointed by the ungrateful and inconstant nature of his human partners. God sends teachers, judges, and prophets to coax and chide the people back to a position of obedience, but these intercessions rarely work. Ultimately, the people must face the consequences of their covenantal infidelity and suffer punishment, usually in the form of losing a war with a foe and being delivered into the hands of their enemies. Only then do the people realize they have strayed from their promises and cry out to God for deliverance. Fortunately for humanity, God is infinitely forgiving and always relents from the punishment of the people after a period of purgation and purification. God then admonishes the people and sets the terms of a new covenant, which they dutifully promise to uphold.

God makes numerous covenants with Israel (the People of God) throughout the Judeo-Christian Scriptures, with the best-known and most-influential in the Hebrew Scriptures being the Mosaic covenant. The covenant struck with Moses comes after God miraculously delivers the Hebrew slaves from their bondage in Egypt under the oppressive rule of the pharaoh. After the slaves cross the Red Sea and the pharaoh's chariots and charioteers are inundated by the waters, Miriam sings her song of deliverance and Moses is led, along with the people, through the desert to Mt. Sinai. There the Mosaic covenant is struck, and God gives the Ten Commandments, along with the other stipulations of the law, to Israel. The People of God transgress the very first of these covenantal commandments even before Moses descends the mountain; he finds them worshipping a metal calf and making sacrifices to it when he returns (Exodus 32:8). Therefore, a pattern is established for the future of divine-human covenantal relationships in the Abrahamic religions.

Biblical covenants, as contracts between God and humans, confer certain privileges and entitlements, which closely resemble what modern political philosophers would call *rights*. Biblical covenants also set out a series of duties, requirements, and responsibilities that closely correspond to what modern political philosophers would understand as laws and expectations of citizenship. In this way, covenants and the relationships they govern function as the forerunners for the modern notion of human rights and the contractual constitutional state.

However, there are limits to this correlation between the ancient and modern given the substantial differences between covenants and modern conceptions of rights.[17] Ancient covenants paired rights with specific duties that spelled out what the inferior partner (people) owed to the higher authority (God). Modern notions of rights are always placed within a theoretical framework of human-to-human relationships, and therefore, equal-to-equal interactions. Rights, in this context, consist of those things one can claim from an equal partner in this larger contractual relationship of the constitutional, democratic state. In addition, ancient biblical covenants begin with the duties the inferior partners owe to the higher authority and then extrapolate from these the rights that the inferior partners can enjoy by performing their duty. The law structures and directs covenantal relationships, stipulating in detail how the duties and rights are fulfilled in specific circumstances.[18]

---

17. For more information about rights and duties in covenantal relationships, see David Novak, "The Judaic Foundation of Rights," in *Christianity and Human Rights*, ed. John Witte and Frank S. Alexander (New York: Cambridge University Press, 2010), 48.

18. Ibid., 49.

The Call to Equality among the Early Christians

An ethic and practice of equality emerged in ancient Christian communities early in their development. This ethic was based on the person of Jesus, whom Christians believed was a manifestation of God—an incarnation in humble, human form who suffered and died. They held that he lived an ordinary life as a carpenter before setting out on a preaching-and-healing mission in the Galilean countryside to reveal the true nature of God. Jesus focused his mission on ordinary Jews, not on Jewish elites or, even less, the ruling Roman elites. For this reason, Jesus can be seen as the ultimate religious populist figure, elevating the lowly and ordinary by choosing their lot in life for his own. Understanding the person of Jesus sheds light on early Christian egalitarian attitudes and behaviors.

Numerous biblical scholars have acknowledged that Jesus orients nearly his entire public ministry toward the healing, teaching, and salvation of the poor, marginalized, and ordinary Jews of first-century, Roman-occupied Palestine. In the Gospels, Jesus almost seems to consciously ignore Jews who hold power and wealth, sometimes even singling them out for ridicule and condemnation. Instead, Jesus scandalizes many by embracing those excluded by Jewish and Roman authorities.[19] The Gospels depict Jesus drawing to himself children, women, slaves, prostitutes, adulterers, lepers, tax collectors and other sinners, ne'er-do-wells, and officially "worthless" people, to the point that his openness to these undesirable elements appalls even his own disciples.

The stories of Jesus include numerous episodes in which he includes a class of people that the wider Jewish culture of this era rejects. One well-known story has people bringing their children to Jesus for his blessing. The disciples rebuke them; children who had not yet undergone the right of passage to adulthood were considered powerless possessions of their parents and, therefore, not worthy of a blessing from a renowned religious leader such as Jesus.[20] In response, Jesus reprimands his disciples saying, "Let the children come to me, and do not prevent them; for the kingdom of heaven belongs to such as these" (Matthew 19:14). This upended social hierarchy considers the children not only worthy of a simple blessing but also the true heirs of the kingdom of heaven. This raising of the lowly signifies a reorientation of common class expectations and humanizes a dehumanized group of people, setting the groundwork for acknowledging the equal value of all persons.

First-century Palestinian Jews considered tax collectors an almost subhuman species and a category of sinner worse than almost any other.[21] Tax collectors in

---

19. One example of this interpretation of Jesus' ministry is Ched Myers, *Binding the Strong Man: A Political Reading of Mark's Story of Jesus* (Maryknoll, NY: Orbis Books, 2008).

20. For a more complete discussion of this passage, see John R. Donahue and Daniel J. Harrington, *The Gospel of Mark* (Collegeville, MN: Liturgical Press, 2002), 301.

21. Ibid., 103.

the occupied territories of the Roman Empire were natives, whose job consisted of extracting payment from the populace to, in essence, fund their own oppression.[22] Tax collectors were hated not just for their association with the Roman occupation but also even more for being traitors who had sold out their own people in order to make money by skimming a percentage off the top of the tax revenue they collected. However, the Gospels reverse the expectations of Jewish readers from that era by showing Jesus in friendly association with tax collectors on numerous occasions. On one such occasion, Jesus asks a tax collector named Levi to come follow him and then invites himself to dinner at Levi's home where he ate and drank and made merry with many tax collectors and other "sinners" (Mark 2:15). Jewish religious leaders were aghast at this act of betrayal, but Jesus responded, "Those who are well do not need a physician, but the sick do. I did not come to call the righteous but sinners" (Mark 2:17). In this instance, like in so many others, Jesus undermines the social hierarchy of his time and place and raises the status of the despised and rejected.

Feminist biblical scholars have pointed out that the Gospels depict Jesus behaving in an unusual way toward women.[23] In fact, almost all of his interactions with women prove exceptional in some regard. First, his status as a teacher among his Jewish followers would have normally shielded him from significant and meaningful interactions with women. Jewish society would have considered it shocking and inappropriate for women to converse publicly with a prominent male religious authority, let alone challenge him in public on moral or theological grounds. Yet again and again, the Gospels portray Jesus as treating women as equals and even occasionally losing a debate to them.

The story of the Syrophoenician woman serves as an example of how the Gospels depict women, and in this case a doubly unworthy gentile woman, debating the teacher, and even winning the debate.[24] The story begins when a gentile woman from the non-Jewish region of Tyre approaches Jesus requesting that he come to her home to cast an unclean spirit from her daughter. Jesus points out that by casting the demon from her child he would be taking food from the children (the Jews) and throwing it to the dogs (the Gentiles). She replies, "Lord, even the dogs under the table eat the children's scraps" (Mark 7:28). In response, Jesus relents and casts the unclean spirit from her child,

---

22. Additional information can be found in Geza Vermes, *The Real Jesus: Then and Now* (Minneapolis, MN: Fortress Press, 2010), 156–58.

23. One example among many rereadings of the story of Jesus from a feminist perspective is Elizabeth Schussler Fiorenza, *Jesus and the Politics of Interpretation* (New York: Continuum, 2000).

24. For a more thorough feminist interpretation of this text, see Elizabeth Schussler Fiorenza, *Sharing Her Word: Feminist Biblical Interpretation in Context* (Edinburgh, Scotland: T&T Clark, 1998), 121–26.

acknowledging in the process the superiority of her initial claims in relation to his own more parochial position.

If these were the only passages in the Gospels showing this kind of reversal of the reigning social hierarchy—a lifting of the lowly and a lowering of the mighty—they could be deemed accidental or inconsequential. However, these role reversals constitute a recurring theme of all four Gospels, to the point that the life of Jesus serves as a kind of symbolic reversal of expectations for the Jewish messiah, who was expected to return as a great, powerful, and wealthy king. Instead, Jesus is born to a humble carpenter and lives a thoroughly unremarkable life right up to the beginning of his public ministry, which he undertook around the age of thirty. Throughout most of his public ministry, the Jewish and Roman authorities generally ignored or dismissed Jesus. When they did finally pay attention, they executed him in the most humiliating and horrific way. Instead of cowering and abandoning Jesus' project, the earliest Christians claimed that Jesus was not only a just and righteous teacher, but also the long-awaited messiah foretold by the Hebrew prophets.

Like the Gospels, other Christian Scriptures embrace the call for equality among early followers of Christ. Letters written by the apostle Paul, as well as those written by others but attributed to him, attest to the early Christian insistence on leveling social hierarchies. Author David E. Aune focuses on one prominent passage in Paul's letter to the Galatians in which Paul claims that Christian unity in the person of Christ erases artificially constructed social divisions.[25] "there is neither Jew nor Greek, there is neither slave nor free person, there is not male and female; for you are all one in Christ Jesus."(3:28)

Aune considers this passage a remarkable testimony to early Christian egalitarianism "that seems to abolish in principle all inequalities based on nationality, social status, and gender."[26] Consistent with portrayals of Jesus in the Gospels, the letters of Paul make explicit what the narratives recounting the life of Christ imply. Christianity worships a God who has embraced all people as his children, and in this singular act of adoption, the social hierarchies of the world have been leveled. All have equal status as siblings who enjoy the parental care of one God.

As Christianity developed over the subsequent three centuries, this initial egalitarian ideal continued to mature. During this Patristic period, many of the greatest figures in the early Christian church express this equality by referring to Jesus as a brother to all believers and claiming that he was especially present in

---

25. David E. Aune, "Human Rights and Early Christianity," in *Christianity and Human Rights*, eds. John Witte and Frank S. Alexander (New York, NY: Cambridge University Press, 2010), 81–98.

26. Ibid., 87.

the poor and oppressed. Gregory of Nyssa, a fourth-century bishop and theologian, for instance, affirms that Christians must acknowledge the true identity of the poor and recognize their special dignity and role in the Christian community.[27] Likewise, John Chrysostom, another bishop and theologian, draws similar conclusions from the identification of Christ with the poor. Chrysostom believes the poor actually represent the person of Christ in a way the rich do not. "Because he is a poor man," Chrysostom argues, "feed him; because Christ is then fed, feed him."[28] Saint Augustine, theologian and Archbishop of Hippo, also exhorts his congregation to recognize Christ in the poor and lowly: "Hold in awe the Christ who is above; but recognize him here below. Have Christ above granting his bountiful gifts, but recognize him here in his need. Down here he is poor; up there he is rich."[29]

This identification of Christ with the poor and oppressed humanized marginalized groups in Christianity and ultimately grounds the notion of universal human rights. Human rights are literally unimaginable in a social milieu that deems some groups of people inferior or even outside the human family, while elevating other groups to a permanent privileged status. Societies marked by an asymmetrical distribution of power and wealth reserve the full litany of entitlements for the privileged, with the remainder forced to accept a more circumscribed version of rights. The early Christian church offered a new, more egalitarian way of imagining the human person that prepared the path for the more expansive, modern notion of human rights.

Catholic Social Teaching on Rights and Responsibilities

The philosophical discussions described earlier had a profound influence on the social teaching of the Church. In fact, Pope John XXIII's encyclical *Pacem in terris* (Peace on Earth, 1963) specifically singles out the UN Declaration on Human Rights for praise, identifying its mission as a uniquely noble one (nos. 142-45). Pope John Paul II did the same twenty-five years later in his encyclical *Sollicitudo rei socialis* (On Social Concern, 1987) (no. 26). The Catholic *magisterium* found inspiration for many of its reflections on human rights and duties from the wisdom of secular theories and practices. In this way, human rights are part

---

27. Johan Leemans, Brian J. Matz, Johan Verstraete, eds., *Reading Patristic Texts on Social Ethics* (Washington, DC: Catholic University of America Press, 2011), 222.

28. John Chrysostom, *Homily XLVIII*, *http://www.catholicprimer.org/chrysostom/matthew/homily048.htm*.

29. William J. Walsh and John P. Langen, "Patristic Social Consciousness—The Church and the Poor," in *The Faith That Does Justice: Examining the Christian Sources for Social Change*, ed. John C. Haughey (New York, NY: Paulist Press, 1977), 132.

a preexisting body of philosophical principles that the Church endorses and further develops with religious principles.

The discussion of rights in CST begins with the relative rights and duties of workers and their employers in Pope Leo XIII's 1891 encyclical, *Rerum novarum*. Catholic theology conceives of most human rights as relative values in that it understands them as, at least in part, earned through the performance of certain duties. This departs from the more unqualified value ascribed to rights in many liberal Western renditions of human rights theory. There, a human right is understood in much the same way Catholic social thought views human dignity—as an innate entitlement based on a person's identity as a person and not on what people do or how they act in society. Therefore, while the notion of human rights in CST does have some foundation in the more universal and inviolable notion of the dignity of the human person,[30] it functions as a practical application of human dignity theory that recognizes the give-and-take character of life in real societies. The Church, in this way, acknowledges that without a strong grounding in the ideal of human dignity, practical campaigns for human rights would lose their power of conviction. Conversely, the absence of the practical and balanced guidelines of rights and duties that help implement the ideals of human dignity in complex and contested circumstances would render human dignity theory an unattainable ideal.

Catholic social teaching also views rights as contextual in the sense that they sometimes exist, not unto themselves, but rather within a specific context, outside of which the rights may or may not apply. Again, this diverges from the universal rendition of human rights found in many liberal Western philosophies. In the late nineteenth century, the discussion of human rights took place in the context of a burgeoning labor movement that, in many cases, had adopted the language and arguments of socialism. Pope Leo XIII saw this as a danger and claimed that it is "no easy matter to define the relative rights and mutual duties of the rich and of the poor, of capital and of labor. And the danger lies in this, that crafty agitators are intent on making use of these differences of opinion to pervert men's judgments and to stir up the people to revolt" (*RN,* no. 2). The right to own property, expressed in *Rerum novarum* and subsequent documents was originally an argument against the radical socialist ideal of eliminating personal property altogether and relinquishing all ownership rights to the collective state.

The reasoning undergirding the right to private property, however, reflects more than just a simple rejection of socialism. It derives from scholastic natural law philosophy developed in the Middle Ages, which affirmed that the

---

30. Vatican Council II, *Gaudium et spes,* no. 26, *http://www.vatican.va/archive/hist_councils/ ii_vatican_council/documents/vat-ii_cons_19651207_gaudium-et-spes_en.html.*

individual was before society and, therefore, society should be ordered toward the advantage of its members and not the other way around.[31]

> Any well-regulated and productive association of men in society demands the acceptance of one fundamental principle: that each individual man is truly a person. His is a nature, that is, endowed with intelligence and free will. As such he has rights and duties, which together flow as a direct consequence from his nature. These rights and duties are universal and inviolable, and therefore altogether inalienable. (*Pacem in Terris*, no. 9)

The natural right to property is contingent upon a prior and more fundamental right of individuals to the fruits of their own labor. This right, in turn, becomes the foundation of the right and duty to work.[32] It also follows logically that the property, thus acquired through one's labor, can be freely disposed of at will. According to Pope John XXIII, *in Mater et magistra* (*MM*, Christianity and Social Progress, 1961), this suggests "that the exercise of freedom finds its guarantee and incentive in the right of ownership" (no. 109).

In this context, the right to engage in productive activity to secure personal property becomes the foundation of the right to marriage and family life. The church casts these rights in absolute terms and understands them as essential elements in a divinely mandated natural order: "In dealing with the family the Supreme Pontiff affirmed that the private ownership of material goods has a great part to play in promoting the welfare of family life" (*MM*, no. 45). For CST, the right to work ultimately establishes "a man's [*sic*] right and duty to be primarily responsible for his own upkeep and that of his family" (*MM*, no. 55).

> For, every man has by nature the right to possess property as his own. . . . It is the mind, or reason, which is the predominant element in us who are human creatures; it is this which renders a human being human, and distinguishes him essentially from the brute. And on this very account—that man alone among the animal creation is endowed with reason—it must be within his right to possess things not merely for temporary and momentary use, as other living things do, but to have and to hold them in stable and permanent possession; he must have not only things that perish in the use, but those also which, though they have been reduced into use, continue for further use in after time. (*RN*, no. 6)

---

31. John XXIII, *Mater et magistra* (1961), no. 109, *http://www.vatican.va/holy_father/john_xxiii/encyclicals/documents/hf_j-xxiii_enc_15051961_mater_en.html*.

32. Ibid., no. 44. See also John Paul II, *Laborem exercens* (1981), no. 16, *http://www.vatican.va/holy_father/john_paul_ii/encyclicals/documents/hf_jp-ii_enc_14091981_laborem-exercens_en.html*.

Catholic social teaching distinguishes between rights derived from nature and rights derived from practical human reason (*RN*, no. 47). *Rerum novarum* comes even closer to affirming a universal notion of human rights when it discusses the right to marriage and family life. In the document, Leo XIII uses traditional natural law arguments to assert that the natural order established by the divine will guarantees this right.

> No human law can abolish the natural and original right of marriage, nor in any way limit the chief and principal purpose of marriage ordained by God's authority from the beginning: "Increase and multiply"(Genesis 1:28). Hence we have the family, the "society" of a man's house—a society very small, one must admit, but none the less a true society, and one older than any State. Consequently, it has rights and duties peculiar to itself which are quite independent of the State. (*RN*, no. 12)

The state may aid families that find themselves in dire distress, but it may not otherwise interfere with the natural patriarchal prerogative to, as the saying goes, rule the castle (*RN*, no. 14).

The document, though, does offer an absolute justification of property ownership. *Rerum novarum* and Catholic social thought, in general, treat all rights as relative and contingent upon the performance of one's duty to society. Therefore, after forcefully defending the right to private ownership, Leo XIII explains how private property always carries a social mortgage (*RN*, no. 22). That is, an individual can legitimately possess private property in excess of immediate needs only to the extent that others in society do not need that property. This is not a law of justice enforceable by the state but rather a law of charity written on the hearts of humans by Christ. It ultimately grounds the idea of the universal destination of the good of creation found throughout CST (*MM*, no. 43).[33] The natural right to private property functions within this larger context of divine providence that is ordered toward universal beneficence and the common good. It highlights the notion in Catholic social thought of "the personal right of all to the use of worldly goods"(*MM*, no. 74). Indeed, as noted in *Mater et magistra*, "Our predecessors have insisted time and again on the social function inherent in the right of private ownership, for it cannot be denied that in the plan of the Creator all of this world's goods are primarily intended for the worthy support of the entire human race"(no. 119).

Catholic social teaching clarifies its understanding of private property and its "social mortgage" over time by weighing the natural right to private property

---

33. See also Paul VI, *Populorum progressio* (1967), no. 22, *http://www.vatican.va/holy_father/ paul_vi/encyclicals/documents/hf_p-vi_enc_26031967_populorum_en.html.*

ownership against the duties imposed by that ownership.[34] Humans have a right to own private property, but that right carries the obligation to dispose of the property in a way primarily ordered toward addressing the needs of the poor and dispossessed. When their needs have been met, any additional wealth can be held or disposed of at the discretion of the owner. This mechanism of disbursement assures that private property will serve the common good, rather than merely a private good or, even worse, self-aggrandizement at the expense of society.

One of the many highlights of *Rerum novarum* is its insistence on the right of workers to form associations of mutual aid, or unions, which was considered a radical and significant expansion of the notion of rights in the West at that time (*RN*, nos. 55–56). The Catholic Church recognizes exceptions to the right of workers to form unions. Most important, these organizations cannot be inimical to the Church or to the spiritual pursuits of its members (*RN*, no. 54). Nevertheless, "such associations may consist either of workers alone or of workers and employers, and should be structured in a way best calculated to safeguard the workers' legitimate professional interest. And it is the natural right of the workers to work without hindrance, freely, and on their own initiative within these associations for the achievement of these ends" (*MM*, no. 22).

Not only do workers have a right to form associations, but also they have the right to strike in the face of unjust wages and working conditions and when other tactics have yielded no progress in redressing the injustice (*LE*, no. 20). Workers who resort to strikes and other extreme negotiating tactics in pursuit of social justice must remain conscious of the common good and how their tactics might harm the greater good of society if done carelessly or taken to an extreme (*LE*, no. 20). The state has a duty to guarantee the right of workers to unionize and strike if circumstances necessitate such tactics. It should guarantee the rights of every citizen, but workers and the poor require special consideration because of their relative weakness and vulnerability to exploitation (*RN*, no. 37).

Catholic social teaching also establishes the right to a living wage and the corresponding obligation of the owners of capital to set their pay scales accordingly. The right to a living wage rests on the precepts of justice and is frequently referred to as a *just wage* in Catholic social thought (*LE*, no. 19). Pope Leo XIII established the concept of the living wage when discussing different elements of the meaning of human labor and referred to it as a moral necessity.

> But our conclusion must be very different if, together with the personal element in a man's work, we consider the fact that work is also necessary for him to live: these two aspects of his work are separable in thought, but not in reality. The preservation of life is the bounden duty of one and

---

34. Pius XI, *Quadragesimo anno* (1931), no. 47, *http://www.vatican.va/holy_father/pius_xi/ encyclicals/documents/hf_p-xi_enc_19310515_quadragesimo-anno_en.html.*

all, and to be wanting therein is a crime. It necessarily follows that each one has a natural right to procure what is required in order to live, and the poor can procure that in no other way than by what they can earn through their work. (*RN*, no. 44)

As it developed through the twentieth and into the twenty-first centuries, and under the influence of the UN Declaration on Human Rights, CST expanded the list of rights a person holds in society. By the middle of the twentieth century, Pope John XXIII included education, health care, and leisure, among others, in his more comprehensive treatment of rights in (*MM*, no. 61).

Two years later, the same pope issued the encyclical *Pacem in terris*, whose lengthy introductory section provided a thoroughgoing treatment of human rights, beginning with the right to life and extending to moral and cultural values, religion and conscience,[35] the right to freely choose one's station in life, a series of economic rights, including the right to work and the right to a living wage,[36] the right of free association, the rights to emigrate and immigrate, and finally the political rights that protect and defend universal participation in the decisions made for a society.[37] Later documents of CST added to this ever-growing menu of human rights in the workplace by including the right to a safe work environment and to a pension (*LE*, no. 19).

Pacem in terris follows up its Catholic "Magna Carta" with an explication of how freedoms, rights, and privileges in society are inextricably bound to the duties of individuals to society.[38] In fact, it asserts that "rights presuppose duties, if they are not to become mere licence" (*CV*, no. 43).

An overemphasis on rights leads to a disregard for duties. Duties set a limit on rights because they point to the anthropological and ethical framework of which rights are a part, in this way ensuring that they do not become licence. Duties thereby reinforce rights and call for their defence and promotion as a task to be undertaken in the service of the common good. (*CV*, no. 43)

Social relationships include reciprocity; individuals contribute to the common good of society in exchange for the rights and freedoms they enjoy (*PT*, no. 30). This explains the insistence in Catholic social thought on pairing entitlements (rights) with duties owed in return for the benefits of citizenship.

---

35. See also John Paul II, *Centesimus annus*, no. 29.1, *http://www.vatican.va/holy_father/john_paul_ii/encyclicals/documents/hf_jp-ii_enc_01051991_centesimus-annus_en.html*.

36. See also John Paul II, *Laborem exercens*, no. 8.

37. See John XXIII, *Pacem in terris*, nos. 11–27.

38. See Ibid., nos. 28–45. See also Benedict XVI, *Caritas in veritate*, no. 6, *http://www.vatican.va/holy_father/benedict_xvi/encyclicals/documents/hf_ben-xvi_enc_20090629_caritas-in-veritate_en.html*.

Every basic human right draws its authoritative force from the natural law, which confers it and attaches to it its respective duty. Hence, to claim one's rights and ignore one's duties, or only half fulfill them, is like building a house with one hand and tearing it down with the other. (*PT,* no. 30)

It follows from this extensive development of human rights and duties that government, or the public authority, has a responsibility to guarantee and protect the rights of its citizens and to ensure that citizens follow through on their obligations to respect the rights and freedoms of others (*PT,* no. 60): "Thus any government which refused to recognize human rights or acted in violation of them, would not only fail in its duty; its decrees would be wholly lacking in binding force" (*PT,* no. 61). In this role, the government must take a balanced approach to the protection of rights, neither favoring any one group in society to the detriment of others nor focusing so exclusively on protecting certain rights that it violates other related rights in the process. In the latter case, the pope refers especially to interventions in the marketplace that attempt to equalize market relations or promote the welfare of disadvantaged groups.[39] In these cases, the pursuit of what under normal circumstances might be considered laudable goals, could infringe on the property and labor rights of other citizens if implemented improperly (*PT,* no. 65). The imposition of a minimum wage set so high as to interfere with business owners' capacity to hire affordable labor offers one example of this kind of state infringement of rights. Governing authorities must protect society against its own potential to impose these sorts of artificial imbalances in the economy.

Because of their innate and unique dignity, humans do not lose their natural rights when their citizenship is compromised or relinquished, such as in the case of refugees. As noted in *Pacem in terris*: "For this reason, it is not irrelevant to draw the attention of the world to the fact that these refugees are persons and all their rights as persons must be recognized. Refugees cannot lose these rights simply because they are deprived of citizenship of their own States" (no. 105). Just as individuals possess rights and duties in relation to one another and society, so too states have reciprocal rights and duties in relation to each other (*PT,* no. 80).[40] Like the individual's right to life that must be respected by other individuals and society as a whole, a legitimate state has the right to be recognized by other states to the extent that its borders are respected.

In addition to addressing major theoretical and practical aspects of rights and responsibilities, official Catholic social documents also explore human rights

---

39. Paul VI, *Populorum progressio* (1967), no. 33, *http://www.vatican.va/holy_father/paul_vi/ encyclicals/documents/hf_p-vi_enc_26031967_populorum_en.html*.

40. See also *Gaudium et spes*, no. 87.

and responsibilities as they pertain to the many communities that make up society. For instance, within the context of the rights of all laborers, Pope John Paul II discussed the rights of disabled workers for the first time in official Catholic teaching in *Laborem exercens* (On Human Work, 1981) (no 52). Ten years earlier, Pope Paul VI addressed the rights of women in the workplace, bringing up their special needs and their critical place in the workforce.[41] The same document raised the issue of racism, describing it as a violation of the basic rights of people within a society to equal and unbiased treatment before the law and in the marketplace (*OA*, no. 16). In recent years, Pope Benedict XVI expanded rights language to include even nonhuman life in the quest to more closely mirror the perfection of the Kingdom of God here on Earth (*CV*, nos. 43–44). In short, the language of rights and responsibilities functions as the practical facade overlaid on the loftier and more abstract undergirding of human dignity and the common good within CST It is the way these broader themes are worked out in policies, regulations, and laws that either violate human dignity and the common good or serve to establish, uphold, and preserve these sublime principles.

Rights and Responsibilities in a Contemporary Business Setting

The discussion of rights has focused on the rights and duties that an individual possesses within the setting of the state. Despite some indirect applications to the kinds of issues corporations face, especially those involving international production and trade, these rights and duties may seem at first glance to offer few lessons to take back to the boardroom or the shop floor. However, a close examination of the headlines in the business section of almost any news source reveals several ways this theme applies to the workplace.

One recent example highlights the applicability of rights and responsibilities: the conflict between Google and the Chinese government in 2009–10 over the censorship of YouTube videos and web searches concerning the protest in Tiananmen Square in 1989. At the time, Google had been in China for four years and had already made a number of adaptations to their services in response to requests from the Chinese government to control and limit the kinds of information Google made available to its end users. During this time, Google engaged in self-censorship by not displaying search results for a list of words and phrases provided by the Chinese government. Instead, users who typed in any of the forbidden words or phrases would see the following message: "In

---

41. Paul VI, *Octagesima adveniens* (1971), no. 13, *http://www.vatican.va/holy_father/paul_vi/apost_letters/documents/hf_p-vi_apl_19710514_octogesima-adveniens_en.html.*

accordance with local laws, regulations and policies, part of the search result is not shown."[42] Many in the media called Google's self-censorship hypocritical because it blatantly contradicted the company's publicly stated principles, especially its commitment to democracy on the web and to doing no evil.[43] In 2010, the company decided to end self-censorship, move its Chinese operations out of mainland China to the island of Hong Kong, and give users the free and unfettered right to information the company had touted since its inception. Google violated what it considered a fundamental right for the sake of establishing itself in China, but ultimately Google chose principle over compromise.[44]

Although not everyone would agree that the human right to liberty encompasses unmitigated access to internet information, in this case, Google had committed its corporate culture to such an interpretation of human liberty. For Google, this was a moment of truth; the company had to choose to either remain true to its founding principles or compromise those principles for the sake of expediency and profit. Google's vacillation and temporary capitulation to Chinese authorities testifies to the pressure it felt to comply. Yet its deference to the Chinese government came at a high cost. Google's discovery that the Chinese government had broken into the Gmail accounts of suspected dissidents and members of the Falun Gong cult was the last straw, and the company announced its intent to end self-censorship and move its Chinese operations to a location in which it would be free of government intimidation.[45]

The case of Google highlights whether corporations should commit their culture to human rights and closely audit overseas operations to ensure that at all points along the production process, from conception to product delivery, remain free of human rights violations. Even companies with renowned corporate codes of ethics, such as Google, can make compromises harmful to basic human rights. Google learned that human rights are morally exceptional principles that do not allow room for violation or even compromise. CST calls for executives, managers, and employees to remain vigilant for circumstances that could lead to human rights abuses or the perception of cooperation with governments, organizations, or other businesses that abuse the rights of their citizens and members. Corporate codes of ethics, according to CST, should prioritize those

---

42. Andrew Jacobs, "Follow the Law, China Tells Internet Companies," *New York Times* (January 14, 2010): *http://www.nytimes.com/2010/01/15/world/asia/15beijing.html?_r=0.*

43. Google's corporate philosophy can be found at *http://www.google.com/about/company/philosophy/.*

44. George G. Brenkert, "Google, Human Rights, and Moral Compromise," *Journal of Business Ethics,* 85 (4): 453–478.

45. For more information on the case of Google in China, see Henry Gao, "Google's China Problem: A Case Study of Trade Technology and Human Rights," *Asian Journal of WTO & International Health Law and Policy,* 6/2 (9/1/2011): 349–87.

parts that relate in some way to human rights and be certain that compliance with those codes is absolute.

Conclusion

Overall, the theme of rights and responsibilities in the Catholic Church's social teaching can offer guidelines for balancing entitlements against responsibilities in social relationships. Because corporations, even relatively small ones, are societies unto themselves, this theme has a lot to say about properly governing a business and distributing burdens and benefits fairly within an organization. All positions in a company aligned with the principles of CST, from the lowest-paid stock workers to the highest-paid executives, receive benefits, entitlements and privileges, and each has corresponding responsibilities, duties, and tasks. The right to a paycheck assumes the responsibility to perform one's job duties to the best of one's abilities. The right to a company car assumes the responsibility to use it only for trips approved by company policy. The right to a break in the workday assumes the responsibility to take that break at a time that does not compromise the business or harm other workers. Although CST addresses only those entitlements serious enough to be properly called *rights*, the thrust of the argument acknowledges that all of human relationships, including those of the marketplace, require some kind of equity and balance.

Case Study

No Hershey's Kisses for Children of Africa

The town of Hershey, Pennsylvania, boasts a magnificent amusement park, a medical center, headquarters for the Hershey Foundation, and the corporate offices for the Hershey Corporation. This iconic setting is a far cry from that of western Africa where the processes of making the sweet, delectable Hershey treats are initiated. Children there are not enjoying chocolate, but the drive for greater profits is biting deeply into their lives and communities. In Ghana, on the west coast of Africa, children are being forced onto cocoa farms. Some children, as young as nine, can spend seven days a week hidden deep in the jungles of Ghana harvesting cocoa beans from pods on trees.[46] These cocoa beans, the key ingredient

(continued)

---

46. "Tracing the Bitter Truth of Chocolate and Child Labour," BBC/Panorama, 2010. *http://news.bbc.co.uk/panorama/hi/front_page/newsid_8583000/8583499.stm.*

Case Study   *(continued)*

in chocolate manufacturing, are then shipped to processing plants to produce the sweet chocolate so many people enjoy. Cocoa, or "black gold" as it is known in Ghana, is the nation's biggest cash crop, employing 1.5 million people—86,000 of them children.[47] In fact, Ghana is the world's largest producer of cocoa after the Ivory Coast.[48]

Because of its proximity to surrounding bodies of water and its strategic placement on western Africa's "Gold Coast," Ghana was regarded historically as the center of the slave trade for that part of the continent. Despite efforts to institute anti-slavery laws, child slavery continues in the cocoa fields of Ghana in modern times. In addition to the long working hours, labor conditions for these children can be quite abusive. Children are forced to work under extremely hot temperatures with no sun protection, engage in physically demanding work practices, and be exposed to all sorts of unhealthy, even poisonous pesticides.[49] There also have been allegations on the farms of physical torture and sexual abuse.

Slavery on these cocoa farms is fueled by the practice of human trafficking in which children are sold by parents in order to generate income for their families, in spite of the fact that, by Western standards, the pay is pathetically low, averaging about 40 cents for twelve hours of hard labor. For these families in western Africa, however, it is an income they desperately need to make ends meet. Increased consumption drives up demand for cocoa, which in turn drives up demand for scarce labor. Cocoa farmers in Ghana claim that they can keep up with this demand only by resorting to child slavery and human trafficking.

Ghana's government acknowledges that child labor on the cocoa plantations is a tragic violation of human rights that needs to be addressed. Leaders in this nation are under pressure to eradicate child labor and restore the right of human dignity to children. Because of their extensive time-consuming work on the cocoa farms, children are unable to attend school. This practice violates the International Labor Organization (ILO) child-labor standards.[50]

(continued)

---

47. "Ghana: Efforts to Reduce Child Labour on Cocoa Plantations Beginning to Pay Off," Integrated Regional Information Networks (IRIN), September 23, 2011, *http://www.refworld.org/docid/4e818b612.html*.

48. "Ghana Investment Promotion Centre: Cash Crops," *http://www.gipcghana.com/page.php?page=207&section=32&typ=1&subs=209*.

49. "16x9 Darker Side of Chocolate," *http://www.youtube.com/watch?v=nLfNDhbQfmk*.

50. "Convention 182—Convention Concerning the Prohibition and Immediate Action for the Elimination of the Worst Forms of Child Labour," 1999, International Labour Organization (ILO) *http://www.ilo.org/public/english/standards/relm/ilc/ilc87/com-chic.htm*.

Case Study

(continued)

Human rights organizations claim that in addition to violating international law, the farmers and the political leaders of Ghana are denying enslaved children a potentially brighter future by depriving them of a proper education. It has been argued that by purchasing cocoa from Ghana and not protesting against these deplorable conditions, Hershey and other multinational corporations participate indirectly in these abuses.

The government in Ghana has made some efforts to resolve the human rights abuses associated with child enslavement. There is evidence to support its claim. In 2001, companies purchasing cocoa from Ghana signed the Harkin-Engel Protocol, which aligned corporate practices with ILO child-labor standards. Many Ghanaian children have been freed from slavery on the cocoa farms and are being placed back in schools. Additional assistance has been given to these children's families to help them understand the value of education.[51]

In concert with these progressive local and international efforts undertaken by human rights organizations such as the World Cocoa Foundation, other groups are stepping up to exert pressure on Hershey and other chocolate producers that have a stake in cocoa production in Ghana (and the Ivory Coast).[52] While there are no concrete *sustainable* steps that the Ghanaian government has taken to fully abolish this cache of human rights abuses, there are consolidated international efforts to mitigate the abuse of child labor. Three NGOs have formed a human rights coalition called, "Raise the Bar, Hershey!" (*www.raisethebarhershey.org/*) in order to hold Hershey accountable for its part in human rights violations in Ghana.

Creation of a supply chain that values human rights and corresponding responsibilities is a major challenge for any multinational company.[53] Hershey may be tempted to model its behavior on other corporations that have overlooked similar exploitative actions in order to maintain financially lucrative supply chains. However, the reputation of the company is at stake as more and more of the abuse and exploitation of human rights at the lower end

(continued)

---

51. "West Africa: Cocoa Industry Moves against Child Labour," *http://www.irinnews.org/Report/32833/WEST-AFRICA-Cocoa-industry-moves-against-child-labour*.

52. World Cocoa Foundation, "Committed to Cocoa-Growing Communities," *http://worldcocoafoundation.org/wp-content/files_mf/2012wcfbrochure.pdf*.

53. Hershey's labor rights violations have also occurred in the United States. The US Department of Labor fined Hershey $283,000 for health and safety violations that they attempted to obfuscate. More specific to this case, however, is that Hershey's plants were also cited for using undocumented foreign students as workers, *http://www.osha.gov/pls/oshaweb/owadisp.show_document?p_table=NEWS_RELEASES&p_id=21852*.

Case Study   *(continued)*

of their supply chain is revealed. As the world's leading confectioner, can Hershey continue to purchase cocoa from sources that have clearly violated international law, while still maintaining that it is "doing well by doing good," as they claim on their webpage? (*www.thehersheycompany.com*)

Meanwhile, Hershey has made identifiable strides toward greater corporate responsibility regarding these issues. Jeff Beckman, Hershey's spokesperson, indicated that the company was involved in partnerships with public and private groups to purge inappropriate labor practices in cocoa communities. As a testimony to Hershey's efforts, a group called Rainforest Alliance believes it can certify that Hershey develops its Bliss chocolate line in accordance with human rights and environmental standards. For its part, Hershey announced in 2012 it was making efforts to ensure that by 2020 all of its cocoa would come from suppliers that meet international labor standards.[54]

Questions

1. Why is it difficult to enforce good corporate behavior in multinational corporations such as Hershey, which depends on a variety of suppliers that are often located in developing areas of the world?

2. Can Hershey be held responsible for the labor practices of its suppliers? To what extent is Hershey being pressured to oversee and regulate the operations of foreign suppliers in ways that mimic the actions that a government ought to take?

3. When people purchase Hershey's products, patronize its amusement park, see a doctor at the Hershey Hospital, or support the company's foundation, are they cooperating in human rights abuses?

4. What kind of ethical responsibility, if any, does Hershey have to Ghana should it no longer need its cocoa?

---

54. Grant Reid, "The Hershey Company Pledges to Source 100% Certified Sustainable Cocoa," October 5, 2012, *http://cocoasustainability.com/2012/10/the-hershey-company-pledges-to-source-100-certified-sustainable-cocoa-2/.*

Case Study

The Bitter Internal Drive of Apple

Apple, Inc. [NSQ: APPL] has revolutionized computing. Apple's brilliant, technologically intuitive devices have become legion throughout the world. While other corporations have attempted to introduce competing products similar to Apple's iPod, iPhone, iPad, and AppleTV, few have been as successful as Apple. In the last fiscal quarter of 2012 alone, people purchased 26.9 million iPhones, 14 million iPads, 4.9 million Macs, and 5.3 million iPods. These numbers of units sold represent significant growth over sales from the previous year. Whether it's the "user experience" that Apple delivers to its customers or the brand appeal, customers keep returning to buy more Apple products as well as to upgrade the ones that they already own.

When Steve Jobs, the masterful engineering genius behind Apple, died in 2011, investors and users speculated about whether Apple could continue with its same creative expansion. Job's successor, Tim Cook, did not disappoint. After the elegies for Jobs were completed, Apple went on to release a new iPad that garnered unprecedented sales. In addition to the new iPad, Apple would follow up with upgrades to the iPhone and the iPad mini.

Apple's stock price ended around $500 in 2012, 31 percent better than only a year before, which demonstrated Apple's dominance as one of the highest-valued companies in the market and a leader in its sector.[55] Apple's market capitalization ($612 billion in 2012) was larger than the gross domestic product of many countries in the world.

As wealthy and powerful as Apple has become, it has not been beyond reproach. In January 2012, stories about harsh working conditions at Foxconn went viral on social media, and ultimately made their way onto mainstream news outlets. Foxconn is a Taiwanese electronics manufacturer to which Apple and other technological giants had outsourced the assembly of their products. Reports of deplorable and reprehensible labor conditions at Foxconn spread quickly. They detailed child labor, an unhealthy, even toxic environment, dangerous physical working conditions, unjust and demanding management, lack of normal access to bathrooms, compromised living quarters, long hours, and low wages.

In a dramatic move in May 2010, Foxconn erected "suicide nets" around its factory buildings after eighteen employees attempted suicide and

(continued)

---

55. Jay Yarow, "Surprise! Apple's 2012 Was Better Than Its 2011," *http://www.businessinsider.com/chart-of-the-day-apple-stock-performance-2013-1#ixzz2UV7GPMUF.*

Case Study   *(continued)*

fourteen were "successful" in this desperate flight from harsh working condi-tions.[56] These workers' deaths at Foxconn factories drew attention from Asia and across the world as the human rights abuses were exposed. Foxconn's Chairman Terry Gou tried to distance Foxconn from these employee suicides and abruptly ended condolence payments to suicide victims' families, after previously claiming that deceased employees' families counted on the death benefits for survival. In response to this scandal, Steve Jobs remarked: "Fox-conn is not a sweatshop. You go in this place and it's a factory, but, by gosh, they've got restaurants and movie theatres and hospitals and swimming pools. For a factory, it's pretty nice."[57]

As pressure was put on Foxconn to produce the iPad 2, employees found themselves subjected to deadly chemicals within the Apple product they were assembling. In May 2011, there was a blast at an iPad 2 plant in south-west China. Three people were killed and fifteen suffered severe injuries.

Meanwhile, Apple became a member of the Fair Labor Association (FLA), which reviews workplaces to uncover any serious labor violations and rec-ommends remedial actions.[58] In February 2012, the FLA investigated Apple's suppliers, and it became evident that Foxconn employees' rights were con-sistently compromised in favor of increased production. The FLA's report confirmed that employees worked more than sixty hours a week—often working seven days a week.

Foxconn made efforts to rectify the harsh working conditions. In con-junction with the FLA, Apple and Foxconn worked together to set up a fifteen-point plan to improve working conditions. The labor conditions, however, only seemed to get worse. In June 2012, one hundred Foxconn workers rioted, and in September, a massive fight involving as many as 2,000 Foxconn employees left many injuries in its wake. Foxconn exec-utives dismissed these as inconsequential disagreements that escalated into large brawls.

Unfortunately, Apple and Foxconn failed to comply with the Fair Labor Association agreement. In October 2012, Foxconn was caught using four-teen-year-olds in its factories, thereby breaking a law that identified sixteen

(continued)

---

56. David Barboza, "After Suicides, Scrutiny of China's Grim Factories," *The New York Times* 6 (2010). Malcolm Moore, "Mass Suicide Protest at Apple Manufacturer Foxconn Factory," *The Telegraph* (2012).

57. "Steve Jobs says Foxconn in China 'Not a Sweatshop' after Worker Deaths," *The Guardian*, June 2, 2010, *http://www.guardian.co.uk/technology/2010/jun/02/steve-jobs-foxconn-china-not-sweatshop*.

58. Worldwide, Improving Workers' Lives, "Foxconn Verification Status Report," 2012, *http://www.fairlabor.org/sites/default/files/documents/reports/foxconn_verification_report_final.pdf*.

Case Study   *(continued)*

as the minimum working age. Foxconn further abdicated its responsibility to civil law by offering proprietary contracts to its parts suppliers.[59]

When media outlets reported on Foxconn's extensive history of compromising the human rights of its employees, there seemed to be an initial groundswell of sympathetic concern for the horrors perpetuated at its factories. Many were disturbed by stories of workers being exposed to lethal chemicals as they assembled Apple's liquid crystal screens but chalked it up to product development "costs." The pictures of "suicide nets" that Foxconn installed on the sides of its factory also heightened public interest for a short period of time, but eventually attention waned and consumers returned to their lives and continued buying Apple products, seemingly unfazed by the controversies at Foxconn.

Questions

1. Foxconn has raised questions about continuing to act as a supplier for Apple, investigating options with other high-tech firms. Foxconn has indicated that it has taken too much of the blame for the human rights abuses that should have been shared with Apple. What degree of responsibility does Apple have in this case?

2. Outsourcing has been an efficient and profitable option for many multinational corporations. What responsibility does the primary producer have to ensure that human rights are fostered and responsibilities are met by the subcontracting company?

3. Many people own at least one Apple product. To what degree are consumers cooperating in the human rights abuses at Foxconn?

4. It could be argued that if it weren't for Apple using Foxconn as its supplier, the people working in these factories might suffer even more from human rights violations. After all, Apple is attempting to remedy violations that the FLA identifies. Further, without Apple's demand for their labor, the workers might not have jobs and might be living lives of abject poverty. Is this supply chain, despite the credible reports of human rights abuses, a "necessary evil"?

59. Charles Riley, "Foxconn in China Bribery Investigation," January 9, 2013, *http://money.cnn.com/2013/01/09/technology/foxconn-china-bribery/index.html.*

For Further Reading

Davila Gomez, Ana Maria, and David Crowther. *Human Dignity and Managerial Responsibility: Diversity, Rights, and Sustainability.* Farnham, UK: Gower, 2011.

Hanlon, Robert J. *Corporate Social Responsibility and Human Rights in Asia.* Abingdon, Oxon; New York: Routledge, 2014

Heinze, Eric A. *Justice, Sustainability, and Security Global Ethics for the 21st Century.* New York: Palgrave Macmillan, 2013.

International Council on Human Rights Policy. *Beyond Voluntarism: Human Rights and the Developing International Legal Obligations of Companies.* Versoix: International Council on Human Rights Policy, 2002.

Karp, David Jason. *Responsibility for Human Rights: Transnational Corporations in Imperfect States.* Cambridge: Cambridge University Press, 2014.

Ruggie, John Gerard. *Just Business: Multinational Corporations and Human Rights.* New York: Norton, 2013.

Sullivan, Rory. *Business and Human Rights: Dilemmas and Solutions.* Sheffield England: Greenleaf, 2003.

Voiculescu, Aurora, and Helen Yanacopulos. *The Business of Human Rights: An Evolving Agenda for Corporate Responsibility.* London: Zed Books, 2011.

Conclusion

A Catholic Understanding of the Nature of Business

Thomas O'Brien

Those tackling questions of business ethics for the first time often make hard and fast distinctions between—and assumptions about—the idealistic world of the ethicists and the real world of business. Many assume that the business "insider" has the correct, factual, and practical perspective and look with disdain upon the impractical, fanciful, and distorted viewpoints of idealistic academics. They believe that ethicists neither understand the deeper value of competition in the marketplace nor recognize that this value comes at the cost of a more brutal, dog-eat-dog corporate environment. Competitive global markets that, with each passing year, supply better goods and services at cheaper prices do so at the expense of pricey and inefficient labor markets in the developed world. Likewise, they argue that ethicists don't understand that there is no "free lunch." Better-paid employees that have better benefits, a cleaner environment, fairer hiring practices, and safer products all come at a cost, and sometimes that cost is prohibitive.

However, these observers rarely look at the discrepancy between the real world and the idealistic world from a third vantage point; that is, from the point of view of those concerned with how businesses conduct themselves. Doing so might yield entirely different results. From the perspective of the ethicist, the unshakable confidence in the idea that unmitigated self-interested behavior will inevitably result in a more efficient and just economy seems unrealistic. Global markets that produce cheaper goods and services do so by exchanging high-wage jobs in developed countries for low-wage, sweat-shop labor in the underdeveloped world. They find it unbelievable that many defenders of the status quo cannot identify the culprit behind the economic collapse of 2008 and the spate of corporate accounting scandals—unbridled self-interest and a corporate culture that nurtures and encourages it at every opportunity.

The Orthodox Theory of the Capitalist Marketplace

Business is the organization of human labor in such a way that it creates value for those who consume the products and services that result. Value is an economic measure of human desire. Business is an engine of human productivity that generates value.[1] Human labor has the potential to add value to an otherwise raw and unmodified natural state of affairs, and this additional value serves as the foundation of the modern theory of private property ownership. John Locke formulated the theory in the seventeenth century, observing that when agricultural intervention improved the otherwise raw state of nature, then the land and its products rightfully belonged to the farmer—the one whose labor made the land productive and valuable.[2] From a theological perspective, God had created an imperfect world with the purpose of offering a challenge to humans who possessed the unique gifts of instrumental reason to solve practical problems and cocreate a new and more perfect world.[3]

The absence of the word *profit* in this definition of business is deliberate; profit is merely a byproduct of business activity. While perhaps the main motivational force behind executive and stockholder decisions, it is not required for a business to exist. Not all businesses are profitable. Indeed, some very good businesses have gone through extended periods of little or no profit. Some business models, even within the capitalist economy, do not require profit generation; that is, nonprofit cooperatives like credit unions.[4]

A just or good society, according to most orthodox versions of capitalism, leads to the maximization of utility. Profit facilitates utility maximization because it greases the proverbial wheels of progress through the reinvestment of excess capital. Its supporters argue that the capitalist system has the greatest potential to maximize utility because it embraces the notion of profit and encourages the progressive reinvestment of this excess capital into the production of future value. The system claims to be "utilitarian" in a broad sense of the term; however, because no one in the system actually assesses all practical options and chooses

---

1. The line of reasoning here is an extension of the argument advanced by Paul Camenisch, "Business Ethics: On Getting to the Heart of the Matter," in *Business, Religion, and Ethics* (Cambridge, MA: Oelgeschlager, Gunn & Hain, 1982). He argues that the "heart" of business is found neither in its productivity, nor in its profits, but in the *kinds* of products it makes. By making products that authentically contribute to human well-being, a business literally and figuratively proves its worth.

2. John Locke, *The Second Treatise of Civil Government*, Chapter 5, Sec. 37, *www.constitution. org—2ndtreat.htm*.

3. Michael Novak, *The Spirit of Democratic Capitalism* (New York: Simon & Schuster, 1982): 39.

4. Max Weber would strongly disagree with both Camenisch and me on this point, claiming that "capitalism is identical with the pursuit of profit." Weber, Max. *The Protestant Ethic and the Spirit of Capitalism* (New York: Charles Scribner's and Sons, 1958), 17.

the one that maximizes utility, it is not utilitarian in the narrow philosophical sense of the term.

Most dilemmas in business, ethical or otherwise, come about as a result of this "utilitarian" foundation, which reduces critical ethical decisions to a cost-benefit analysis. One can point to countless famous business ethics cases to highlight crude versions of this kind of calculus that, on the one hand, seem to make perfect business sense, yet on the other, offend the moral sensibilities of most who read them. In the Ford Pinto case, for example, the company faced a decision between making costly revisions to the design of their subcompact car that would delay the release of this strategically important automobile or ignoring the problem and accepting the probability that the company would face costs associated with lawsuits and bad press. The company chose to forego any changes to the Pinto and to take their chances with the current flawed design. This decision, based on a cost-benefit analysis, seemed to place a monetary value on the life of a human person.

Most people seem to instinctively understand something is wrong with this strictly materialistic view of the human person and society. They deem it grossly immoral to place a monetary value on human life. From the perspective of the cost-benefit analysis, *value* is understood as an entirely tangible quantity that can be maximized. This rendition of *value* includes nothing subjective or immaterial; the model ignores or trivializes values other than material wealth. Herein lies the moral conundrum faced by contemporary business ethicists: How does one inject a more comprehensive theory of value into a discussion that has been systematically purged of such ideas?

Contemporary business ethicists suggest that the very inception of capitalist theory—Adam Smith's *Wealth of Nations* and his "invisible hand" argument— offers a logical place to start this discussion. Most capitalist theorists point to this work as the foundation of market theory and interpret it as defending a raw type of self-interest that is frequently indistinguishable from unadulterated selfishness. However, a thorough and critical reading of Smith's entire corpus yields a very different conclusion. Smith's theory of the invisible hand really represents a kind of natural law—a belief that God so ordered the universe that even when people behave in such a way as to achieve only their own good, they nevertheless—by means of the mysterious and wonderful invisible hand of providence—end up achieving the greatest good of all. Therefore, Smith concluded, it is possible that an unrestricted competitive marketplace filled with individuals pursuing the maximization of their own personal utility (without consideration of the good of others or society as a whole) will result in the common good much more effectively than any other system—especially those that make lofty altruistic claims.

Smith's capitalist interpreters often truncate their descriptions of the invisible hand, leaving the impression that Smith would endorse a rapacious form of economic and social Darwinism in which individuals in a society are cast against one another in a dog-eat-dog competition for scarce resources. Numerous experts of Smith's entire corpus have reacted to this characterization of his principle of the invisible hand using his earlier work, *The Theory of Moral Sentiments,* to inform a more nuanced interpretation that suggests Smith understood the self-interest of the individual within the context of the individual's ethical responsibilities to others.[5] In other words, self-interest did not mean selfishness to Smith; it described a natural tendency that normally would result in the good of all but sometimes needed to be checked against the moral claims of others.

Taken to its extreme, the belief that pursuit of self-interest in free competitive markets will inevitably lead to the common good can be a very naive perspective, one that ignores the accumulation of power and its application. Wealth itself is a form of power that can manipulate markets so that they do not serve the greater good but only serve the relative advantage of a small group of elites. Monopolies provide one example of power accumulation that often leads to high prices, inferior products, and the wielding of dictatorial power by the monopolistic firm.[6]

Even some defenders of democratic capitalism acknowledge the problems associated with accumulated power in capitalist markets. One such defender, Michael Novak, acknowledges four valid objections commonly made by socialists to capitalist markets:

> (1) Markets resolve problems according to the purchasing power of those who have money. One dollar may be analogous to one vote, and those who have more dollars have more votes than those who have fewer. (2) Modern advertising distorts the judgments of those who have money, so that market decisions are far less rational than they should be. (3) Large corporations are able to place administered prices on their goods, either in collusion with other suppliers or through their power over particular markets. (4) Markets work in such a way that the rich get richer and the poor get poorer.[7]

One can see the effects of accumulated power in modern North American markets: What—other than distortions in power relationships in the

---

5. Harvey S. James and Farad Rassekh, "Smith, Friedman, and Self-interest in Ethical Society," *Business Ethics Quarterly* 10, no. 3 (July 2000): 659–674. See also Stephen Young, *Moral Capitalism: Reconciling Private Interest with Public Good* (San Francisco, CA: Berrett-Koehler Publishers Inc., 2003), 34–35. For more on interpreting Smith from the perspective of his earlier works, see also Michael Novak, *Three in One: Essays on Democratic Capitalism, 1976–2000* (New York, NY: Rowman & Littlefield Publishers Inc., 2001), 34. See also James R. Otteson, *Adam Smith's Marketplace of Life* (New York, NY: Cambridge University Press, 2002), 2–11.

6. See John McMurtry, *The Cancer Stage of Capitalism* (Sterling, VA: Pluto Press, 1999), 38–49.

7. Michael Novak, *The Spirit of Democratic Capitalism* (New York, NY: Simon & Schuster Publications, 1982), 106.

market—explains the disparity in pharmaceutical prices between the United States and Canada where the price for identical medications is frequently two or three times lower? What else explains the dearth of criminal convictions after the financial debacle of 2008 and, alternatively, the subsequent toothless legislation that barely passed in the wake of the collapse of financial markets? Wealth is powerful. Wealth can hire lobbyists to prevent real legislative reform. It can also hire the best legal teams to prevent aggressive investigations and convictions of the richest criminals. It has the power to insulate an entire class of citizens from the repercussions of their misdeeds and allow them to exist in a stratum somewhere above the law. To actively ignore the power of wealth and its increasing accumulation by elites constitutes a moral failure when this kind of power is being wielded in unprecedented and harmful ways.

A Catholic Critique of Orthodox Capitalist Market Theory

> The purpose of a business firm is not simply to make a profit but is to be found in its very existence as a *community of persons* who in various ways are endeavoring to satisfy their basic needs, and who form a particular group at the service of the whole of society. (*Centesimus annus*, no. 35)

In Catholic thought, the orthodox or neoclassical theory of the capitalist market, and the purpose of the business firm functioning within these markets, philosophically shortchanges itself in two ways. First, the theory confuses one byproduct of business activity (the accumulation of profit) with the final purpose of business enterprise (to create valuable products and services). Secondly, it erroneously equates excellence with mere quantity maximization. Such a confluence of errors is analogous to mistaking the actual purpose of eating (nourishing the body) with one of its byproducts (food accumulating in the stomach), and then subsequently evaluating the excellence of this effect based solely on its quantifiable maximization. Needless to say, if successful eating is merely a matter of food accumulating in the stomach, and one equates excellence in this case with quantity maximization, then the result will be gluttony, obesity, and disease—precisely the opposite of the intended purpose of eating.

The purpose of eating is nourishment, not simply food maximization in the stomach. Therefore, people evaluate eating using complex quantity and quality measures in order to see how each contributes to a proper balance of health. The quantity measures seek moderation in order to avoid malnourishment on the one hand and obesity on the other. Qualitative measures—such as freshness, amount of processing, exposure to harmful chemicals, methods of preparation, and so forth—serve as a filter in this process of feeding the body. Individuals measure successful eating not by the amount of food in the stomach, but by other, more vital, signs of overall health.

Analogously, the tenets of Catholic social teaching suggest that business theorists should focus far less on the single quantitative measure of maximum profit and far more on other quantitative and qualitative measures that better reflect overall corporate health. One can find many good examples of businesses taking care of their corporate (body) health, recognizing that the overall vitality of the business depends on much more than simply profit and acknowledging the importance of the various communities that exist within and around the corporate body.[8]

Another theoretical shortcoming of the philosophy of capitalist markets pointed out by Catholic social teaching has to do with how Adam Smith's theory of the pursuit of self-interest is narrowly interpreted and anachronistically applied. That exclusive pursuit of self-interest will inevitably conflict with the good of others at some point and in some significant ways is well-established in experience and common sense. Most learn that lesson from parents, teachers, coaches, and other authority figures at a young age. Some were taught that self-interest, in and of itself, was an evil, only to discover later that pursuit of self-interest helped them achieve many good things for themselves, their families, and their communities. In truth, people naturally pursue self-interest and, under normal circumstances, doing so results in some marginal good for them and those in their identity group. However, the virtues of sharing, cooperation, and solidarity have demonstrated their value when the interests of society as a whole interfere with the pursuit of individual interests. Under these relatively unusual circumstances people need ethical resources to help them identify the shortcomings of self-interest and raise questions about how they pursue personal ends, while still contributing to, or at least not interfering with, the good of others and the good of society as a whole.

When people of relatively equal political, economic, and social power pursue self-interest within transparent legal and governmental structures in which everyone follows the rules and acknowledges the legitimate interests of others, then this enlightened self-interest likely results in a greater good for everyone. However, this context is rarely, if ever, achieved. Political, economic, and social inequalities abound in every society the world has known. Legal and governmental structures have never been perfectly transparent or immune from manipulation by powerful individuals and organizations. Daily news stories report on individuals who circumvented the rules or simply broke them because they believed they were entitled to do so. To enshrine self-interest as a guiding ethic does not reflect the reality of contemporary economic and political structures. One can only maintain

---

8. See Jeffrey L. Seglin, "How Business Can Be Good (And Why Being Good Is Good for Business)," *Sojourners* 29, No. 1 (Ja-F 2000): 17–19.

a thoroughgoing belief in the ethic of self-interest in the context of a utopian society that ensures perfect equality, liberty, and fraternity.

The Tragedy of the Commons

According to Catholic social thought, the good achievable through business activity is a type of common good because it is achieved in community for the sake of those in that community and for society as a whole. Solely stressing self-interest and profit maximization tends to obscure the communal nature of the corporate enterprise. It tends to equate the corporation with the shareholders and owners, treating other constituencies as externalities of one sort or another. For instance, some boardroom discussions regard workers as just another operating cost, reduce customers to mere consumers, and treat the broader communities within which the corporation operates as anonymous and interchangeable realities, like theater sets. Such a perspective ignores important bonds of solidarity that develop between workers, customers, managers, and the larger community. This type of ignorance can affect the health of a corporation through loss of credibility and good will.[9]

The corporate capitalist worldview also tends to privilege some groups in the corporate family, while treating others as expendable or even problematic. At its core, this attitude is elitist, says Marjorie Kelly in her article "The Divine Right of Capital." She identifies six principles of economic aristocracy that go largely unchallenged in contemporary culture:

1. Worldview: In the worldview of corporate financial statements, the aim is to pay stockholders as much as possible and employees as little as possible.
2. Privilege: Stockholders claim wealth they do little to create, much as nobles claimed privilege they did not earn.
3. Property: Like a feudal estate, a corporation is considered a piece of property—not a human community—so it can be owned and sold by the propertied class.
4. Governance: Corporations function with an aristocratic governance structure, in which members of the propertied class alone may vote.
5. Liberty: Corporate capitalism embraces a predemocratic concept of liberty reserved for property holders, which thrives by restricting the liberty of employees and the community.
6. Sovereignty: Corporations assert that they are private and the free market will self-regulate, much as feudal barons asserted a sovereignty independent of the crown.[10]

---

9. Marjorie Kelly, "The Divine Right of Capital," *Tikkun* 15, no. 4 (Jl-Ag 2000): 33–39.
10. Ibid., 14.

Kelly also identifies six principles of economic democracy that clearly harmonize with the principles of Catholic social theory.

1. Enlightenment: Because all persons are created equal, the economic rights of employees and the community are equal to those of capital owners.

2. Equality: Under market principles, wealth does not legitimately belong only to stockholders. Corporate wealth belongs to those who create it, and community wealth belongs to all.

3. Public Good: As semipublic governments, public corporations are more than pieces of property or private contracts. They have a responsibility to the public good.

4. Democracy: The corporation is a human community, and like the larger community of which it is a part, it is best governed democratically.

5. Justice: In keeping with equal treatment of persons before the law, the wealthy may not claim greater rights than others, and corporations may not claim the rights of persons.[11]

6. Evolution: As it is the right of people to alter or abolish government, it is the right of the people to alter or abolish the corporations that now govern the world.[12]

The first six principles associated with economic aristocracy find a home in the current culture of global capitalism, in which the ultimate good in society is the consumption of utility achieved through market exchange and in which the owners of capital have dictatorial power over management and distribution. In this system, the corporation and its managers act as agents for the owners of the business, pursuing their interests, which are always narrowly construed, and making decisions that maximize the owner's marginal value (profits).

Catholic social theory serves as a corrective influence and a reminder that the ultimate good in society is the common good and not merely the aggregation of all those goods that are individually and rapaciously pursued. The principles espoused by this theory closely match those outlined by Kelley as just and democratic. This book has explored how systematically applying the principles of Catholic social teaching would alter the current reigning economic system. It would require discarding many grounding principles cherished by staunch advocates of the current system for new ones that advocate more equal distribution and democratic governance; however, it turns out that capitalism itself could still survive and even thrive in this new moral environment. In other words, it is not

---

11. Of course, this principle contradicts the recent "Citizens United" decision of the US Supreme Court, *http://www.supremecourt.gov/Search.aspx?FileName=/docketfiles/08-205.htm*.

12. Ibid., 15.

impossible to conceive of a just and equal and yet, at the same time, competitive and productive marketplace.

Establishing these new kinds of business in this new kind of market does not require relinquishing everything known and cherished about the current system, but it will require moral imagination and the courage to change the usual order of business. At base, the marketplace is not the product of impersonal and inevitable laws of nature; it is made up of the choices people have made collectively over the centuries. Reforming the market today entails making new and different choices based on human dignity, the common good, and the other principles discussed in this book. The potential benefits to humanity are enormous, but the marketplace also gains under this new regime by becoming more universally beneficial and, consequently, more sustainable in the long term. In this way, this book is as much about the enduring health of the marketplace through good business practices, as it is about justice for all and an equal distribution of goods. In the end, the interests of business and the interests of justice are not inimical but mysteriously intertwined. Maybe Adam Smith's invisible hand theory has been pointing in this direction all along: good business demands justice and good moral practice—and a firm moral foundation will result in good business.

Index